The Athletics of Philadelphia

The Athletics of Philadelphia

Connie Mack's White Elephants, 1901–1954

by

DAVID M. JORDAN

McFarland & Company, Inc., Publishers
Jefferson, North Carolina, and London

Cover: Crowds outside Shibe Park in July 1948. *Urban Archives,
Temple University, Philadelphia.*

British Library Cataloguing-in-Publication data are available

Library of Congress Cataloguing-in-Publication Data

Jordan, David M., 1935–
    The Athletics of Philadelphia : Connie Mack's white elephants,
1901–1954 / by David M. Jordan.
        p.   cm.
    Includes bibliographical references and index.
    ISBN 0-7864-0620-8 (sewn softcover : 50# alkaline paper) ∞
    1. Philadelphia Athletics (Baseball team)—History.   2. Mack,
Connie, 1862–1956.   I. Title.
GV875.P43J67   1999   99-18627
796.357'64'0974811—dc21   CIP

Manufactured in the United States of America

*McFarland & Company, Inc., Publishers
    Box 611, Jefferson, North Carolina 28640*

To Sarah

Contents

Preface		1
Prologue: The Quaker City at the Turn of the Century		5
1.	New Man in Town	11
2.	A Pennant for Philadelphia	21
3.	Top Dogs	30
4.	Interlude, 1906–1908	37
5.	Shibe Park and the First Dynasty	42
6.	A Stick in John McGraw's Eye	51
7.	Rollercoaster	63
8.	Rock Bottom	75
9.	On the Way Again	87
10.	Top of the Mountain	95
11.	Another Dynasty	107
12.	Back to the Basement	115
13.	The War Years	130
14.	New Day Coming	140
15.	A Surprising Pennant Race	151
16.	Jubilee	164
17.	The Road to Kansas City	172
Epilogue: The Wanderers		187
Notes		191
Bibliography		207
Index		21

Preface

This work is a labor of love. I was an A's fan growing up in Philadelphia, at a time when our numbers were decreasing. It took some strength of character, I thought, to root for the Athletics (admittedly the same was true of the Phillies, too), because what we got for our loyalty was Connie Mack, whose better days were long behind him, and a team that never had enough money or front-office imagination.

My father took me to Shibe Park to see my first A's game when I was eight years old, and they were shut out on two hits by Hal Newhouser. They won the second game of that day's doubleheader, behind a knuckleball pitcher named Roger Wolff, and I was hooked. I immediately became a staunch fan of the Athletics and of Hal Newhouser and went to see my team as often as I could. There were afternoon games through the summers and doubleheaders on Sundays, so I could get down to 21st and Lehigh frequently. It always gave me a little jolt of pleasure to come up the ramp into the sunlight, to see the green walls and the green grass, the infield dirt and the sparkling white uniforms of the home team.

The A's lost a lot of games that I saw, but there were highlights as well. I sat through all 24 innings of their 1-1 tie with Detroit in 1945, and I had the joy of watching my team shut out the hated Yankees twice on Memorial Day 1947. I remember them beating Bob Lemon on a rare Elmer Valo shot over the lofty rightfield fence. The 1948 pennant contender is still my all-time favorite team, even though it eventually faded to fourth place. Over the years I cheered for Dick Siebert, Ferris Fain,

1

Frankie Hayes, Lum Harris, Eddie Joost, Joe Astroth, Lou Limmer, Bobby Shantz and the rest. In 1954 I may have been the only person in the whole Philadelphia area to take seriously the mayor's "Save the A's" campaign. I went to see about 45 games, and I think that DeMaestri, Renna, Portocarrero and the others lost 40 of them. Most were not even close.

After that I suffered through the awful trauma of having my team wrenched away from me, sold off to Kansas City despite several last-minute attempts to keep it in town (which never really stood a chance of succeeding). The loss produced a feeling similar only to that of being abandoned by one's true love. It took a while to recover, to realize that my team was irrevocably gone, that it was never coming back to Philadelphia, that what was left was … the Phillies.

The Athletics and Phillies enjoyed a strange symbiotic relationship in the Quaker City. Mack and the A's had, of course, feasted on the Phillies' talent in 1901 and 1902, helping to denude the National League team of most of its best players. The Phillies won in court, but even those victories had not brought back the star players who had left the team. After peace between the leagues was established, the two clubs each operated with a wary eye on the other. For most of the time the two teams shared the city, the Athletics were dominant. The opening of Shibe Park in 1909 helped to demonstrate how inadequate Baker Bowl was. The A's won more pennants, had bigger stars, and almost always drew far more fans to their games than the Phillies did. They even became the Phillies' landlords in 1938. They were no real threat to the Phillies' existence, however, even in those years when Gerry Nugent was muddling along with no cash and little talent. It was the Athletics' misfortune that the injection of DuPont money into the Phillies came just as the economic realities of baseball were changing, with two-team cities soon passing from the baseball map. The A's, like the Braves and Browns ahead of them, found themselves forced to leave a town they used to own.

I had a good deal of assistance in writing this book. I want to thank the staffs of the newspaper division of the Free Library of Philadelphia and the National Baseball Library for all their help, as well as the folks at Urban Archives at the Temple University Library, where the morgue of the defunct *Evening Bulletin* is now housed. The contemporaneous newspaper account usually beats the recalled memory for accuracy in what really happened. My daughter Diana went over the manuscript with a critical and helpful eye, and my friend Paul Shein has refreshed my recollections in some areas. I want to thank my friend Kit Crissey for permission to quote from his book on wartime baseball, *Teenagers, Graybeards, and 4-Fs*. Bill Marshall and Jeffrey Suchanek of the University of Kentucky Library made available to me transcripts or tapes of Bill's interviews with A's players of the '40s.

There is a temptation in writing about the Philadelphia Athletics to concentrate almost exclusively on Connie Mack. I have tried to avoid that, while still giving him his due. After all, Connie Mack never played a game for the Athletics. That privilege was left for the real heroes of this book, Rube Oldring, Lefty Grove, Squiz Pillion, Bob Hooper, Wally Moses, Eric McNair, and the rest. The Athletics won 3841 games over their years in Philadelphia, they lost 4171, and they even played eighty ties. For most of that time they were the best show in town.

David M. Jordan
Jenkintown, Pennsylvania

Prologue: The Quaker City at the Turn of the Century

In 1900, the year before Connie Mack and his Athletics came to town, Philadelphia had a population of 1,293,000 and was the third largest city in the United States. But census figures alone cannot describe a large American city, with its own peculiar geography, ethnic makeup, and personality. What was it that made Ban Johnson, with his new American League, feel sure that Philadelphia would support another baseball club, even though the Phillies of the National League had been established there since 1883?

Philadelphia in 1900 was defined by its location between two rivers, by its port some hundred miles up the Delaware River from the sea, by its site at the far southeastern corner of a sprawling agricultural and mining state whose inhabitants were often suspicious of the large metropolis. It was defined by its Quaker heritage, by its commercial and social rivalry with New York, and by the peculiar development of its populace, shaped by both internal and foreign immigration. It was defined by its commerce and particularly by its industry, as well as by its culture and its social practices.

The city in the period from the beginning of the Civil War to 1900 had been transformed into an industrial giant, "the center of heavy industry, of iron and steel, coal and oil, America's foundry ... chief port for the foundry, nerve center of transportation, producer of finished goods of an enormous variety but particularly of steam engines and steamships."[1] The resultant metropolis, often blanketed with smoke and soot, may not have been as pleasant a place to live as William Penn's "greene Country Towne," but it made money and provided employment for thousands of workers. Money in the pockets of the kind of people who would go to baseball games was what the founders of the American League were looking for.

Philadelphia's industrial prosperity rested upon three bases, iron and steel, railroads, and coal. The symbol of this prosperity was the mighty Pennsylvania Railroad, the foremost enterprise in the city itself and the single largest corporation in the country, led by its president, Alexander Cassatt.

The engineering feats of the Pennsylvania Railroad, exemplified by the famous Horseshoe Curve in the mountains near Altoona, were legendary. The lofty Broad Street Station, across from City Hall, was the mark of the Pennsylvania writ large across the face of downtown Philadelphia, and the Main Line, the series of suburban communities built along the railroad's trunk line westward, was similarly a creation of the Pennsylvania Railroad which transformed Philadelphia's hinterlands. Generations of children in Philadelphia memorized "Old Maids Never Wed And Have Babies" to keep in mind the westering stations of the Main Line: Overbrook, Merion, Narberth, Wynnewood, Ardmore, Haverford and Bryn Mawr. Railroad executive Henry Houston developed a far northwestern area of the city known as Chestnut Hill, which, with the Main Line, attracted many of Philadelphia's wealthier residents.

The Reading Railroad, which ran into Philadelphia from the upstate coal regions, was always a poor relation to the Pennsylvania, especially after financial crises delivered control of the road into the hands of New Yorkers. The fiscal imprudence of its early president, Franklin B. Gowen, drove the line into bankruptcy by 1880. Nevertheless, in 1900 the Reading was transporting 447,000 tons of anthracite into Philadelphia in a year.

Among the greatest manufactories of the world at the turn of the 20th century were two of the brightest stars of Philadelphia's industrial constellation. The Baldwin Locomotive Works produced three times as many locomotives as any other factory in the world. The Cramp Ship-building Company, whose shipyard stretched for fifty acres along the Delaware at Kensington, was the premier shipbuilder of the day.

In addition to the Baldwin and Cramp industrial behemoths, Philadelphia was home to numerous other manufacturers turning out products as diverse as wheelbarrows, telephones, parasols, water closets, cigarettes, and false teeth. Leading the way was the manufacture of tex-tiles and carpets, in which Philadelphia outpaced the country. Some 35 percent of Philadelphia's 229,000 workers were employed in textile plants.

Shipping to and from the port of Philadelphia was still a major enterprise for the city, with its five miles of wharves along the Delaware and four miles along the Schuylkill. While Philadelphia no longer stood first in shipping, having slipped behind New York, the port on the Delaware maintained a virtual monopoly on the export of coal.

Philadelphia in 1900 remained the largest city in area in the coun-try, its 129 square miles home to almost 300,000 families. They lived in numerous defined communities like Frankford, Manayunk, Ger-mantown, and South Philadelphia. Philadelphia was a city not of packed tenements but of long streets of mostly one-family row houses. Elec-tric street railways, which had replaced horse-drawn trolleys in the last decades of the 19th century, facilitated movement around the city, mak-ing it convenient to go to a ball game.

Philadelphia was an anomaly politically, for it was a one-party Republican town at a time when most large cities were controlled by Democrats. Bosses like Boies Penrose, David Martin, Israel Durham, and the Vare brothers in South Philadelphia frequently competed among themselves for power. However, the machine they led controlled gov-ernment and politics in the Quaker City, making graft and corruption a standard way of life. That brought Philadelphia notoriety across the land for its seamy public culture.

Philadelphia's population was more homogeneous than that of most other large cities. As late as 1890, 59 percent of the city's foreign-born denizens came from the British Isles, half of them from Ireland. There were substantial numbers of Italian and Russian Jewish immigrants, but far fewer from other parts of eastern and southern Europe. Philadelphia had a reputation as a skilled worker's town; unskilled immigrants usually passed it by for Pittsburgh, Reading, Wilkes-Barre or Scranton.[2]

There were so many British immigrants in 19th-century Philadelphia that cricket became a popular sport. When millworkers from Midlands textile towns like Nottingham and Lancaster poured into Philadelphia they brought cricket with them. More than two hundred cricket clubs were organized in and around the city. Cornelius Weygandt, a famous English professor at the University of Pennsylvania, recalled growing up in Germantown in the 1870s and 1880s: "There was baseball on corner lots, but more than half of the town's boys, both mill hands' sons and sons of the 'carriage folks,' played cricket." Matches at the Germantown Cricket Club were well attended, because the club's original grounds in Nicetown and its second home off Wissahickon Avenue were close to many of the textile mills. In addition, collegians from Haverford College and Penn became avid cricketers, and the sport flourished. As it did, its skills with bat and ball were easily transferred to that other blossoming game with which it shared roots, baseball.[3]

Symbolic of the increasing taste of the populace for pleasure and entertainment was the creation of two "amusement parks," Woodside Park, which opened in West Philadelphia in 1897, and Willow Grove Park, in the suburbs north of the city. Both were located at the end of trolley lines designed to convey the public to these new meccas. Willow Grove, even with its Ferris wheel and scenic railway, had its greatest attraction in concerts given by such eminent musicians as John Philip Sousa and Walter Damrosch. Foremost among the entertainments embraced by the public, however, was the game already known as "the National Pastime."

Philadelphia had been a baseball town from the earliest days of the game. Baseball in Philadelphia started in much the same way it started elsewhere in the northeastern part of the United States, deriving from an old English game called "rounders," itself an offshoot of cricket. Baseball was a game played by young men with free time, young men who eventually formed clubs to play it on a regular basis. The Olympics, organized in the early 1830s, constituted one of the earliest ball clubs in Philadelphia. The Olympics were soon joined by such other local teams as the Minervas, the Equity, the Mercantiles, the Keystones, and the Swiftfoot, and even some clubs made up of black men, such as the Excelsiors, the Orions, and the Pythians.

In 1860 U.S. Marshal James N. Kerns established a club called the

Athletics, which quickly became the outstanding team in the area. When the leading clubs organized the first professional league in 1871, the Athletics were the Philadelphia club invited to join the new league, to be called the National Association of Base Ball Players. Playing at a structure at 25th and Jefferson Street, known as the Jefferson Street Grounds, the Athletics won the league championship in the first year of its existence. In 1873, a second Philadelphia team, called the Quakers, joined the league.

When a Chicago booster named William Hulbert pulled eight teams out of the National Association in 1876 to form a new and more businesslike organization called the National League, the Athletics were once again the representative from the Quaker City. Near the end of the first National League season, however, the money-losing Athletics refused to make their final western trip, hoping to cut their losses. Hulbert booted the club from the league, and the Athletics resumed an independent existence.

Another new league, called the American Association, was formed in 1882, and again the Athletics were the team from Philadelphia. With slugger Harry Stovey and pitching star Bobby Mathews, the Athletics won their only Association pennant in 1883, the same year that the failing Worcester franchise in the National League was transferred to Philadelphia, where it became known as the Phillies.

Philadelphia continued with two teams (three in 1884 and 1890, when short-lived third leagues challenged the National League and the American Association) until the Association died after the 1891 season, taking with it the Athletics. The Phillies' owners, Colonel John I. Rogers, an attorney, and Alfred J. Reach, one of the legendary fathers of the game, contributed a large share of the $50,000 paid to the Wagner brothers, the owners of the Athletics, to extinguish their territorial rights in Philadelphia. The Phillies soldiered on in mediocre fashion in what now became a 12-team league, despite possessing for several years what may have been the best outfield ever to play together. Ed Delahanty, Billy Hamilton and Sam Thompson have all been enshrined in the Hall of Fame.

The National League maintained a baseball monopoly in the 1890s. Having beaten back the players' Brotherhood in the 1890 trade war the League owners utilized their power to cut labor costs in order to maximize their profits. "Labor costs," of course, meant players' compensation. Led by magnates like John T. Brush of Cincinnati, Arthur Soden of Boston, Andrew Freedman of New York, and Rogers of the Phillies, the League took an increasingly hard line with its players, who had no place else to go if they wanted to play big-time baseball. By 1894 the owners had fixed a $2400 ceiling on annual wages, leaving the players little choice but to submit.

The latter part of the 1890s saw the National League owners come up with such ideas as "syndicate" baseball. It featured common ownership of two teams with all the better players placed on one team. This was done with St. Louis and Cleveland and with Brooklyn and Baltimore, to the great distress of the fans in Cleveland and Baltimore, who got the leavings. Proposed by New York's Freedman was a baseball "trust" in which the league would consist of one big corporation, with the majority of the stock to be controlled by Freedman and his three allies. "Only a blackguard could think up such a thing!" exclaimed the Phillies' Rogers, and the "trust" scheme was finally scuttled.[4]

Following the 1899 season, the League did agree to Freedman's plan to "lop off the dead wood," and the franchises in Louisville, Baltimore, Cleveland, and Washington were dropped. This marked the end of "syndicate" ownership, and it eased travel requirements somewhat, but the $104,000 payout made to the expiring franchises had to be raised somewhere. The National League went back into debt, and it left inviting openings for a possible challenger to its monopoly. There would not be a long wait for one to appear.

CHAPTER 1

New Man in Town

Connie Mack was 38 years old in 1901. Born in East Brookfield, Massachusetts, on December 22, 1862, young Cornelius McGillicuddy worked in a shoe factory until he found that baseball represented an escape from industrial toil. McGillicuddy's first professional job was catching for Meriden in the Connecticut State League in 1884, at $80 a month. He quickly moved up through the Eastern League to the big leagues. Toward the end of the 1886 season his contract was purchased by the Washington National League team, for whom he caught ten games and hit .361.

Connie Mack, the name McGillicuddy adopted for baseball purposes,[1] was tall and thin as a rail. It was his catching skills rather than his hitting which made him a valuable professional. He played for Washington the next three years until 1890 when he and many of his peers jumped to the Players League, the outlaw league fostered by the Brotherhood of Professional Baseball Players. The Players League grew out of the increasingly bitter resentment of players against the franchise owners, particularly the arrogant owners of clubs in the National League. Signing with the Buffalo franchise, Mack put his own money into the venture, as other committed players did, and when the league folded after one season his assets were gone.

Connie Mack was a cute operator as a catcher. He perfected the technique of tipping the bat with his mitt in such a way that his interference went undetected but the batter's timing was destroyed. He also learned to flick his glove with his bare hand so that the umpire thought he heard a foul tip. Mack was no saint; he was a professional ballplayer with a strong desire to win, and he felt no moral inhibitions against a little minor chicanery to accomplish that result.

In the shake-out after the collapse of the Brotherhood's league, Mack landed a job with the Pittsburgh National League club. After almost four years with the Pirates, he was named manager with 22 games left in the 1894 schedule. The Pirates had winning records the next two seasons under Mack, but they were nowhere near the top of the league so the owner, W. W. Kerr, let him go, after two years of second-guessing him. Mack learned a lesson about how unreasonable and interfering an owner-employer could be.

Mack then hired on as manager of the Milwaukee club in the Western League. The league president was a former baseball writer with big ideas, a feisty, hard-drinking, pugnacious man named Byron Bancroft Johnson. It would be difficult to find more of a contrast to the gentle, abstemious, soft-spoken Mack than Ban Johnson, but the two men were close over the years.

Johnson had revived the old Western League in 1895, with franchises in Detroit, Kansas City, Indianapolis, Grand Rapids, Toledo, Sioux City, Minneapolis, and Milwaukee. After the 1899 season, Johnson changed his circuit's name to the American League. He then moved clubs into Cleveland (just vacated by the National League Spiders, ousted when the big league trimmed down from 12 teams to eight) and Chicago, where Charles Comiskey's team was permitted to move into territory already occupied by the Nationals, so long as it stayed on the south side of town. For 1900, Johnson's organization remained a minor league, but Ban had bigger things in mind. He had financial backing from a Cleveland coal baron named Charles W. Somers, among others, and he was ready to take on the established league.

After the close of the 1900 season, Johnson let it be known that his league would not sign the National Agreement for 1901 and that he was expanding into the East, into Baltimore, Washington, Buffalo, and Philadelphia, with a veiled threat to move into Boston. He was soon engaged in negotiations with representatives of the National League, but no accord on the status of the American League could be reached, because Johnson wanted equality. The talks ended in early December, and on the 4th James A. Hart, owner of the Chicago National League

Connie Mack in the late 1940s (The Falvey Collection, courtesy Philadelphia A's Historical Society Archives).

club, said, "The National League is willing to be fair, but it will not be trampled upon."[2]

The next day, Colonel John I. Rogers, treasurer and co-owner of the Phillies, said that Johnson "cannot expect us to consent to a lot of carpet-baggers coming into our territory," for which the Phillies had paid handsomely at the end of the wars in the early 1890s. Rogers continued: "The rumor is, I believe, that the American Leaguers intend to import a Western club to this city. Now, the Philadelphia Club ... could hardly agree to take the new-comers in on equal terms with itself."[3]

On December 11, 1900, Johnson arrived in Philadelphia with Somers and declared his organization a "major" league, which would battle the National League for players and customers. The American League would not recognize the "reserve" or "option" clause in National League contracts, the crucial clause which bound a player to a team for another year after the term of his contract. It would go head to head with the old league in Chicago, Boston (replacing Buffalo), and Philadelphia. Johnson's teams would not go after any players actually under contract with a National club, but they served notice that players who had simply had a unilateral option exercised by a club were not to be considered under contract. Johnson's five other clubs were in Milwaukee, Detroit, Cleveland, Washington, and Baltimore. The latter three of those cities had seen their National League franchises disappear in 1900; Detroit had been without big league ball since 1888.

The National League's response, orchestrated by John T. Brush, the controversial owner of the Cincinnati franchise, was to announce on January 5, 1901, the creation of a new minor league to be called the American Association, with teams in the American League cities. That this would have meant *three* teams in Philadelphia, for example, did not seem to bother the old league's magnates. Rogers of the Phillies insisted that the new Association team had to play in the Phillies' park, at an annual rental of $5400. The reaction to this heavy-handed maneuver was so bad—one reporter, for instance, called the Association plan "a regular bunco game"—that on February 27 the Nationals announced that there would be *no* support for the new minor league. It quickly faded away.[4]

Ban Johnson wanted Connie Mack, the quiet and genteel Irishman, to run the new club in Philadelphia, so he talked him into leaving Milwaukee. Mack put up between five and ten thousand dollars and received 25 percent of the stock in the new franchise. The team was called the Athletics, an honored name in Philadelphia baseball, though the new team obviously had no connection with the old Athletics of the American Association and before. Cleveland money man Somers put up the rest of the cash, more than $30,000.[5]

Ban Johnson could not afford to pass up a challenge to the old league in Philadelphia. Although this was the "corrupt and contented" period about which muckraker Lincoln Steffens wrote, the industrial giant which Philadelphia had become was too tempting a situation for a man on the make like Johnson to ignore.

As Philadelphia grew, the city's character had crystallized into "contentment, conformity, and conservatism ... [where] imagination and innovation were suspect." Philadelphia, it was said, was "safe and sound, prosperous and potbellied."[6] Nevertheless, Philadelphia extended hospitality to new businesses and hard-working entrepreneurs of the right sort. Atwater Kent with electrical equipment, the Stephano brothers with Turkish cigarettes, Christian Schmidt with his beer, Bayuk cigars, Bassett's and Breyer's ice cream, John B. Stetson and his hats, soap maker Joseph Fels, and a myriad of textile manufacturers were examples. These ventures and venturers were brothers under the skin to Connie Mack and his upstart baseball team.

Mack arrived in Philadelphia after the 1900 season, moved into the Hotel Hanover, and set about organizing his team. Two local sportswriters, Samuel "Butch" Jones of the Associated Press and Frank Hough of the *Philadelphia Inquirer*, worked with Mack to locate a spot for a ballpark. After a couple of false starts they found a vacant lot at 29th and Columbia in Brewerytown, and secured a ten-year lease on it. Mack contracted with a builder named James Foster to put up a 12,000-seat wooden grandstand and bleachers. He called it Columbia Park.[7]

Mack's sportswriter allies introduced him to local businessman and baseball fan Benjamin F. Shibe. A 68-year-old native of the working-class section of Philadelphia known as Fishtown, Shibe was a partner of Al Reach in the sporting goods concern A. J. Reach & Co. One of the greatest of pioneer baseball players Reach was then part-owner of the Phillies. Shibe was a mechanically minded man who came up with many innovations in the manufacture of sporting equipment. After the Civil War he was a partner in a hardware firm which soon specialized in baseball equipment. When he joined his manufacturing know-how with Reach's salesmanship in the late 1870s, the business boomed. Now Shibe became a target of Connie Mack, who was seeking local investment in the new franchise.

When Mack and Shibe met in December 1900, Mack invited the

manufacturer to invest in his ball club. As a sweetener, Mack offered to have the Reach company's baseball chosen as the official ball of the new major league. Shibe, who had once had a small investment in the old Athletics club in the American Association, was tempted. His sons, Tom and John, who were in the business with him, urged their father to become involved.

Ben Shibe hesitated. A new club in competition with a popular and prosperous established team represented a considerable risk. Besides, he was Al Reach's partner, and how would that look? Reach, though, was having problems with the overbearing Colonel Rogers and was quickly losing interest in the Phillies. He too urged Shibe to invest in Mack's team, and Ben was convinced. He put up an undisclosed amount of cash, enough to buy out the interest of Charles Somers, and wound up with 50 percent of the club's stock. Mack held 25 percent, and the two newspapermen, Hough and Jones, shared the remaining 25 percent. On February 19, 1901, Benjamin Franklin Shibe was elected president of the new ball club, with the *Inquirer* asserting that "the very fact that Mr. Shibe has accepted the presidency of the local club is a sufficient guarantee that it will be run on straightforward business principles."[8]

Frank Hough was also Mack's emissary to ballplayers in the older league. Hough let them know what the Athletics were prepared to pay those who jumped their teams and signed with Connie Mack. He found a lot of dissatisfied players who were ready to bolt.

The best of them all was the Phillies' Napoleon Lajoie, a big Frenchman from Woonsocket, Rhode Island, a standout second baseman who had averaged .345 over his four and a half seasons in Philadelphia. "What a ballplayer that man was!" outfielder Tommy Leach said of Lajoie. "Every play he made was executed so gracefully that it looked like it was the easiest thing in the world."[9]

Since 1893 the monopolistic National League had enforced a salary cap of $2400 per man, and this limit rankled many players. There were many *sub rosa* violations of the cap, and before the 1900 season Lajoie and slugger Ed Delahanty had agreed not to sign with the Phillies unless they received more than $2400. Rogers agreed to bend the rules, and he signed Lajoie for $2600, telling Nap that he would pay Delahanty the same. In fact, Delahanty signed *his* contract for $3000.

Rogers, of course, was foolish in thinking this discrepancy would not come to light, and when Lajoie saw one of Delahanty's paychecks he was furious. He demanded the extra $400, but Rogers refused. Thus, when Hough came around offering Lajoie $4000 to play for the Athletics, the star second baseman had little hesitancy in signing.[10]

The Athletics offered a like amount to Delahanty, but Rogers matched it. Big Ed did not jump to the new league until the next year, when he went to Washington. Mack did sign three of the Phillies' pitchers, Chick Fraser, Strawberry Bill Bernhard, and Wiley Piatt, and infielder Joe Dolan who came over after the start of the season.

In his autobiography Mack wrote: "Our rivals, the Phillies, were not happy over our invasion of Philadelphia."[11] Indeed not. Colonel Rogers hired eminent Philadelphia lawyer John G. Johnson and went to court on March 28 to enjoin Lajoie and the other jumpers from playing for the Athletics. Two other high-priced barristers, William Jay Turner and Richard L. Dale, represented Lajoie and the Athletics. In Philadelphia Common Pleas Court No. 5, the Phillies' case, after being heard for a couple of days by the court *en banc*, was thrown out by Judge Robert Ralston on the grounds that the standard baseball contract lacked "mutuality," since the club could terminate it on ten days' notice while the player had no such right. The Phillies promptly filed an appeal to the state supreme court.

The test of the new Philadelphia Athletics, of course, would be on the playing field—and in the grandstands. Connie Mack, as manager, did not wear a uniform or go out onto the field. When he hung up his glove with Milwaukee in 1897, Mack decided there was no point in wearing a uniform to manage.[12] Soon the dark suit, stiff collar, and straw hat of the Philadelphia skipper became an easily recognizable trademark. So too did the uniform of the new team, the usual white for home and gray for the road, with a large blue "A" on the left breast and dark blue stockings.

It was an oddity of the franchise that over its entire tenure in Philadelphia there was never an indication on the team's uniform of its connection with the city. There was usually the large "A" on the shirt, with later an "A" on the cap, for some years an elephant, and in the final year the word "Athletics" in red and blue script, but never a hint of the city's name or even the simple letter "P."

The Athletics unveiled their team and opened their new ballpark on April 8 with an exhibition victory over a semi-pro team. Mack and Shibe were elated to see more than a thousand people show up for the occasion despite cold and wet weather; "the success of the new League in this city," the *Evening Telegraph* predicted, "is assured."[13]

In the third week of April, preparations were underway for the formal debut of the new baseball team in Philadelphia. It had been an eventful winter and spring: Queen Victoria and former president Benjamin Harrison had passed away; the great Australian soprano Nellie Melba had come to the Academy of Music to sing Marguerite in Gounod's *Faust*, with Edouard de Reszke as Mephistopheles, prompting the *Inquirer* to salute Melba as an "exquisite singer and admirable artist"; President William McKinley had been sworn in for his second term on March 4, with his new vice-president, Theodore Roosevelt of New York. Jacob Reed's Sons, at 1412-14 Chestnut Street, was offering winter topcoats for $10, housecoats and smoking jackets at $5 to $22.50. Miss Phoebe Davis was performing in "Betsy Ross" at the Chestnut Street Opera House. But on April 24, the eyes of Philadelphia were on 29th and Columbia, where Connie Mack's Athletics would open their official league season.[14]

Gettysburg Eddie Plank, winner of 285 games for the A's.

April 24, however, was a very rainy day; the Athletics game with Washington had to be postponed. The Phillies, also opening in Philadelphia, were rained out too. On the 25th the story was about the same; the rains stopped but the playing fields were too wet. Ah, but the 26th was the day! "If there ever was a time in the young life of Connie Mack [he was 38 years old when his A's came into being], when his heart was effervescent with joy and he felt at peace with all the world," wrote one lyrical and imaginative scribe, "that time was this afternoon when the American League base-ball season was opened in this city."[15]

"Never was there a more auspicious base-ball opening in this city," it was written. The crowds began to arrive before two o'clock, and the trolley cars were jammed. The First Regiment Band entertained the early arrivals, and by three o'clock "there was not a vacant seat left and standing room was at a premium." In attendance were Ban Johnson, Somers, and a host of other notables (not including, of course, Colonel Rogers, "who neither sent flowers, his regrets, or a basket of bricks"). At four o'clock Mayor Samuel H. Ashbridge threw out the first ball and the crowd settled back to watch baseball. Unfortunately, the Senators, who were just as brand-new as the Athletics, scored a run in the fourth against A's starter Chick Fraser, two in the sixth, and one in the seventh before the home team tallied its first run. Ralph Seybold had the first base hit in Athletics' history, a second-inning single, but it went for naught in the 5-1 defeat.[16]

The next day, the Athletics, with another large crowd on hand, lost again, as Washington beat lefthander Wiley Piatt, 11-5. On the 29th, however, Mack's team knocked off Boston, 8-5, behind Bill Bernhard, and the Athletics were on their way.

Although not a pennant winner the first Athletics team had a winning season with 74 wins and 62 losses, finishing in fourth place. Lajoie was sensational; he led the new league in hitting, with a tremendous .422 average, in home runs with 14, and in runs driven in, with 125.

Mack had some problems at first base. He originally signed a first sacker named Pat Crisham, who never made it to the starting gate and was replaced by Charlie Carr. After two bad games Carr was gone, his spot taken by Ralph Seybold, who came in from the outfield. On April 29, Mack signed the veteran Hugh Jennings, but Jennings was coaching at Cornell (where he was also a law student) and could not join the Athletics until the end of the Big Red's season in June. By then, Mack had remembered a first baseman named Harry Davis who had played for him in Pittsburgh; he talked Davis out of a bank position to return to baseball, and Davis did a fine job, hitting .306. There was no need for Jennings.

A little infielder named Lafayette Napoleon Cross, nicknamed

"Lave," jumped from Brooklyn and hit .331 for the Athletics at third base. Cross, when he appeared with the A's, completed a unique cycle, being the only man who played for Philadelphia franchises in the American Association, the Players League, the National League, and the American League.

Mack had another hard hitter in the outfield, a 30-year-old Ohioan named Ralph "Socks" Seybold. Seybold had played in the National League briefly a couple of years earlier, but mostly he had been in the Western League. Seybold hit .333 for the Athletics and pounded out eight home runs. Dave Fultz started the season in the infield but was soon given outfield duty, where he performed well and batted .295.

The pitching for the new club was led by two of the ex-Phillies, Fraser with a record of 22-16 and Bernhard with 17-10. A young left-hander with a sweeping delivery, which he called his crossfire pitch, was signed on the recommendation of his Gettysburg College coach. The young man was named Eddie Plank, and he won 17 games for Mack in 1901—and hundreds more for him over the next thirteen years. Plank was noted for rarely throwing over to first to hold runners. "There are only so many pitches in this old arm," he said, "and I don't believe in wasting them throwing to first base."[17]

Plank was the first of many college-trained players to star for Connie Mack's Athletics. Later came such performers as Jack Coombs, Eddie Collins, Jack Barry, Mickey Cochrane, Bill McCahan, George Earnshaw, and Sam Chapman. "These boys," Mack said, "who knew their Greek and Latin and their algebra and geometry and trigonometry, put intelligence and scholarship into the game."[18]

Handling the pitching staff was Michael "Doc" Powers, a 30-year-old who had had training as a physician. Powers was a very bad hitter—his .251 in 1901 was an aberration, to be overshadowed by five straight seasons with averages of .190 or below—but he was an excellent catcher and a man who could keep his pitchers' heads in the game.

The Athletics, with their new club, their new ballpark, their crisp white uniforms, were a success in their first season. They had a winning team, exciting players like Lajoie, Seybold, Plank, and Fraser, and a new spirit. They drew more than 206,000 customers, which almost matched the 234,000 drawn by the long-established Phillies. The new man in town had become established very quickly.

CHAPTER 2

A Pennant for Philadelphia

Preparing for the 1902 season, Connie Mack signed several more players from the Phillies' "option" list: hard-hitting, speedy outfielder Elmer Flick, pitcher Bill Duggleby, and shortstop Monte Cross. Rogers and the Phillies lost most of their team's top players when Washington picked up third sacker Harry Wolverton, slugging star Ed Delahanty, pitchers Al Orth and Jack Townsend, and the St. Louis Browns signed hurler Red Donahue. The Phillies faced disaster as they scrambled to fight off the National League and the Athletics too.

Finally, Rogers received a break. The Pennsylvania Supreme Court, on April 21, 1902, handed down its opinion in the case of *Philadelphia Ball Club, Limited, v. Napoleon Lajoie et al.* The court's opinion, by Justice William P. Potter, reversed the lower court's decision that Lajoie's contract with the Phillies lacked "mutuality." Potter agreed with the club's argument that Lajoie was unique and impossible to replace easily: "Lajoie is well known, and has great reputation among the patrons of the sport, for ability in the position which he filled, and was thus a most attractive drawing card for the public." Lajoie "may not be the sun in the baseball firmament," held the court, "but he is certainly a bright, particular star." In conclusion, the opinion directed that "the court cannot compel the defendant to play for the plaintiff, but it can restrain him from playing for another club in violation of his agreement."[1]

The baseball world was stunned. Rogers and other National League leaders joyously quoted from the court's opinion; the president of the Chicago Cubs said, "I cannot see it in any other light than a fatal blow to the rival league." Prompted by his lawyers, Ben Shibe argued that the decree applied to Lajoie alone, because of its language stressing his particular value.[2]

While Rogers announced that he would direct Lajoie, Fraser, and Bernhard "to report to the club at once," Connie Mack said calmly, "The American League and the Athletics are here to stay, whether Lajoie is with us or not." He said that his signing of Lajoie was "in good faith," and, asked about the other players who had left the Phillies, said, "Sufficient unto the day is the evil thereof, and we will play them until enjoined from so doing."[3]

There now commenced a month and a half of confusion, caused in part by Justice Potter's emphasis in his opinion on the unique value of Lajoie, as well as by public posturing on both sides and by a series of fruitless legal moves. Rogers made numerous pronouncements on the effect of the decision, while Ban Johnson and Charles Somers issued statements every few days or so regarding the determination of the American League to litigate to the last lawyer.

Early on April 22, Rogers showed up in the office of the pro-thonotary of the Supreme Court, to make sure the record in the Lajoie case was certified promptly back to the lower court. The next day he applied to Judges Ralston and Davis in the Philadelphia court for an injunction against Lajoie's playing for any club but the Phillies. Meanwhile, Billy Shettsline, manager of the Phillies, said he had met with Bernhard and Flick; he claimed that both had agreed to return if they could not play for the Athletics.

On April 23, opening day for the Athletics, Judge Ralston issued a temporary restraining order against Lajoie, rebuffing the efforts of the Athletics' lawyers. He refused Rogers's request to include Bernhard and Fraser in it because the state supreme court decision applied so specifically to Lajoie alone. When Ralston asked Rogers how this injunction would affect a player "out of this jurisdiction," Rogers confidently assured him that it would be operative "anywhere else in the United States."[4]

When the A's took the field that day in Baltimore, Lajoie assumed his familiar spot at second base, as if nothing judicial had transpired.

Just before the ninth inning, however, Mack was handed a telegram from the club's counsel informing him that the court in Philadelphia had issued a temporary injunction banning Lajoie from performing with the Athletics. Mack hastily replaced his star.[5]

Before a packed courtroom on April 28, Ralston continued the injunction against Lajoie. After hearing lengthy testimony on the talents, accomplishments and value of Fraser and Bernhard, he issued injunctions against the two pitchers as well. On May 2, the attorneys for the Athletics took appeals of the three injunctions back to the state supreme court and asked for bond to be fixed, so that after the required security was posted the three men could continue playing until the appeals were decided. On May 5, lawyers for the two sides squabbled over whether a bond for a *supersedeas* was appropriate, and Judge Ralston took the matter under advisement.

Duggleby returned to the Phillies on May 5 and Fraser on May 16, but they were the only ones. Mack allowed Elmer Flick to join the American League club in Cleveland, near his home, on May 7. Flick had played eleven games for the Athletics but was concerned about being involved in a legal tangle. Monte Cross was never joined in any litigation (nor was Flick), and he stayed put with the Athletics.[6]

The big prize, of course, was Larry Lajoie, who became the centerpiece of a peculiar bidding war. Colonel Rogers assumed Lajoie must come back to the Phillies, so when he met with Lajoie on May 15 to discuss the terms of the second baseman's return he announced that Larry must first pay a hefty fine for jumping the club. Lajoie, who had that day cleaned out his locker at Columbia Park, walked out of the meeting determined not to return to the Phillies. He then entertained offers from MacNamara of Detroit and Comiskey of Chicago before agreeing to a generous offer from Cleveland—all with the consent of Connie Mack, who still had a contract of some validity with the big Frenchman. Charles Somers, ostensibly the owner of the Boston franchise but still quite closely involved with Cleveland, came to Philadelphia and offered Lajoie "the largest salary ever paid to a ball player, the contract calling for a term of years," Somers's lawyers first having satisfied themselves that the injunction against Lajoie applied only in Pennsylvania. After several days of consideration, Lajoie agreed to sign with Cleveland, as did Bill Bernhard. Lajoie played his first game for

Cleveland on June 4. For the rest of the 1902 season. Lajoie had to make himself scarce when Cleveland came to Philadelphia to play. Rumor had it that Napoleon cruised on down to Atlantic City.[7]

As apparent recompense for his allowing Flick, Lajoie, and Bernhard to go to Cleveland, Mack on May 23 signed catcher Ossie Schreckengost, released by Cleveland. On June 11 he signed Cleveland team captain Frank Bonner, the erstwhile second baseman who was made wholly superfluous by the arrival of Lajoie.

With the signing of Lajoie and Bernhard by Cleveland, the flurry of litigation died away, with the exception of an unsuccessful effort by the Phillies to have their injunctions enforced by an Ohio court. With ballpark crowds down, one writer said, "That the public, the court of last resort, is heartily weary of the present complications is shown in the attendances all over the country." This was a message that the baseball magnates could and did read.[8]

The year 1902 turned out, in spite of the victory in the Supreme Court, to be just about as bad for the Phillies as it looked before the season began. They finished seventh, while the Athletics won the American League pennant and outdrew them, 442,000 to 112,000. (In fact, the A's easily outdrew everyone in both leagues.)

For the Athletics, it was a wildly successful year, despite the shock with which it began. Mack received good production from several areas. Davis at first base hit .307, and Lave Cross at third hit .342. Shortstop Monte Cross batted .231 and played well in the field.

Second base was a problem after Lajoie's sudden departure. Rookie Jud Castro, a native of Colombia, played the position for a while, until Bonner came over from Cleveland. Bonner, though, was a great disappointment, batting only .182 in his brief stint. In mid-season, Mack purchased the contract of Danny Murphy, a local boy, who had been with the New York Giants in 1900 and 1901 and was tearing up the Connecticut League in early 1902. Murphy made his debut on July 8, and he did it with a flair, banging out six hits in six at-bats, including a grand slam home run. Murphy was not the fielder at second base that Lajoie was, and he was certainly not Napoleon's equal as a hitter, though he did average .313 for the A's in 1902. Nevertheless, he was far better than anyone else they tried at second base after the Frenchman, and he solidified Mack's infield.

Across the outfield the A's had Socks Seybold, who led the league with 16 home runs, Dave Fultz, and little Topsy Hartsel, a 5'5" speedster from the Chicago Nationals whose 47 stolen bases were high for the league. Behind the plate Schreckengost took over the bulk of the duties from Powers, and the pitching was led by Eddie Plank, with a record of 20-15, and a strange young lefthander named George Edward Waddell, known as "Rube," who won 24 and lost 7.

Born in western Pennsylvania in 1876, Waddell was probably mentally handicapped, although baseball charitably called him "eccentric" or "carefree," at least as long as he pitched well. One longtime observer said Waddell "lived as his emotions told him to live, without much thought of the consequences."[9]

Sam Crawford, who played with Rube in the Western League, told of Waddell pouring ice water on his pitching arm. "I've got so much speed today," he would say, "I'll burn up the catcher's glove if I don't let up a bit." He would then go over to the water barrel in the dugout, dip the ladle in, and pour ice water over his left arm and shoulder. "That's to slow me down a little," he'd say, and then he would take the mound and start firing. "How good he'd have been if he'd taken baseball seriously," Crawford said, "is hard to imagine."[10]

"I believed that Rube, a kindly fellow, could be persuaded to concentrate his great abilities on the game," Mack said, having handled him at Milwaukee in 1900, so he bought the southpaw's contract. Waddell was pitching in California when Mack acquired him, and he showed little interest in coming back east until Mack sent a couple of Pinkerton detectives to bring his new pitcher to Philadelphia.[11]

In each of his six seasons with the A's, Rube led the league in strikeouts, and he won 96 games his first four years in Philadelphia. He had a blazing fastball, a sharp curve, and good control, although he was a very bad fielder. Nevertheless, no one was ever able to predict when Waddell's cravings for booze, women, fishing, and fire engines were likely to cause his disappearance. At one time he took it into his head to take up alligator wrestling. There were occasional hints, although nothing was ever substantiated, that he was sometimes controlled by gamblers. Connie Mack displayed more patience with the erratic southpaw than any other manager he worked for, but even Mack's patience had a limit.

Besides the contributions of Plank and Waddell, the champion Athletics got 14 wins from Pete Husting, a former football and baseball star at the University of Wisconsin, seven from local boy Howard "Highball" Wilson, and five from Fred Mitchell, obtained early in the season from Boston. Another pitcher named Lewis "Snake" Wiltse won eight games before he was sent to Baltimore at mid-season.[12]

The club even picked up an icon, courtesy of John McGraw. Midway through the 1902 season McGraw deserted the faltering Baltimore Orioles in the new league and hooked up with the New York Giants. From his new vantage point with the old establishment, McGraw told the press that Shibe, in Philadelphia, would find that he had a "white elephant" on his hands. Mack quickly adopted the White Elephant as the symbol of his club. It was an enduring symbol, one which lasted as long as the Macks owned the franchise and can still be found on the sleeves of the present-day Oakland Athletics. In 1902 it provided a rallying point for Mack and his team as they fought for the pennant.

Early in the season, the Athletics bounced into and out of first place several times, exchanging the position with the St. Louis Browns. In June Charles Comiskey's White Stockings took the lead and held it for some time, opening a gap of several games. But the Athletics, with Murphy's bat leading the way, stayed close. Once Waddell arrived he won game after game to put them at the top. Calm and steady, Connie Mack had patiently put his club back together and kept it winning ball games.

Heading into the September home stretch, the Athletics held a slim lead as they struggled through a tough western trip. They lost two straight doubleheaders at St. Louis, and after the second of these, on Labor Day, their lead was only a half-game over the Browns and one game over Boston. Even Waddell, "the Rube," as he was called in the papers, was beaten, and this did not happen often in 1902. ("With the Rube in there was one game that looked to be cinched.") Still, as one reporter put it, "That bunch of Connie's is out for the flag, and they are not to be stayed because of a couple of reverses."[13]

Besides, the Browns were using underhanded tactics, it was inferred; Mack thought he spotted a man sitting in front of the centerfield scoreboard giving signals to the St. Louis batters. "Such a contemptible, tin horn trick has no place in legitimate base ball," complained the *Inquirer*'s correspondent; "square sportsmen never play with marked cards."[14]

The A's had another reverse in store; at 4:35 in the morning of September 2, the train carrying the team from St. Louis to Detroit collided with a freight train near the Wabash River. No one was injured but many were shaken up, and they all had a long wait in the dark before the trip could be resumed. When the Athletics straggled onto the field at Bennett Park in Detroit that afternoon, the *Inquirer* noted that "they were a pretty woebegone set of athletes." Nonetheless, they regrouped for a five-run seventh inning and won the game, 5-1, behind Waddell.[15]

Two more wins at Detroit were followed by a 10-7 loss at Cleveland, with Howard Wilson taking it on the chin. The Athletics still held just that half-game lead over St. Louis and two games over Boston. On September 6, Waddell hooked up in a battle with the Cleveland Bronchos' sensational rookie Addie Joss and came out on top when the Athletics put together a Hartsel walk and successive hits by Fultz, Davis, and Lave Cross for three sixth-inning runs and a 3-2 victory.

After an off-day on Sunday the 7th, the Rube beat Cleveland again on the 8th, 8-5, and the Athletics headed home from their western trip with a two-game lead over the Browns and Boston. Connie Mack exulted: "Those Western clubs lay in wait for us. They made up their minds to drive us from first place, but we fooled them." A large and enthusiastic crowd greeted Mack and his men at the Broad Street Station, and no one was happier than Ben Shibe, who said the club's position was "the result of clean, honest ball playing."[16]

Mack was happy to be home, but he knew he was not home free. Pete Husting, it was said, had caught a cold in his pitching arm standing around in the night air the evening of the train wreck, so the club was now juggling Plank and Waddell and trying to get what it could out of Wilson, Mitchell, and the ailing Husting. Seven games remained with Jimmy Collins's Boston Americans, and they could decide the race.

The Athletics swept two doubleheaders from Baltimore, Plank and Wilson each winning a game and Waddell winning two in relief, with Topsy Hartsel contributing a game-saving catch in the outfield. Then it was off to Boston for three important games.

On the 13th, before a crowd that included art collector and Boston society leader Isabella Stewart Gardner, the famous "Mrs. Jack," Waddell lost to Cy Young, 5-4, as Buck Freeman singled home the winning run with two out in the ninth, cutting the Philadelphia lead to three games.

Rain on Saturday the 14th forced a postponement, but good news came in from the shores of Lake Erie, where Cleveland took two games from St. Louis. A glum Jimmy McAleer, manager of the Browns, admitted that the pennant would likely go to Philadelphia. The Athletics made this a little surer on the 16th, when they took two from Boston. Plank beat Bill Dinneen 6-4 in the opener, and Waddell beat Young 9-2 in the second game. This result left the lead over the Browns at four games, with Boston one game further back.

Three wins over Washington, behind Wilson, Plank, and a rookie called Jack McAllister (an assumed name for a pitcher who turned out later to be Andy Coakley), had the *Inquirer* promoting a mammoth parade to celebrate the coming championship.

On September 20, the Boston Americans came to Philadelphia for four games they had to win to stay in contention, but the Athletics were in no mood to let up. Waddell beat Cy Young again, 6-4, in the opener, as Danny Murphy drove in the two runs to win it in the eighth. The next day a huge crowd of 23,897 packed Columbia Park, and Eddie Plank pitched the White Elephants to a 7-2 win over Tully Sparks.[17]

After the usual Sunday off (required by Pennsylvania law, which barred the playing of professional baseball on the Lord's Day), the two teams met again in a Monday doubleheader. Dinneen bested the rookie McAllister 5-1 in the first game. Not to be denied in the nightcap, Rube Waddell beat Nick Altrock 5-3 before 16,922 happy fans. With a five-game lead over St. Louis, the Athletics were now almost there; Boston slipped to fourth place behind the White Sox.

Plank beat Baltimore, 4-2, the next day, and a reporter wrote, "That flag is as good as won. Mr. Shibe might as well order the pole." On September 25, the Athletics won two more from the Orioles and clinched their pennant. McAllister won the first game, and Wilson won the clincher, 5-4. In the ninth inning, with the score tied, ex-Athletic Snake Wiltse walked Hartsel and Fultz, and little Topsy scored the winning run on a wild pitch. Philadelphia had its first champion since the old Athletics, related in name only to Mack's team, had won the American Association pennant in 1883.[18]

Ben Shibe said, "The boys made a magnificent showing against great odds." Referring to the stunning setback when the club lost Lajoie, Fraser, Duggleby, Bernhard, and Flick, he said, "Broken up at the beginning of the season, they pulled themselves together and played ball the like of which has never been seen in this city." Connie Mack said simply, "Just say for me that we tried and we landed."[19]

Given the circumstances, Mack's managing job in 1902 was one of the best ever. He had to rebuild his team on the run, overcoming the adverse court decision which took away two Hall of Famers in the prime of their careers and his two best pitchers. There were many strange seasons, many losing seasons, in the long years ahead, but in 1902 Connie Mack was a great manager.

On the night of September 29, a huge parade, with local ball clubs, marching bands, and marching citizens, moved down Broad Street from Girard Avenue to Vine. The focus of attention for the cheering thousands along the sidewalks was the group of carriages bearing Waddell, Plank, Seybold, Hartsel, and the other Athletics. For their adoring fans, it made little difference that the baseball war prevented any showdown with the Pittsburgh Pirates, winners of the other league. The Athletics were the toast of Philadelphia. They were the champions.

CHAPTER 3

Top Dogs

Peace came to the major leagues after the 1902 season when the National League recognized that it could not continue a war which it was clearly losing. An agreement between the two leagues was concluded early in 1903. A National Commission, consisting of the two league presidents and Cincinnati president Garry Herrmann, was set up to oversee the operation of the game. Herrmann, while a National League clubowner, was actually closer to Ban Johnson, who became the most powerful figure in baseball for many years to come.

Unable to repeat their 1902 success, in 1903 the Athletics finished a distant second to Jimmy Collins's Boston club. Thus Boston became the first American League representative in the modern World Series. Plank won 23 and Waddell 21, but each lost 16 as well.

The most noteworthy addition to Connie Mack's team was a 20-year-old righthander named Charles Albert Bender. One-fourth Chippewa Indian and a product of the Carlisle Indian School and Dickinson College, Bender was known as "Chief." To all, that is, except Connie Mack, who always called him "Albert," and who frequently called him "my greatest clutch pitcher." Rube Bressler, who pitched for the A's a few years later, called Bender "one of the kindest and finest men who ever lived." The Chief, in 1903, won 17 and lost 15.[1] In 1904 Mack's team slipped to fifth place with 81 victories and 70 defeats. Waddell won 25 and lost 19, Plank was 26-16, Weldon Henley was 15-17, and young Bender won ten and lost 11. Waddell set a seasonal record of 349 strikeouts that lasted for 61 years until broken by Sandy Koufax in 1965.

The dependable Chief Bender (National Baseball Hall of Fame Library, Coop-erstown, N.Y.).

Harry Davis was Mack's only .300 hitter, and he led the league with ten home runs. But the departed Lajoie had a splendid year for Cleveland, hitting .381 and leading the league in batting, hits, doubles, total bases, and runs driven in. Second baseman Danny Murphy hit .287 with seven home runs for the A's, but they could have made good use of the big Frenchman.

Even finishing 12⅓ games out of first, the Athletics reached a new high in attendance, drawing 512,294 paying customers. This figure was far more than the Phillies could draw; their attendance dropped to 140,771 as they fell into last place.

The following year the Phillies moved up to fourth place, but the favorites of the Quaker City in 1905 were Connie Mack's White Elephants. The Athletics of 1903 and 1904 had been disappointments, but the fans who had fallen in love with the champions of 1902 had high hopes of another flag.

Still, it looked like a dogfight, and it turned out to be one. Boston, under the guidance of third baseman Jimmy Collins, had won two straight pennants. With their pitching staff led by the redoubtable Cy Young, Boston was confident. The resurgent Chicago White Sox under Fielder Jones had little power, but their pitching, featuring ex-Phillie Doc White and a youngster named Ed Walsh, put them in contention. And Cleveland still had Napoleon Lajoie, now the club's manager, Elmer Flick, Harry "Deerfoot" Bay, and a young pitching star named Addie Joss.

Indeed, it was the Cleveland Naps who built up a big lead through May and June. However, just as visions of a pennant started dancing over League Park, disaster struck the front-runners. On July 1, Lajoie was spiked on his left foot, and the dye from his colored stocking caused an infection which turned into blood poisoning. Suddenly doctors were talking about the possibility of amputation, and Napoleon was coming to games in a wheelchair. The infection cleared up, but Lajoie was effectively through for the season. With their great second baseman gone, and with subsequent injuries to Flick, Joss, Bill Bradley, and Bay, the Naps fell below the other contenders, as the Athletics surged into the lead on August 2. Lajoie tried a comeback at the end of August, playing four games against the Athletics. He was far below form, and his efforts were unable to prevent a sweep by the Mackmen; Cleveland fell 8½ behind.

Boston could not mount any threat, as Cy Young slumped to a record of 18-19, but the White Sox were another story. Fielder Jones's team battled the Athletics tooth-and-nail through September, and by the 28th they were in a virtual tie for first place with the A's as they arrived in Philadelphia for three games.

Mack had a solid aggregation awaiting the invaders from Chicago. Harry Davis, the club's leading hitter, held down first base; his eight home runs led the league for the second year in a row, and he also led in runs batted in, with 83. Danny Murphy played at second and Lave Cross at third. The veteran Monte Cross wound up with the job at shortstop. Socks Seybold, Danny Hoffman, and Topsy Hartsel manned the outfield, with rookie Bris Lord, the elegantly named Bristol Robotham Lord, in reserve. Ossie Schreckengost did the catching; Schreckengost roomed with Waddell and, legend has it, forced the club to put a clause in the Rube's contract forbidding him to eat crackers in the bed they shared.

The 1905 Athletics had great pitching. This was the deadball era, and good pitching abounded; still, the Athletics' staff was exceptional. The eccentric Waddell was the leader, finishing with a 26-11 record and an earned run average of 1.48. Plank was right behind him, with 25 and 12, and young Andy Coakley, from Holy Cross College, won 20 and lost only 7, with an ERA of 1.84. Behind these three came Chief Bender, who was 16-10. Weldon Henley, who won 27 games for Mack the two previous seasons, won only four and lost 12. But he gave up fewer than three runs a game, and his 6-0 win over the Browns on July 22 was a no-hit game, the first ever for the Athletics.

The most serious problem confronting Connie Mack as the crucial series began was the absence of Waddell. Early in September, Rube engaged in a scuffle with Coakley and injured his pitching arm. There were hopes for his early recovery, but he could not pitch against Chicago. Even without Waddell, however, Mack had two other future Hall of Famers to throw at the Sox.

Plank subdued the visitors by a 3-2 score on Thursday, to give Philadelphia the league lead by a game over the White Sox, and Bender won 11-1 the next day to stretch the lead to two games. Even though they lost to Chicago on Saturday, Plank going down 4-3 before a turnaway crowd of 25,187, the Athletics held a one-game lead with eight to go.[2]

The best news to come out of Saturday's events was "a good work-out" by Waddell, with the Rube reporting no pain. A skeptical Connie Mack, who had heard that before, put on a mitt and caught a few of Waddell's pitches himself. He decided that he would try to use Waddell briefly in one of the remaining games.[3]

After the obligatory Sunday off, the A's took on Jimmy McAleer's last-place Browns on Monday afternoon and beat them 5-0 on Andy Coakley's shutout pitching. Coakley, a reporter said, "has pitched uniformly good ball all season, and ranks as the Athletics' winning pitcher."[4] Davis hit a two-run homer, and Seybold's triple in a three-run seventh inning nailed down the win. At Washington, the White Sox lost, 3-2, and the Philadelphia lead was increased to two games. The Athletics beat the Browns on Tuesday, 5-2, behind Henley, and again on Wednesday, 4-1 with Plank, in the team's last home game. Chicago won both days as well, but the White Sox were running out of games, trailing by two with only five left.

On October 5, Chicago was idle, but the Athletics won two from Washington on a blue-ribbon day for Chief Bender. The Chief won the first game, 8-0, scattering seven hits. When Coakley struggled in the nightcap, Mack pinch-hit Bender for him in the third inning. Bender tripled and scored and then told the manager that his arm felt so good he could finish the game on the mound. He did so and won it by a 9-7 score. "One more victory," wrote the *Inquirer* reporter, "and then for the Giants and the world's championship!"[5]

The next day, October 6, Fred Glade of the Browns beat Chicago by the score of 6-2, and the pennant for Connie Mack and his men became official. The Athletics lost, 10-4, at Washington, but most interest centered on Rube Waddell when he relieved Coakley in the third inning. In his brief appearance, Waddell was wild, not unusual after a long layoff.

The following day Waddell started the first game of the final doubleheader at Washington but departed after the first inning; "it was evident ... that he was not right," wrote one reporter.[6] With his injured arm still not fully recovered, Rube Waddell could not be counted on for the world championship series against John McGraw's New York Giants.

Mack and his champions were greeted on their arrival home by a big crowd at Broad Street Station. The fans buzzed with anticipation over the upcoming series with the Giants and the manager who had sneered at the A's as "white elephants." New York was the betting favorite. The first game was scheduled for October 9 at Columbia Park, with Plank to start against Christy Mathewson. "It should be a fight to the bitter end," wrote the baseball man for the *Public Ledger*.[7] A big crowd was anticipated, even though ticket prices had been raised to 50 cents in the bleachers, $1 for general admission, and $2 for reserved seats.

"Never in the long history of the national game has there been such universal interest manifested in a series of games as there is in the coming clash," wrote one fevered observer.[8] In addition to the baseball championship at stake, it was the city of Philadelphia against arrogant, overbearing New York, and it was kindly Connie Mack against rowdy John McGraw and his swaggering Giants. Philadelphia supporters vied with New York adherents to get money down on their favorite team.

When Lave Cross and McGraw met with the umpires to present lineup cards, Cross gave McGraw a package "which, when unwrapped, proved to be an effigy of a white elephant." As the crowd roared with laughter, McGraw placed the elephant on his head.[9]

McGraw had a surprise of his own for the Athletics: the Giants appeared in special black uniforms, with white "NY" lettering. More importantly for the Giants, they put Christy Mathewson into one of them. Plank pitched a good game in the opener but he was no match for McGraw's ace, who won it, 3-0. The Philadelphia hitters, the *Public Ledger* man wrote, "were as clay in the hands of that pitching marvel, Mathewson."[10]

The next day, though, the same reporter could write, "Great is Bender. Mighty his arm, cunning his skill, inspiring his name."[11] For the Chief matched Mathewson's four-hit shutout with one of his own, defeating the Giants at the Polo Grounds by an identical 3-0 score. Bris Lord drove in two runs as the Athletics evened the series, defeating Joe McGinnity. Rain the next day put off Game Three, back in Philadelphia, for a day, to October 12.

The third game, though, was no contest. The A's committed five errors, three of them costly ones by Danny Murphy, and the Giants scored nine runs (only two earned) against Coakley. The errors hardly mattered, for "Big Six," Christy Mathewson, was on the hill again for New York, and he held the Athletics to four hits and no runs once again.

The two teams went back at it the next day at the Polo Grounds, with Eddie Plank facing McGinnity. "Poor Plank," wrote the *Ledger* correspondent. "His superior work merited a better result." In the fourth inning, Monte Cross fumbled a ground ball, and his error led to a run. This run loomed larger and larger as the game went on. In the top of the eighth, Hartsel led off with a walk, but Lord lined out after failing to get a bunt down. After Davis popped up to third, Lave Cross hit a single that could have scored Hartsel had he been on second base. It was the major threat for the A's, but Seybold stranded the two runners, and when the Mackmen were blanked in the ninth, McGinnity had his 1-0 victory. The Giants had a 3-1 stranglehold on the series.[12]

On the 14th, again at the Polo Grounds, Mathewson threw his third shutout of the series at the A's, winning 2-0 to wrap up the title for the Giants. Bender pitched an excellent game, but a touch of wildness led to two New York runs, and they were all Mathewson needed. The world championship crown settled upon the heads of McGraw and his New Yorkers, and the Athletics went home to lick their wounds.

Afterwards, a Philadelphia reporter wrote, "Too much importance cannot be given to the fact that the Athletics entered the series in the poorest form they had shown during the season. While no one was actually incapacitated by reason of injury save Waddell, the great mental and physical exhaustion that followed the severe fight necessary to win the American League pennant left the players almost a wreck in every respect."[13] Perhaps. This litany was repeated down through the years by A's supporters as the reason for the loss of the 1905 World Series. The reason may be a simpler one: the Athletics were overmatched by a Christy Mathewson at the peak of his powers.

CHAPTER 4

Interlude, 1906–1908

In 1906 Mack's team was in the chase most of the year and in fact led the league until August. A slump then coincided with a 19-game winning streak by Fielder Jones's Chicago White Sox—a group known to history as "the Hitless Wonders"[1]—and the A's ultimately fell to fourth place. Harry Davis led the league with 12 home runs and 96 runs batted in, and Seybold and Murphy hit over .300, but as a whole the team did not hit well.

The pitching staff fell off considerably—Waddell's total of wins dropped from 26 to 15, Plank's from 25 to 19, and Coakley's from 20 to 7. Chief Bender held up his part with 15 wins. Mack unveiled a new righthanded pitcher, a collegian named Jack Coombs from Colby College in Maine who went 10-10 and gave promise of good things to come.

Two more youngsters who would have an impact made their first appearances for the Athletics in 1906. One was a 22-year-old New Yorker named Rube Oldring, who hit .241 in 59 games, mostly at third base. He seemed to be nothing special. When Mack switched him to center field the next season, however, Oldring found a regular position he would hold a long time. He had speed and a quick bat, and he was a keeper.

The other newcomer was a slightly built kid who played football at Columbia. He appeared in six games for the A's under the name of Eddie Sullivan, in a vain effort to preserve his amateur status for the Lions of Morningside Heights. They caught on to him anyway, and he played no more football. When next he played for the Athletics, he did it under his own name, Eddie Collins.

Collins later told the story that he had been playing ball at Platts-burg, New York, in the outlaw Northern League in the summer of 1906, when a scout for the Athletics talked him into going to New York to meet with Connie Mack. When he did so, Mack signed him for the fol-lowing year and then suggested he join the Athletics for a couple of weeks to "get an idea of big league atmosphere." When Collins showed up at the Athletics office Mack leaped up, shouted, "Hello, Sullivan!" and pushed the mystified young man back through the door. There was a writer who covered college baseball in the office, and Mack did not want Collins recognized. Ironically, the reporter never saw Collins, but Columbia took away his eligibility because he had played at Plattsburg, not for the A's. To the Athletics players, though, he was Sullivan; Collins said "the following year I had a hard time convincing Socks Seybold and Murphy that it wasn't my right name."[2]

Not until 1908 did Collins settle in as a regular at second base, where he would play a total of 2650 games over 21 years, becoming in the process one of the all-time greats. Nicknamed "Cocky," because he was smart and self-assured, he had the physical ability to do whatever had to be done and the confidence that he would do it. He stood close to the plate, seldom swung at a bad pitch, and hit to all parts of the field. His natural talents combined with his intelligence and quickness made Collins a great player.

Over his long career Eddie Collins achieved a lifetime batting aver-age of .333, with 3311 base hits and 743 stolen bases. In addition, he won universal respect as a man of character and quality. When he played for the 1919 Chicago Black Sox, the crooks and fixers knew enough to stay far away from Eddie Collins.

When his playing days were about over, Collins came back to Philadelphia and worked as a coach for Connie Mack for several sea-sons. In 1933, when Thomas A. Yawkey bought the Boston Red Sox, he asked Eddie Collins to serve as his vice-president and general manager. Collins remained with Yawkey and the Sox until his death in 1951. In the meantime, he was elected to the Hall of Fame in 1939.

The Athletics were back in the pennant race in 1907. In late Sep-tember, they were locked in a struggle with Detroit, the White Sox, and Cleveland. It finally boiled down to Mack's team and the Tigers of Hughie Jennings, tied for the lead as Detroit came into Columbia Park for a three-game series on September 27. The Tigers were led by their sensational young outfielder, Ty Cobb, veteran Wahoo Sam Crawford, the great leadoff man Davy Jones, and pitchers Wild Bill Donovan, Ed Killian, and George Mullin.

The Athletics' hitting strength was spread among Davis, who led the league once again in home runs (his fourth year in succession), Murphy, Seybold, old-timer Jimmy Collins (obtained from Boston in June), Oldring, and a journeyman infielder named Simon Nicholls, who had the only good year of his career, hitting .302 to lead the club. Nicholls, a Maryland farmer, filled in at second while Murphy was injured and then replaced Monte Cross at shortstop. Bender and Coombs had arm trouble in September, and Waddell was ineffective, but Plank and young Jimmy Dygert, a slim spitball specialist from Utica, each won more than 20 games.

The first game of the crucial series with Detroit went to the Tigers as Wild Bill Donovan outpitched Plank, 5-4. The game scheduled for the 28th was rained out, and a doubleheader was put on the books for Monday. More than 24,000 people crammed into Columbia Park, where they spilled over into the outfield, held back by a rope from the field of play.

Dygert opened the first game, and the Athletics took an early 7-1 lead over Donovan, pitching on short rest. When Dygert booted a couple of balls in the second inning, Mack took him out in favor of Waddell. The Tigers crept back against the Rube, getting four runs in the seventh when errors by Oldring and Nicholls were followed by Crawford's ground-rule double into the roped-off crowd. Detroit was within two runs. The A's scored one in the seventh, and the Tigers matched it in the eighth. Crawford led off the ninth with a single, and Cobb then belted a homer over the right-field wall to tie the score. Legend has it that Connie Mack was so keyed up that he fell off the bench on Cobb's blow. Plank replaced Waddell, while Donovan continued on the mound for the visitors.

Both teams scored runs in the tenth, but the game was still tied when Harry Davis led off the bottom of the 14th with a long fly to center. The ball landed in the crowd behind the ropes, but Crawford got tangled up with a policeman in trying to make the catch and umpire Silk O'Loughlin ruled Davis out because of spectator interference.

The Philadelphia players and fans were outraged, and even Connie Mack protested. (It was years before he spoke to umpire O'Loughlin again.) Fighting broke out on the field. Donovan and first baseman Claude Rossman traded punches with Waddell (now in street clothes) and Monte Cross, and the police arrested Rossman and hauled him out of the park. Nevertheless, Davis was still out. When order was restored, Murphy hit a solid single which would have scored Davis had he been on second, where the A's felt he rightfully belonged. The game proceeded on to a 17-inning tie, called on account of darkness, and of course the nightcap was canceled as well.

The Tigers, with the win and a tie, left town in first place and moved on to Washington, where they swept a four-game series. The Athletics won two games from Cleveland, but when they lost to Walter Johnson at Washington while Detroit was beating the Browns, the Tigers clinched the pennant. The Athletics won no championship, but they had the satisfaction of setting a club record for attendance in 1907, drawing 625,581 fans to Columbia Park.

The A's attendance was way down the next year, to 455,602, as the team dropped to sixth place, with a losing record of 68-85. Mack tired of trying to handle Waddell and shipped him off to the Browns. A journeyman righthander named Rube Vickers led the staff with a record of 18-19. Plank won 14, Dygert 11, and Bender only eight, as the club trailed the league in hitting with a .223 team average.

Schreckengost was sold late in the season to Chicago, and Mack started working younger players, like Collins, rookie shortstop Jack Barry, another collegian out of Holy Cross, and a farm kid from Maryland named Frank Baker into his lineup.

Baker was a shy, quiet, very strong young man who swung a bat that weighed an incredible 52 ounces. A lefthanded hitter, Baker had a good 1908 season for Reading in the Tri-State League with Mack bringing him up for nine games at season's end. Baker was an uneven fielding third baseman, but there was never any doubt that the young man could hit. In 1909, his first full season, Frank Baker led the American League with 19 triples. Over a 13-year major league career he batted .307.

It was a good thing for Connie Mack that he had the future development of young men like Collins, Baker, and Barry to look forward to, for his 1908 White Elephants were none too inspiring. Davis, Hartsel, Murphy, Jimmy Collins, Oldring, Schreckengost—all had off years with the bat, making for a long season. Uptown, though, Ben Shibe's pet project—a new ballpark—was coming along nicely, promising to combine with Mack's youngsters to give the Athletics an exciting future.

CHAPTER 5

Shibe Park and
the First Dynasty

The new American League team was making a lot of money. Ben Shibe's reluctant investment was paying off very nicely, and his partnership with the soft-spoken Cornelius McGillicuddy was working out well. The division of responsibilities among Shibe, who stuck with the sporting goods business, his sons Tom and John, who ran the business end of the franchise, and Connie Mack, who took care of the baseball team, resulted in each doing what he was most comfortable doing.

Once the war between the National League and the interloping Americans ended, there was little to stand in the way of a well-run baseball team making money. The Athletics put good, exciting squads on the field and as a result had excellent attendance figures. The Shibes made a tidy profit—from 1902 to 1913 they made almost $350,000—and Mack himself did well. In 1906 his salary was a handsome $15,000, and he tacked on to that each year his share of the club's profits.

It was time, Ben Shibe decided, for a new ballpark. The wooden park at 29th and Columbia had seen its best days, and there was new technology available for an up-to-date stadium. The development of reinforced concrete—steel rods embedded in concrete—permitted the building of a structure of great strength at a reasonable cost. As a bonus, the Athletics' new park would be fireproof; no longer would there be the ever-present danger of fire as with ballparks made of wood.

On a site farther up town, between two areas rather informally called Swampoodle and Goosetown, Shibe planned a new steel-and-concrete ballpark, covering an entire city block bounded by Lehigh Avenue, 20th Street, Somerset Street, and the extension of 21st Street. Since trolleys ran up Broad Street and over Lehigh Avenue, and both the Reading Railroad and the mighty Pennsylvania had stations nearby, spectators could easily reach the new park. The city's Hospital for Contagious Diseases, the dreaded "smallpox hospital," was a block away on Lehigh Avenue—not a very nice neighbor for a ballpark to which one hoped to attract large crowds of people—but Shibe had learned that the city was planning to close the dilapidated facility, which it did in June 1909.

The neighborhood surrounding the proposed new ballpark was one of small working-class rowhomes, with an immigrant blue-collar population composed primarily of Irish with smaller numbers of people of English, German, and Italian extraction. Among the salient features of the area were Saint Columba's Church, at 24th and Lehigh, the Freihofer bakery, and a plethora of saloons.

Ben Shibe started quietly putting together title to his square block early in 1907. He picked up the parcels of land through a complicated series of acquisitions, preventing price inflation by masking his intentions and paying a total of $67,500. In February 1908 he arranged to strike from the city plan two paper streets which ran through the block, and in April he broke ground.

Under the aegis of the building firm William Steele and Sons, a pioneer in the erection of steel-and-concrete buildings, construction proceeded rapidly. The facade of the park was done in an ornate French Renaissance style, complete with arches, vaultings, and Ionic columns. The walls were brick with terra-cotta ornamentation.[1]

The most striking feature of all was an octangular tower topped with a dome at the 21st and Lehigh corner of the building, behind where home plate would be located. This tower housed the Athletics' offices in its upper levels, and on the ground floor it served as an elegant main entrance lobby for customers entering the park. Carved into the front of the tower, about 30 feet above street level, was the name of the new facility: SHIBE PARK. Bobby Shantz, a latter-day Athletic, wrote that the park's "entrance behind home plate looked almost like a church."[2]

A young fan several decades later remembered his first venture into

Shibe Park, "into the most beautiful sight I'd ever seen." The ballpark, he said, "was totally green. Besides the greenest grass ever seen anywhere, it had green seats and olive-green walls, unadulterated by advertising. The color scheme was in fact broken only by crisp white numbers, 331 in right, 334 in left, and 468 in dead center. Perfect."[3]

Shibe Park was the first concrete-and-steel baseball park, a splendid forerunner of others like it. It would soon be followed by seven more, all privately financed: Wrigley Field and the original Comiskey Park in Chicago, Fenway Park in Boston, Forbes Field in Pittsburgh, Ebbets Field and the Polo Grounds in New York City, and Navin Field (later Briggs, now Tiger, Stadium) in Detroit. Ben Shibe and the Steeles initiated the "golden age of ball parks."

The new park's listed capacity of 20,500 dwarfed the 13,600 of Columbia Park; the only reminder of the club's former home was the transplanted sod. Construction of his new park cost Shibe $301,000, but he had no doubt that the erection of the facility was "a shrewd business move." At the end of the first season in Shibe Park, 1909, attendance had jumped from 455,000 to 675,000, a Philadelphia record.[4]

The first game played in Shibe Park was on April 12, 1909, with the Boston Red Sox helping the locals to open the season. After noon, the gates were unlocked, and a huge crowd of more than 30,000 poured into the park. The roofs of houses on 20th Street, overlooking the low right field wall, were filled with onlookers (and a new Philadelphia business was born). It would not be long before the homeowners would put up bleachers on their roofs, a source of friction and contention with the club management for years to come.

Mayor John E. Reyburn, who called the new park a "pride to the city," threw out the first ball, and at about 3:00 p.m. the game began.[5] Eddie Plank was in full command that day easily subduing the visitors from Boston, 8-1. A new era for Philadelphia and the Athletics had begun.

First, though, there was tragedy. The opening-day catcher for the A's was 38-year-old Michael "Doc" Powers, who had been with the club since its creation. After going 1-for-4 in the game, Powers was rushed to Northwestern General Hospital with an intestinal infection. Over the next two weeks his condition steadily worsened, as peritonitis developed and three operations failed to arrest his sharp decline. On April 26, to the shock and consternation of the city and all of baseball, the popular Doc Powers died.

Putting the Powers tragedy behind them, the young Athletics set about making their mark on the 1909 pennant race. Mack's team had not been figured as a contender. At best it was an unknown quantity, and some observers even consigned the A's to the cellar. A seasoned and aggressive Detroit team, led by stars like Cobb, Crawford, Donie Bush, and George Mullin, under manager Hughie Jennings, was looking ahead to the World Series, where it had been a loser each of the prior two years. But Connie Mack's A's would give the Tigers all they could handle.

Mack switched Danny Murphy to the outfield and installed young Eddie Collins at second base. He revamped the left side of his infield by giving the shortstop job to Jack Barry, the speedy youngster from Holy Cross, and third base to Frank Baker. Collins hit .326 as a regular, Baker hit .305, and Barry hit in the clutch and played good shortstop. Murphy batted .281 as a regular outfielder. The veteran Harry Davis continued at first base with the catching handled by Ira Thomas and Paddy Livingston.

Mack's pitching was outstanding, as he got strong work from Plank, Bender, and a rookie lefthander named Harry Krause. The three of them, along with Cy Morgan, a spitballer picked up from Boston, had earned run averages under two. Krause's 1.39 led the league. Plank had a record of 19-10, Bender and Krause were each at 18-8, Morgan won 16 and lost 11 and Jack Coombs was 12-11.

The Athletics held the American League lead into late August. The Tigers moved past them in a hard-fought series in Detroit in which the dangerous Cobb spiked Baker, cutting him on the forearm, and later knocked over Collins at second base. An angry Mack called Cobb the dirtiest player in baseball history. Jennings retorted that Mack was a "squealer." Baker was not seriously injured, but the Athletics' pennant hopes were, as Detroit won the first game, 7-6, the second game, 4-3, when Donovan outpitched Plank, and the finale, 6-0, behind Mullin.

On September 16, the swaggering Tigers came into Shibe Park for a four-game series. Still only four games behind, the Athletics had hopes of catching the front-runners. The Philadelphia fans turned out in huge numbers for this series, in part because of the exciting pennant race, in part to vent their feelings upon the hated Ty Cobb. Passions had been pumped up by a series of inflammatory articles about Cobb by the *Bulletin*'s Horace Fogel. The Tiger star received several death threats with the result that he was escorted to and from the park by police bodyguards.[6]

Eddie Plank won the series opener for the A's by a 2-1 score. In the second game, Detroit ace Mullin beat the rookie Krause, as the Tigers stole seven bases. When Cobb stole third, Baker shook his hand, easing the explosive tension and terminating the so-called feud.

Mack sent Bender out for game three and was rewarded with a 2-0 victory; Plank's 4-3 win in the final game cut Detroit's lead to two games. Momentum seemed to be riding with the Athletics, until they lost their next game, to the woeful St. Louis Browns, and saw the Tigers' lead go back to 2½ games. The A's could get no closer in the remaining few games, and they finally finished second, 3½ games behind Detroit. Nevertheless, the Athletics had served notice that they would be contenders in the future.

Mack and his team opened the 1910 season in Washington, in a game attended by President William Howard Taft. The portly chief executive honored the game of baseball by throwing out the first ball, setting a precedent which was followed by his successors until the expansion Senators deserted Washington after the 1971 season. Inspired perhaps by the presidential presence, the Senators' Walter Johnson held the Athletics to one hit in posting a 1-0 victory. The defeat was hardly an indicator of things to come for the Athletics, however, as Mack's team proceeded to roll over the rest of the American League.

The Athletics started slowly but took the league lead in the first week of May. The New York Highlanders went into first place briefly in the second week of June, but the A's soon built up a commanding lead and never looked back.

They were shown the way by Jack Coombs, who, after four seasons in which he won 35 games and lost the same number, compiled a spectacular record of 31-9, with 13 shutouts and a 1.30 earned run average. The righthander's overhand curve developed into a nearly unhittable pitch. During one stretch he threw 46 consecutive scoreless innings.

Bender, Morgan, and Plank had fine years, and the staff's collective earned run average was 1.78. Collins, Murphy, and Oldring all hit at .300 or better, and Baker knocked in 74 runs to rank second on the squad behind Collins's 81.

In 1908 and 1909 an illiterate lefthanded-hitting outfielder named Joseph Jefferson Jackson, from Brandon Mills, South Carolina, had played a total of ten games for the Athletics. In late July 1910, Mack had a chance to reclaim Bris Lord from Cleveland. Lord had played three earlier seasons with the Athletics before slipping away, and Mack recognized that Bris would fit in well with his 1910 team. On July 25, he traded Jackson, then playing with New Orleans in the Southern League, to Cleveland in exchange for Lord, who played 72 games for the 1910 A's and batted .278.

Mack knew that Jackson could hit—he led the Carolina League in 1908, the Sally League in 1909, and he would lead the Southern League in 1910—but he felt that Lord could give him more immediate help. Mack was no doubt pleased for Cleveland owner Charles Somers, who had helped to bankroll the Athletics back at the beginning of the American League, when Shoeless Joe Jackson, as he came to be known, hit .387 for the Naps in 20 games at the end of the 1910 season. (We might note that Cleveland received from the A's three Hall of Famers, Lajoie, Flick, and Jackson—who certainly would have gone to Cooperstown but for the Black Sox scandal—and Somers got his money back besides. The Athletics must have been the most grateful organization in sports history.) Mack may have had second thoughts about the trade when Jackson hit .408, .395, and .373 in his first three full years with Cleveland.

On August 12, the Athletics beat the Tigers 7-4 at Bennett Park in Detroit; Lord saved the game for Plank with a leaping one-handed catch at the fence. The loss dropped the third-place Tigers 13½ games behind, and a correspondent wrote in the *Inquirer*, "It is all over. Ty Cobb concedes the championship to the Athletics, certainly a most gracious admission on his part."[7]

On September 2, with an 11-game lead, Mack said that from then on he would concentrate on sharpening his team for the World Series against the Chicago Cubs, who were dominating the National League much as the Athletics were the American.

On September 21, Plank beat Cleveland, 6-3, and the second-place Highlanders lost to Chicago, 3-0, which stretched the A's lead to 17 games and clinched a tie for the pennant. When the Sox beat New York again the next day, the flag was won.

On October 1, Coombs won his 31st with a 4-1 win over Boston and Smoky Joe Wood. It was the club's 99th win, setting a new American League record. The next day Clarence "Lefty" Russell, whom Mack had purchased for $12,000, made his big league debut with a 3-0 win over Boston, for the team's 100th victory. It was the only major league game Lefty Russell ever won.[8] Two more triumphs over the Red Sox gave the Athletics a final record of 102-48, 14½ games ahead of New York.

The American League season ended on October 9, but the National League schedule stretched on for another week. In the meantime, speculation about the upcoming World Series with the Cubs ran wild. Both teams were crippled. A's leftfielder Rube Oldring broke his leg in August, and his place was taken by 21-year-old Amos Strunk, a native Philadelphian. Chicago second baseman Johnny Evers, middleman in the Cubs' fabled Tinker-to-Evers-to-Chance double-play combination, broke his fibula sliding into the plate at Cincinnati on October 2; he was replaced by Heinie Zimmerman, a slightly stronger hitter than Evers but nowhere near him as a fielder or as a leader.

More than 5,000 enthusiasts from out of town arrived in Philadelphia for the October 17 opener, many of them with money they were anxious to wager on the Cubs, favorites at 10 to 7 to win the series. The National League champions, winners of the 1907 and 1908 Series, were led by first baseman-manager Frank Chance, "the Peerless Leader," and featured Joe Tinker, Frank "Wildfire" Schulte, Jimmy Sheckard, veteran catcher Johnny Kling, and a pitching staff paced by Mordecai "Three-Finger" Brown, Orvie Overall, Ed Reulbach, and a tall rookie named Leonard "King" Cole, who had gone 20-4.

The day before the opener, the occupants of the houses on 20th Street were notified by the Bureau of Building Inspection that they would not be permitted to have their roofs occupied during World Series games. The residents were predictably outraged. They blithely ignored the edict.

In Game One of the Series, Chief Bender was in full command at Shibe Park, holding the Cubs to three hits in a 4-1 victory. The A's struck quickly against Overall, with two second inning runs and another in the third. Baker's third hit and second double brought Collins home in the eighth, and the 4-0 lead easily stood up against the lone Chicago run in the ninth. A crowd of 26,891 went home happy, the names of Bender and Baker most prominent on their lips.

A throng of 24,597 packed Shibe Park on October 18 and saw Eddie Collins steal the show as the Athletics pounded out a 9-3 win over 25-game-winner Three-Finger Brown. Collins had two doubles and a single, stole two bases against the formidable arm of catcher Johnny Kling, and dazzled in the field.

The A's, leading 3-2, put the game away with six runs in the seventh. Davis, Murphy, and Strunk had key two-base hits, and Jimmy Sheckard of the Cubs allowed the final run when he dropped Lord's fly ball. Coombs, who walked nine and gave up eight hits, had less than his best stuff—"John Coombs was in wretched form," one demanding observer wrote[9]—but he managed to find the right pitch at the right time, stranding 15 Cubs on base as he went the route.

Mack took his men off to Chicago, all of them being careful not to gloat over their two decisive victories. The battered Cubs checked back into town; at the railroad station an onlooker shouted, "Lemon, lemon!" at Frank Chance. Assuming that the epithet was not meant to be flattering, the Peerless Leader had to be restrained from plunging into the crowd after him. With bad weather forecast for the third game the Cubs hoped for a postponement.[10]

Instead, there was a light mist up until game time, when the weather turned cloudy and cold. After the travel day, Mack trotted Jack Coombs out again as his starter on the 20th, this time against Ed Reulbach, before 26,412 fans at the West Side Grounds.

Both clubs scored a run in the first and two in the second. With the score 3-3, Chance lifted Reulbach for the third inning in favor of righthander Harry McIntire. It was not a good move. McIntire gave up a three-run homer to Danny Murphy as part of a five-run inning, and Chance was ejected from the game for arguing vehemently that the hit should have been ruled a double. The A's scored four more in the seventh, and Coombs coasted to a 12-5 win.

On October 21, the Cubs finally got their rainout.

The next day the Athletics came close to attaining a four-game sweep, as Bender took a 3-2 lead into the bottom of the ninth. The Cubs tied it on a Schulte double and Chance triple. In the tenth, Jimmy Archer doubled, and Sheckard hit safely over second to bring him home and end the game.

The Chicago win simply delayed the inevitable. On October 23, Mack gave the ball once again to Coombs, and Colby Jack responded with his third victory, outpitching Mordecai Brown for a 7-2 win. The A's broke a 1-1 tie in the fifth, when Jack Lapp singled home Murphy. They held the 2-1 lead into the eighth, when singles by Coombs and Murphy, doubles by Lord and Collins, and shoddy play by the Cubs scored five more runs and sent most of the Cub rooters home.

Chicago scored a run in the eighth to make it 7-2, but Coombs was in command. Archer singled with two out in the ninth, but pinchhitter Johnny Kling grounded to Jack Barry, who stepped on second to end the Series.

"It's all over," crowed the *Inquirer.* "The Athletics are champions of the world, and there is not a flaw to the title." In truth, they had dominated Chance's men in every aspect of the game as their first world's championship was achieved in very convincing fashion.[11]

On October 24, the team returned to Philadelphia, to be greeted by roaring thousands upon their arrival at Broad Street Station. At a banquet to celebrate the players that evening, Mayor Reyburn said, "They deserve all the honors that can be given them. They have worked faithfully to bring the pennant and world's championship to this city. They have accomplished it. It means much to Philadelphia."[12]

CHAPTER 6

A Stick in John McGraw's Eye

For the 1911 season, Connie Mack made one major lineup adjustment to his world's champions. First baseman Harry Davis, 37 years old, had shown his advancing age in 1910. So Mack moved shortstop John "Stuffy" McInnis, a young man from Gloucester, Massachusetts, who had played in a handful of games for the Athletics in both 1909 and 1910, to first base. Stuffy was only 5'9½", short for the position, but with his good hands and quick feet he soon made himself into an excellent first baseman.

The 1911 campaign did not start well for the Athletics. With a spring training marred by bad weather, they were slow to round into shape and played indifferently at the opening of the season. The Tigers came into the season red-hot, winning 20 of their first 22 games and moving far ahead. Eventually, the A's started winning and cutting into Detroit's lead; the Athletics had a stretch in which *they* won 20 of 22 games. They seized first place on July 4 when they won a doubleheader from New York, only to yield the lead to Detroit again the next day.

When the A's returned home from an injury-plagued western trip in late July they were four games back. With great hitting from Collins, Baker, McInnis, Murphy, Oldring, and Lord, and excellent pitching of Plank, Coombs, Bender, and Cy Morgan, the club was soon performing at top efficiency. They recaptured first place with a doubleheader sweep of the Browns on August 4, never relinquishing the position after that.

By the end of August the Athletics had a 4½ game lead over the Tigers. When they started September with Bender and Plank beating Boston by 1-0 and 3-1 scores, a Philadelphia reporter wrote that "the only question now to be decided is the number of games by which they will ultimately win out from Detroit." Then, wrote the Old Sport in his *Inquirer* column, looking at the lead McGraw's Giants held in the National League, would come "the effacement of the calamity of 1905."[1]

A hot September resulted in a pennant clincher on September 27, an 11-5 win over the Tigers before 10,000 happy fans at Shibe Park, with Frank Baker banging out two doubles and two home runs. When Jack Coombs, the winning pitcher, fanned Jim Delahanty for the final out, joy reigned supreme in Philadelphia.

When the regular season ended a week and a half later, Mack's team had a record of 101-50 and a 13½ game edge over second-place Detroit. Coombs finished with 28-12, Plank was 22-8, Bender was 17-5, and spitballer Morgan was at 15-7. The splendid Eddie Collins led the team with a .365 average, but five other men hit well above .300, and Baker led the league with 11 home runs and drove in 115.

The coming World Series meeting with John McGraw's New York Giants gave the Mackmen an opportunity to avenge the still-galling 1905 loss. The Giants were led by Laughing Larry Doyle, Chief Meyers, Fred Merkle, Fred Snodgrass, and Buck Herzog. In Mathewson and the sensational southpaw Richard "Rube" Marquard, who won 26 and 24 games respectively, they had two great pitchers.

The A's had a major question mark in Stuffy McInnis, who had been hit on the right wrist three weeks earlier by Detroit's George Mullin. If McInnis could not play the Athletics had the experienced Harry Davis to fill in. A reporter asked Bender whether McInnis could play. "He can't with such a wrist as he's got," the Chief replied.[2]

Mack took his team over to New York on the 4 p.m. train the day before the series began, so they could enjoy a quiet night of rest in their hotel before the opener. The Giants were established as 6 to 5 betting favorites, but the Athletics paid no attention to that. *They* were the champions, and McGraw's men would have to beat them.

The World Series opener was played on October 14, before a sell-out crowd of 38,281 at the Polo Grounds. McGraw pulled a surprise by decking his players out in replicas of the all-black uniforms with white lettering which the Giants had worn for the 1905 Series. The ploy received much attention from the press but had little discernible effect on the psyches of the contestants. Mathewson and Bender faced one another, just as they had in the 1905 finale. The A's scored first, with Harry Davis, playing first base in McInnis's absence, singling home a run in the second inning. The Giants tied it in the fourth when Snodgrass scored on an error. A run-scoring double by Josh Devore in the seventh gave Mathewson a 2-1 lead which held up. Mathewson was still a tough pitcher to hit against.

Two days later, 30,000 people jammed Shibe Park to see their Athletics tie the Series with a 3-1 victory. Plank was at his best, and the only New York run scored as a result of Oldring misplaying a Herzog fly ball into a double. The score was tied 1-1 in the sixth when, with Collins on base, Baker pounded one of Rube Marquard's fast balls for a home run. Plank, the *Inquirer* reported, "had his speed, terrific at times, and ... command of the crossfire and curve balls."[3]

An interesting feature of the 1911 World Series was the number of participants on both sides who lent their names to ghostwriters for columns of analysis following each game. After the New York loss in Game Two, there appeared under Mathewson's name an article chiding Marquard for throwing a fast ball to Baker after Matty had warned him about it. Needless to say, Marquard hardly appreciated this journalistic second-guessing.[4]

Back at the Polo Grounds the next day the A's won another one, this time 3-2 in 11 innings as Coombs outpitched Mathewson. As fortune would have it, Frank Baker came to bat in the top of the ninth, with one out and a 1-0 New York lead, and slashed one of Matty's offerings into the rightfield stands to tie the score. In the 11th, hits by Collins, Baker, and Davis combined with two New York errors to produce two runs for the Athletics. The Giants scored an unearned run in their half, but the game ended when Beals Becker was thrown out stealing by catcher Jack Lapp.

Mathewson's newspaper article after the game whined about the umpiring, about his pitching opponent ("We have been beating better pitching than Coombs showed all season in the National League"), and about the way Baker played third base. Marquard, of course, was quoted as being "satisfied ... now that Baker hit Matty for a home run," after

Mathewson's earlier criticism. Philadelphia writers complained about Snodgrass, writing that he had intentionally spiked Baker twice. Poor Frank Baker seemed frequently to be getting in the way of someone's spikes.[5]

On October 18, it rained in Philadelphia and the game was washed out. The Athletics were disappointed, as they now had the momentum of two straight wins plus Chief Bender ready to pitch. There was much more comment on Snodgrass, with even Connie Mack (or his ghostwriter) criticizing the Giant outfielder. Hal Chase, first baseman and manager of the New York Highlanders, he of the gifted feet and twisted mind, wrote in *his* column in the *New York Evening World* that Snodgrass's spiking of Baker "was the most cowardly and dirty piece of ballplaying I ever witnessed."[6]

It rained again on October 19, and on October 20, and on October 21. "There is nothing but mud and water at Shibe Park," an *Inquirer* reporter wrote. "The field is absolutely flooded now and ... a good hot sun and strong wind are the necessary dryers to sop up the wet spots."[7] There was no game scheduled for Sunday, October 22, but one could not have been played anyway. On the 23rd the field was still too wet for play, but both clubs worked out and there was hope of playing on the 24th.

When the sun finally came out the Series resumed after a full week's hiatus. Bender faced Mathewson once again, but this time the outcome was the reverse of the opening game. The A's won their third game, 4-2, as they piled up ten hits, seven of them doubles, against the Giants' ace. Jack Barry had three hits, and Collins, Baker, and Murphy had two apiece. In the sixth inning the Athletics pulled off a delicious double play: Doyle on first broke for second as the batter hit a foul popup to Baker; Barry duped Doyle into thinking he was fielding a grounder, so Doyle slid into second as Baker was throwing to first to double him up. It was a McGraw-type play, so sweet to execute against McGraw's team.

On October 25, the teams squared off in Game Five at New York, with Marquard opposing Coombs. When Oldring hit a three-run homer in the third inning, McGraw lifted his starter and brought in Leon Ames, who pitched four scoreless frames. Coombs, who had pulled a ligament in his groin, weakened in the seventh and yielded a run. He seemed to be in pain, and catcher Ira Thomas suggested that he leave the game.

Coombs insisted he could still pitch, and he retired the Giants in the eighth. Pitching in obvious discomfort, Coombs struggled in the ninth, giving up two runs with two out, and left with the game tied. Plank came on in the tenth. Doyle doubled and beat Plank's late throw to third on a bunt by Snodgrass. Plank got Murray, but Merkle hit a fly down the short right field line. Murphy caught the ball and fired home, but Doyle appeared to beat the throw. Lapp picked up the ball and left the field. Bill Klem, umpiring at the plate, made no call at all as the fans surged onto the field.

After the game, Klem said Doyle never touched the plate and he would have been called out if Lapp had tagged him. Mack later said that he too noticed Doyle's failure but said nothing for fear of starting a riot with the Giant fans all over the field. Imagine Billy Martin, for example, or Gene Mauch in such a situation. The mind reels.

Regardless, the Giants were still alive, but barely, down three games to two and returning to the City of Brotherly Love. On the strength of his four good relief innings the day before, Ames was called on by McGraw to start Game Six. Opposing him was the redoubtable Chippewa, Albert "Chief" Bender.

The Giants scored once in the first but the Athletics tied the game in the third on a double by Bris Lord. In the fourth, the A's took command. Baker and Murphy singled, and Baker came home when Doyle hesitated too long in making a play on Davis's grounder to second. When Barry bunted, Ames picked up the ball and his throw hit Barry in the head, with Murphy scoring. When rightfielder Red Murray threw wildly trying to get the ball back to the infield, both Davis and Barry came around. The A's led, 5-1. Hooks Wiltse came on to pitch next for New York, and he gave up a run in the sixth. When the home side pushed seven more runs over the plate in the seventh, against Wiltse and Marquard, it was all over.

Bender scattered four Giant hits, although he yielded a second run to New York in the ninth. With two out in the last inning, Mack lifted Davis and installed the wounded Stuffy McInnis at first base. Art Wilson hit a grounder to Baker, who threw to McInnis for the final out in the 13-2 clincher. The Athletics were world champions for the second year in a row. It was sweet revenge for 1905 and, as always, a joy to Philadelphians to put a stick in New York's and John McGraw's eyes.

Baker's .375 average, on 9-for-24, led all hitters, and his well-publicized slugging earned him a nickname: henceforth he was "Home Run" Baker. Barry, Murphy, and Collins contributed mightily to the offense, and the three pitchers, Bender, Coombs, and Plank, who worked the entire series, each had earned run averages under two. The mighty Giant pitching stars had been treated with disrespect. McGraw even took himself off the coaching lines when the A's took the lead in the last game: let someone else absorb the hoots and catcalls from the joyous Philadelphia fans.

Two pennants, two 100-plus-victory seasons, two world championships in succession—there was no doubt that this Athletics team was a great one. Its infield of McInnis, Collins, Barry, and Baker picked up its own nickname: "the $100,000 infield," an appellation which, in those pre-war, pre-inflation days, simply meant "beyond price." The three great pitchers, Coombs, Bender, and Plank, had won a total of 137 games among them in two years, and Morgan added another 33. Presiding over it all was the slim, somberly dressed Connie Mack.

As Philadelphians celebrated their world champion Athletics, there were signs that they might also be attempting to shed the label Lincoln Steffens had fastened upon the city. Philadelphia was spreading out, spurred in part by the rapid growth in the number of automobiles registered in the city.

In 1907, the Market Street Subway opened from 15th Street to the Schuylkill River, the town's first underground railway. The portion of the subway running east to the Delaware opened the following year. Its connection with the Market Street Elevated brought the center city area into easy contact with 69th Street in far West Philadelphia. The Torresdale water filtration plant opened in 1908, bringing a vast improvement in public health and a great decrease in the toll taken annually by typhoid fever. In 1914, a seven-mile length of the Northeast Boulevard opened. Later renamed for Theodore Roosevelt, it led to development of the northeastern section of the city.

In late September, 1911, reform candidate Rudolph Blankenburg, a Quaker and a dry-goods merchant, won the Democratic and Keystone parties' nominations for mayor. George H. Earle, Jr., won the GOP nomination by some 20,000 primary votes over William S. Vare, in a contest between two rival segments of the Republican organization. Earle was backed by bosses Boies Penrose and James P. McNichol because they feared loss of their party leadership if the Vare brothers, with their solid control of South Philadelphia's votes, should take over City Hall. Blankenburg's nomination on a fusion ticket was considered interesting but nothing more, since Philadelphia, as everyone knew, always voted Republican.

In the end, Earle's inept campaigning, the fact that he really resided outside the city, and the less-than-enthusiastic support of the Vares in South Philadelphia combined to enable the small reform element to combine with the (even smaller) Democratic party to elect as mayor the elderly but respected reform leader, Blankenburg. Historian Lloyd Abernethy wrote that "Blankenburg set a standard for responsible city management during his four years in City Hall that has rarely been equalled in Philadelphia."[8] Typically, after four years of reform, City Hall was easily recaptured by the Republican organization.

One other event which took place in 1912 was actually a very surprising development for conservative Philadelphia (where Connie Mack in his high starched collar was regarded as the most exciting fellow in town). That was the hiring by the Philadelphia Orchestra, a fledgling organization which had received little attention in its first 11 years, of a young Polish conductor named Leopold Stokowski. The flamboyant and innovative Stokowski was to lead the Philadelphia Orchestra to the musical heights in his 26 years of command, although stodgy Philadelphia was not always happy about it.

Connie Mack assumed that 1912 was to be another successful year for his ball club. Indeed, he was sometimes quoted in the years ahead as saying that his 1912 team was his best ever. Obviously his players felt that way. After getting off to a typical slow start, the A's still felt that when they put their minds to it they could take charge of the American League. It didn't happen. When they put the foot to the pedal, there was little response.

The great infield had another great season: McInnis hit .327, Collins .348 with 63 stolen bases, Barry hit .261, and Baker batted .347 and led the league in home runs (10) and runs batted in (130). Cocky Collins twice stole six bases in a game. Oldring and Amos Strunk had good years, as did Jack Lapp. Plank won 26 and lost 6, and Coombs was 21-10.

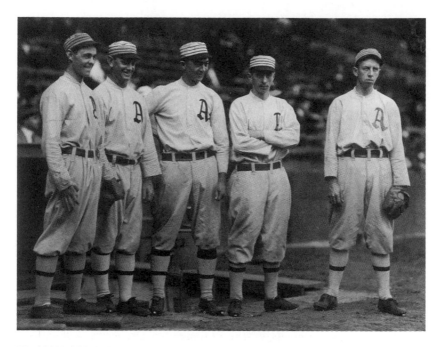

The $100,000 infield (plus one): left to right, first baseman Stuffy McInnis, outfielder Danny Murphy, third baseman Frank "Home Run" Baker, short-stop Jack Barry, and second baseman Eddie Collins (National Baseball Hall of Fame Library, Cooperstown, N.Y.).

But Chief Bender won only 13 games, and Cy Morgan was down to three. The former phenom, Harry Krause, was 0-2 and was sold to Cleveland. A Jerseyite named Carroll "Boardwalk" Brown won 13 and lost 11. An 18-year-old lefty named Herb Pennock, from Kennett Square, out in the Chester County mushroom country, was 1-2; he would make his mark, but not in 1912. With 90 wins the Athletics finished third, 15 games behind Jake Stahl's Boston Red Sox, who had the great Hooper-Speaker-Lewis outfield and Smoky Joe Wood's incredible 34-5 season.

Still smarting from the third-place finish, the Athletics took care of some necessary business during the off-season. On November 16, Frank Hough and Sam Jones, the two sportswriters who had owned 25 percent of the Athletics' stock since the club's inception, agreed to sell their shares to Connie Mack, along with their interests in the real estate at 21st and Lehigh. "It did not take long," Mack said, "for us to come to an agreement as to what their shares were worth." They were paid $113,000, the proceeds of a loan to Mack by Ben Shibe.[9]

To protect his own investment, Shibe wanted to make sure that Connie Mack did not listen to the siren songs of other clubs. Connie's transaction left him holding a 50 percent interest in both the franchise and the ball park. By this deal Shibe insured Mack's adherence to the Philadelphia Athletics. What he also insured, although it never occurred to anyone at the time, was that Connie Mack would stay on as manager no matter how awful his teams were, no matter how many years the bad teams persisted, and in fact no matter whether Connie Mack retained his mental faculties or not.

The downside of guaranteeing Connie Mack's tenure was not an issue in November 1912 because having Mack to run the team seemed to have nothing but upside. Ben Shibe felt "no one had a better right to purchase the stock than the man who had spent so many years in bringing championships to Philadelphia."[10] Clearly, Mack had few peers in the ability to put together a winning team: the triumphs of 1902, 1905, 1910, and 1911 demonstrated that. In addition, the image that the non-swearing, teetotaling manager presented, in his collar and tie and dark suit, had a value in itself, giving respectability to a sport that craved acceptance but still had some rough edges.

Besides, the image was not a false one: Connie Mack was just about as good a man as he appeared to be. He was considerate of his players, solicitous of their welfare, kindly, gentle, and restrained. Rube Bressler said, "Connie Mack. There was a wonderful person. A truly religious man. I mean *really* religious. Not a hypocrite, like some are. He really respected his fellow man. If you made a mistake, Connie never bawled you out on the bench, or in front of anybody else. He'd get you alone a few days later, and then he'd say something like, 'Don't you think it would have been better if you'd made the play this way?'" Sam Crawford called him "a very considerate man." Roger Cramer said, "Whatever you would want in a man, Mr. Mack was it." Jimmy Dykes once said that Mack looked "like a deacon who'd wandered into the ball park by mistake," but he was a deacon who turned out winning ball clubs. Ben Shibe wanted to make sure they continued to be Philadelphia teams.[11]

The Athletics felt that they had loaned the American League championship to Boston for a year, but it was clear to Connie Mack that they would have to approach the 1913 season with a different attitude. In spring training he drummed into his players the necessity of avoiding the vices of complacency and overconfidence, and he brought them into the season ready to play ball.

The A's moved into first place in April, and they stayed there for the rest of the season. They won 96 games and easily outdistanced Washington by 6½ lengths. Mack confronted a problem with his pitching staff and converted it into a plus. Jack Coombs was suffering from typhoid fever, and he missed the entire season. Mack had a bunch of young pitchers, and he had Plank and Bender. Mack decided that, while Plank and Bender would continue as starters, they would also be used as relievers after his youngsters had pitched as long as they could.

The Chief won 21 and lost 10, but six of those wins were in relief. Plank was 18-10, and four of his victories were out of the bullpen. Boardwalk Brown had an excellent season, with a record of 17-11 and 11 complete games. But Byron "Duke" Houck, with a 14-6 mark, completed only four, and rookie Bullet Joe Bush, a fastballing righthander, had a 14-6 record with five complete games. Another rookie with a bright future, righthanded Bob Shawkey, won six and lost five.

The young hurlers were carried along by a hard-hitting offense. The "$100,000 infield," the oldest member of which was Baker at 27, had another fine year. McInnis hit .326 with 90 runs batted in, Collins hit .345, Barry batted .275, and Baker hit .336 to go along with his home run and RBI titles.

Two young lefthanded hitters, Eddie Murphy and Jimmy Walsh, took over outfield spots flanking the veteran Oldring. Switch-hitting Wally Schang shared the catching chores with Lapp. Schang, a good hitter and a smart, smooth-fielding receiver, would soon develop into one of the best catchers in the business.

Waiting for the Mackmen in the World Series once again were McGraw's Giants. To their aces Mathewson and Marquard were added young Jeff Tesreau, who won 22 games, and Al Demaree, with a record of 13-4. The Series opened at the Polo Grounds on October 7, with Bender opposing Marquard.

The A's won the opener, though Bender did not have his good stuff as the Giants banged out 11 hits against him. New York scored first, but the Athletics came back with three in the fourth inning; triples by Collins and Schang the key blows. In the fifth, there was a bit of *déjà vu* as Marquard served up a two-run homer to Frank Baker. The Giants tallied three in the bottom of the fifth, but Bender settled down and, with another A's run against the Giants relievers, hung on for the 6-4 win.

The next day, in Philadelphia, Plank and Mathewson matched scoreless innings through regulation play. The A's had men on second and third with no outs in the ninth, but Mathewson reached back for something extra and Lapp, Plank, and Eddie Murphy were unable to get a run home. In the tenth the Giants broke through for three runs, and Mathewson had a 3-0 victory.

Back in the Polo Grounds on October 9, Mack selected Bullet Joe Bush as his starter against the Giants' Tesreau. The Athletics scored five times in the first two innings, and Bush held the New Yorkers to five hits. Wally Schang helped out with a home run, and the A's had an easy 8-2 win to take a one-game edge.

Game Four, in Shibe Park, saw the return of Bender, this time matched with Al Demaree. Baker doubled home a run in the second inning, and three more scored in the bottom of the fourth on hits by Strunk, Barry, Schang, and Oldring, along with a Giant error. Rube Oldring made a sensational diving catch in the fifth of a drive to center with two runners on base to stymie the Giants, a catch long regarded as one of the great defensive plays in World Series history.

Schang singled home two more runs in the fifth against Marquard, making the score 6-0, and things looked easy for the Athletics. But Fred Merkle's three-run homer in the seventh and two runs in the eighth made the score 6-5 and put the tying run on third. Bender made sure to keep it there by retiring Red Murray on a ground ball. The Chief then set the Giants down in order in the ninth, and the A's had a 3-1 lead in the Series.

They put it away on October 11. Plank opposed Mathewson in the Polo Grounds, and Gettysburg Eddie was never better. The A's touched Matty for a run in the first inning, and two more came over in the third. Plank held the Giants hitless until Larry McLean's run-scoring single in the fifth inning, but McGraw's men could gather only one more hit and no more runs after that. Plank won the clincher, 3-1, and the Athletics had won their third world championship in four years.

Baker hit .450 for the Series, and Collins was not far behind at .421. Mack used only 12 players in the entire series, including his three pitchers, Plank, Bender, and Bush. In contrast to the regular season, in which he had been lavish in his use of relievers, Mack made no pitching changes at all.

Whatever questions the 1912 failure might have raised, there could be no doubts now: the Philadelphia Athletics, the boys of Benjamin Shibe and Connie Mack, were alone at the top of the baseball world.

CHAPTER 7

Rollercoaster

The years 1914 and 1915 were as hectic and eventful as any two years in Philadelphia's long baseball history. The A's were up; the A's were down. The Phillies were down; the Phillies were up. An exciting and startling time, its headliners were some of the greatest names in the town's saga: Eddie Collins, Pete Alexander, Frank Baker, Chief Bender, Gavvy Cravath, Dave Bancroft, Eddie Plank, and of course Mack and Pat Moran, the new manager of the Phillies. The giddy events of these two seasons left the Philadelphia baseball fan feeling as if he were riding a loop-the-loop.

The player raids of the Federal League, which declared itself a major circuit in 1914 and initiated aggressive efforts to sign established stars, left the world champion Athletics relatively unscathed. The only loss suffered by the A's in 1914 was that of the veteran Danny Murphy, who jumped at the age of 37 to the Brooklyn Federals. Murphy, after 12 years in Philadelphia, could still hit, but his playing time had been reduced to 40 games in 1913. He would be missed, but his departure in itself did not have a major impact upon the team.

The significant aspect of Murphy's defection was the fact that he kept in contact with his old teammates on the Athletics, and he soon had several of them listening to Federal League overtures. The club became riven with pro-Federal and anti-Federal factions. As Mack would learn, and as baseball leaders as disparate as Charles Comiskey and Tom Yawkey would learn, a divided club is headed for trouble.

On the surface, the Athletics of 1914 looked as powerful as any of their predecessors. Wearing new pin-striped home uniforms, still featuring a large blue "A" on the chest, they took over the league lead at the end of May and never gave it back, eventually beating second-place Boston by 8½ games. Eddie Collins hit .344, Baker .319, and McInnis .314. Baker led the league with nine home runs, and he and McInnis, with 97 and 95 respectively, were runners-up to Wahoo Sam Crawford of the Tigers for RBI honors.

The pitching staff was effective and deep. Chief Bender won 17 and lost 3, with a 2.26 earned run average. Bob Shawkey, a righthander in his second year with the team, was 16-8, Bullet Joe Bush put up a mark of 16-12, Plank was 15-7, and a 19-year-old southpaw named Raymond "Rube" Bressler won ten, lost four, and did it with a 1.77 earned run average. A couple of years earlier Bressler had been pitching for a Pennsylvania Railroad shop team at Renovo, Pa., where he worked, and he beat a barnstorming team managed by Earle Mack, Connie's son. Mack had him pitching for Harrisburg in 1913 and he came up to the A's in mid-year 1914. Jack Coombs was out for another full season with illness, but he was hardly missed.

After the Athletics shut out the Yankees on October 5, with three innings of scoreless pitching each by Bush, Bressler, and Shawkey, a reporter wrote: "Some one said that 'there's no joy like the joys of anticipation,' but when any ball club has to anticipate facing this pitching, with Bender and Plank added to it, the chances are there won't be many outbursts of raucous mirth from said ball club."[1]

"Said ball club" and the A's World Series opponent was the improbable Boston Braves squad of George Stallings, winner of Boston's first National League championship since 1898. The Braves, in last place as late as July 18, had come on with a rush and won the flag easily. Boston was led by the pitching of Dick Rudolph, Bill James, and George "Lefty" Tyler, the middle infield combination of Johnny Evers and Rabbit Maranville, and the steady catching of Hank Gowdy. Short of big-name power hitters, the Braves won on pitching, defense, and hard-nosed hustle.

The Braves had long played in a bandbox on Walpole Street, the South End Grounds, but it was considered inadequate for World Series play. They moved out in mid-August while their new park, to be called Braves Field, was being erected for April 1915 occupancy. In the interim and for the World Series, they called Fenway Park home. Both clubs were permitted to charge $5 for box seats for the series, with reserved seats at $3 and $2, and general admission for a buck. The Braves also had some 50 cent seats in far center field, but the Athletics eschewed that price level.

"On form and past performances," wrote the Old Sport in the *Inquirer*, "the Athletics, a veteran team and victors in three World's Series, are the logical favorites over Boston.... If ever there was a popular champion ball team it is the Athletics." Mack's team was a solid betting favorite at 8 to 5, but there was little money being wagered on the Series because the A's were considered such a sure thing.[2]

The chances of the Braves appeared dimmer when, in their last regular season game, third baseman James Carlisle "Red" Smith, who had been purchased from Brooklyn on August 14 and hit .314 down the stretch, broke his ankle sliding into second base. Charlie Deal, a .210 hitter who'd lost the third base job to Smith, would replace him in the Series.

On October 8, Stallings first got into a fistfight with an A's fan in the Hotel Majestic lobby, then, essaying some gamesmanship, accused Connie Mack of reneging on a promise to let the Braves work out at Shibe Park, with which most of them were unfamiliar. "He is a poor sport and a cheap sport," Stallings blustered. "I'll punch his head in.... Why Mack assumed this attitude I do not understand. My men know of it and they are more determined than ever to win the series."[3] Philadelphia had had some experience with Stallings: he had managed the Phillies in 1897 and 1898 before his players rose in revolt against his harsh and vitriolic style and got him fired. Philadelphia could take him in stride.

What did rile up the locals was a poorly handled distribution of tickets for the games at Shibe Park. They were put on sale at the Gimbel's department store ticket office at 9 a.m. on the morning of October 7, and things quickly got out of hand. Speculators bought up large quantities of the precious ducats, and some 6,000 unhappy fans went home without any.

The Philadelphia players said little publicly, but they were highly confident. "The members of the Athletics," wrote a *Bulletin* reporter, "do not think they can be beaten by any National League club." Mack asked Bender to take some time off to scout the Braves the last week of the regular season, but Bender felt it was a waste of time. All he had to do to beat bush leaguers like the Braves, the Chief told his manager, was to toss his glove onto the field. There might be dissension in their ranks, but the A's players knew it had been no impediment to their easy triumph in the American League.[4]

Despite the heavy sentiment in favor of the Athletics, the rules said the games had to be played, so the two teams took the field for the World Series opener on October 9 before a capacity crowd of 20,562 at Shibe Park. The Braves touched up Chief Bender for two runs in the second inning, but then the Athletics scored one. The A's were back in the game, their fans felt, and their great righthander would settle down after his shaky beginning. Not so. The Braves, hitting the Chief almost at will, picked up another run in the fifth and drove Bender from the game with three more in the sixth. Rudolph, throwing slow stuff and breaking balls, coasted to a 7-1 triumph.

"Gloom radiated from every wrinkle on the countenances of the Mackian multitude," wrote one hyperbolic reporter, and indeed the fans were troubled by the inability of the A's to gather more than five hits off Rudolph, with Baker's double the only extra-base blow. Boston's lanky catcher Hank Gowdy smashed out a single, double, and triple all by himself.[5]

For the shocked Bender, it was the first time he had been knocked out in ten World Series starts. Jack Barry, writing a column for the *Evening Bulletin*, said "the 7-to-1 score was a great surprise to us—even greater to us than to our many loyal supporters." Nevertheless, he concluded, "Our fellows are just as confident of winning now as before the game was played and we expect to reverse the score today, and then continue through the series without further interruption." It was, after all, just one game.[6]

On October 10, another capacity crowd came out to see Eddie Plank subdue the upstarts from Boston. And indeed Eddie did just that. Unfortunately, his teammates were unable to touch the fast balls of Bill James, and the game was still scoreless going into the ninth inning. With one out in the Braves' half, Charlie Deal, the fill-in, hit a fly ball to center which Amos Strunk misjudged. Deal got a double out of it, and one out later he scored when Les Mann hit a little flare into short center field which fell just beyond the lunging reach of Eddie Collins. The Athletics put two men on with one out in the bottom of the inning, but Murphy hit into a double play to end the 1-0 game, called by the *Inquirer* reporter "one of the most heartrending world's series conflicts ever witnessed." The valiant Plank gave up only seven hits, including the two cheapies in the ninth, but the A's could garner only two, a Collins single and a Schang double, against James.[7]

Mack's players were stunned as they headed off to Boston, down by two games and suddenly in a teamwide hitting slump. They arrived in Boston, "determined," as a Philadelphia writer reported, "to win back some of their lost laurels tomorrow." Mack told the press that Rudolph and James had shown them "pitching entirely different from what we are accustomed to. That is why the Athletics have not been hitting." Some of his players complained about the umpiring, but Barry wrote that "every member of the team feels just as I do, that we cannot and will not lose."[8]

The third game, of course, was crucial. Win it, and the Athletics were down just a game with momentum shifting in their direction. Lose it, and their deficit would be virtually insurmountable. This was "the Mackmen's Armageddon, as they desperately tried to rally their forces," reporter Edgar Wolfe, using his pen name "Jim Nasium," wrote. If they lost, they would be left "nothing but a quivering mass of mangled remains." More than 35,000 roaring Bostonians packed Fenway Park to watch Bullet Joe Bush take on Lefty Tyler in a game that would be long remembered, "probably the most exciting and nerve-racking contest" of any World Series game ever, one writer said. Bush did his job; he pitched a fine, gutty game, but his mates once again failed to hit Braves' pitching, and the outcome was a 5-4 Boston victory in 12 innings.[9] Each team scored twice in the first four innings, but the pitchers settled down after that and the 2-2 score carried into extra innings. In the tenth, the Athletics broke through, with the help of a mental error by the usually impeccable Evers.

Wally Schang singled to left. Bush struck out trying to bunt, but Eddie Murphy hit a ball near the mound on a hit-and-run. Tyler's throw to second was too late to get the fast-breaking Schang, and Evers's return throw to first was too late to get the batter. Rube Oldring was out on a ball to Tyler, but Collins walked to load the bases. Frank Baker hit one in the hole toward right field; Evers just got to the ball but could not make a throw as Schang scored. While Evers tossed the ball angrily in his hand, the alert Murphy caught him napping and scored a second run on what was ruled a steal of home.

If ever the "Miracle Braves" were to be tested, the moment had come. Leading off the bottom of the tenth, Hank Gowdy boomed one out of the park for a center field home run. Josh Devore pinch hit for Tyler and struck out, but ex-Athletic Herb Moran walked and Evers singled him to third. Outfielder Joe Connolly's fly ball to center was deep enough to get Moran home, and the game was tied again.

With Bill James on the mound for Boston, the Athletics could not score in the 11th or 12th. Gowdy led off the bottom of the 12th with a ground-rule double into the field seats in front of Fenway's left-field wall, and Mann ran for him. After an intentional walk, Moran topped a nubber down the third base line. Bush pounced on the ball, whirled, and threw toward third. The ball sailed past Baker into left field while Mann picked himself up and scored the deciding run. The Braves now led the series, three games to none, and most of the fight drained out of the once-mighty Athletics.

A reporter noted that the unfolding debacle seemed to be taken more to heart by the players' wives than by the A's themselves. Many of these young women, he said, "were in tears when they stepped from the taxicabs on their return to the hotel" after the third game, perhaps because they had already planned how they would spend the anticipated winners' share of the Series proceeds. Nevertheless, Barry wrote in his column that, confident in the ability of Chief Bender, "we will be out there this afternoon, fighting all the way."[10]

Many times in years to come, Connie Mack, when asked who was his greatest clutch pitcher, would answer, "Albert Bender." For the fourth game of the 1914 World Series, however, a game he had to win to keep his team alive, Mack surprised his players and baseball people everywhere by passing over a well-rested Bender and giving the ball to 23-year-old Bob Shawkey. "[T]he selection of that pitcher did not fill the fans with ... confidence," the *Inquirer* writer said, "but as Connie Mack's judgment cannot be questioned every one is satisfied that Shawkey was the one best bet under the circumstances." Stallings sent out Dick Rudolph again.[11]

In the fourth inning, the Braves scored a run on two slight misplays, not charged as errors, by Collins. In the fifth, Jack Barry beat out an infield hit, advanced on Schang's out, and scored on Shawkey's double to left to tie the game. It was the last gasp of the Athletics.

In the bottom of the fifth, after Shawkey retired two batters, pitcher Rudolph banged a hit to center field. Moran doubled past Oldring, and when Evers hit a long single to center both runners scored, for a 3-1 Boston lead. Young Herb Pennock pitched the last three innings for Philadelphia and kept the Braves from scoring any more, but the A's could not touch Rudolph. The Boston ace threw only nine pitches to retire the side in the final frame, as Collins struck out, Baker grounded to second, and McInnis hit the first pitch to third baseman Deal, who threw him out to end the series.

A Philadelphia writer commented on the final game: "Toward the end there wasn't a flutter of the Mackian fighting spirit left." It was the first four-game sweep in World Series history, and it left the Philadelphians and their followers with hardly a thing to say. "Hard luck," said Ben Shibe, when he greeted the team upon its return to Philadelphia. "There is not much use in trying to frame an alibi for a team that loses four straight games," Barry wrote.[12]

Connie Mack returned to his adopted city to consider what he was going to do with his ball club. He read Ty Cobb's comment that the Series "marks the crumbling of the great Mack machine."[13] He knew that the operatives of the Federal League were hovering around several of his players. He had recently learned that the club's home attendance, even with a pennant-winner, had plummeted, from 571,896 in 1913 to an astonishing 346,641 in the season just completed.

Mack knew that he and the Shibes had lost money in 1914; indeed, the losses caused Mack to turn down Jack Dunn, the owner of the minor league Baltimore Orioles, in the first week of July, when the hard-pressed Dunn offered to sell him pitcher George Herman "Babe" Ruth and two other players for $23,000. Mack knew that Ruth was a great talent. He did not need Ruth to win in 1914, and, as he told Dunn, he simply did not have the money to buy the young pitcher for the future. He suggested that Dunn contact Red Sox owner Joseph Lannin.

Mack may have heard, too, whispers about possible gambling influences on some of his players in the World Series, although these never became any more than whispers. Stories, never confirmed, floated around that the A's had "lain down" in the Series; certainly the business of passing by Bender in the final game looked odd, although the reason for that decision was most likely Mack's suspicion that Bender was headed for the Feds and would not have his head in the game. But there was no doubt that his club had been solidly outplayed by the surprising Braves in the championship match.

On the last day of October, the baseball world was startled to hear that Mack had asked for waivers on three starting pitchers, Chief Bender, Eddie Plank, and Jack Coombs. Mack, confirming this report, said that he had requested waivers on the three players in order to give them their unconditional releases. "I am going to shift things around before springtime comes," Mack said, "and will have a few more surprises for the fans before it comes time for baseball again."[14]

Mack said that one of the three, whom he did not name, had told him that he had been offered big money by the Federal League. He knew, too, that Plank had turned up a few days earlier in New York City, where the Federal League owners were meeting. Plank denied, not very convincingly, that he was going to sign with the Federals; he was going hunting, he said, with his buddy Danny Murphy. Mack, always an American League man, felt that if he made the pitchers free agents some other club in the league might be able to match the Federal dollars. (He knew that *he* could not.) As it turned out, both Bender and Plank signed to pitch in the Federal League, and Jack Coombs joined the Brooklyn Dodgers, for whom he pitched well.[15]

Early in December, Bob Shawkey, on his honeymoon, ran into a reporter in Butler, Pennsylvania, and answered a few questions about the release of the three pitchers. "Well, I think he did it to cut down expenses," Shawkey said; "you know they had a bad year at the box office last season." Unfortunately, he did not leave it at that. Bender and Plank, he said, were always used against weak teams, teams that Mack knew they could beat. "Both of them are bothered a whole lot with rheumatism," Shawkey went on, "and will probably never again pitch winning ball in the American League."[16]

Bender was furious: "If Shawkey really said that, then I stand convinced there is no gratitude in baseball among players. I taught Shawkey all I knew about pitching." The Chief, in announcing that he had signed with the Federal League, said, "I worked faithfully twelve years for the Athletics, gave them the best there was in me and do not think the summary way I was treated a month ago the right kind of treatment for my years of labor." He added, though, that he held no grudge against Connie Mack.[17]

On December 8, just when the sensation from the release of the three pitchers was dying down, Mack astounded everyone by announcing the sale of Eddie Collins to the White Sox for cash, rumored to be $50,000. Bender, Plank, and Coombs were getting along in years, but Collins, universally regarded as one of the two best players in the game (with Cobb), was in his prime.

Mack said, "As for my reasons for selling Collins, they are my own, and I wouldn't have sold him if I did not think I was doing the right thing." This time, though, there could be no doubt that the reason was economic.[18]

Prior to the 1914 season, Collins had signed a three-year contract for the princely annual salary of $14,000; this contract was the club's protection against a jump to the Feds. With the financial losses sustained by the Athletics, Mack wondered how he could possibly pay Collins in 1915. It all came down to the bottom line, and the Philadelphia Athletics, the Shibes, and Connie Mack did not have the resources, or chose not to risk their resources, to fill their ledgers with red ink.

An *Inquirer* reporter wrote, "With Collins, Bender, Plank and Coombs wiped off the slate and one or two more high salaried men to follow, the pay roll will be reduced to a sensible proportion and the club placed in a position whereby it can realize something on its investment for the season."[19]

Mack planned to fill the spots of the departed stars with players who would cost him much less. The sportswriters and fans expected the Athletics to field a contender, although it could not be as strong with the four stars gone. "Connie evidently intends to sweep clean for 1915 and beyond being a baseball man of acknowledged ability, he must have something up his sleeve....[T]he Athletics next year will not be left flat to wander after the field in the 1915 race," it was written. The touching faith of Philadelphia in Connie Mack was about to be shattered, although even he never expected what happened in 1915.[20]

On December 9, 1914, Mack squelched a rumor that he and the

Shibes were going to sell the club and he was going to manage the Yankees. Nothing to such a story, he said; "I expect to be right here on the job piloting the Athletics during 1915 and a few years more." At the same time he said he had "no doubt as to Frank Baker's loyalty" and fully expected to have him at third base in 1915. "Baker will be with us next year and you can make that as strong as you like."[21]

Baker was already under contract for 1915, but because of the money being thrown around by the Federals he asked for a salary increase. The Athletics refused. What could Baker do? He could play under his existing contract, or he could not play at all. Much to the astonishment of the Shibes and Mack, Baker chose not to play. He refused to report to spring training until his contract was adjusted, and he never did report.

Frank "Home Run" Baker sat out the entire season, working on his farm in Maryland. Mack had made conscious decisions to shed Collins and the three pitchers, and he had worked out in his mind before doing so how to make up for their absence. His plans may not have panned out as well as he expected, but at least there were plans. The unexpected subtraction of Baker was a stunner for which he had no answer, and it magnified his problems for 1915.

With those player losses the Athletics opened the 1915 season much changed from the team which had closed 1914. Out-of-town experts picked the A's to finish in the second division, some as low as seventh, but local people could not subscribe to such gloomy views. They knew Connie Mack, after all. The squad would not be up to 1914 standards, said the *Bulletin*, "but nevertheless it is a good ball club."[22]

On Opening Day, Herb Pennock beat the highly regarded Boston Red Sox, 2-0, pitching no-hit ball until Harry Hooper's infield scratch with two out in the ninth. Who needed Chief Bender? Unfortunately, that game was the high point of the season. The bottom dropped out in a hurry, and the Athletics soon showed themselves to be a truly bad baseball club.

As the losses mounted, attendance dropped sharply from the disappointing levels of the season before. With 1915 evidently a lost cause, Mack acted decisively. In June, he sold Pennock and then Barry to the Red Sox for cash. On July 7, Shawkey was sold to the Yankees for $18,000, and on July 15 Eddie Murphy went to Chicago for $13,500.

There was no longer the pretense that the Athletics were a competitive team. Mack had picked up Larry Lajoie from Cleveland, but the Frenchman was 39 years old and nearly stationary around second base. On April 22, Lajoie made five errors in one game; after the game, Mack said to him, "Stick with it long enough, Larry, and you'll get one."[23]

Wally Schang, one of the game's best catchers, played most of the season in the outfield or at third base. Dependable Stuffy McInnis still hit .314, and Amos Strunk got his share of base hits, but the offense suffered. The club's batting average fell from .272 to .237, and the total of runs scored for the season fell by 196. Bad as the offense was, however, it was not the team's main problem.

The pitching staff was horrendous. Its earned run average was a full run higher than that of any other team in the league. The staff leader was young Bucknell man Weldon Wyckoff, with a record of 10-22. Bush won 5 and lost 15, and Rube Bressler was 4-17. A total of 27 different hurlers pitched for the Mackmen that season, many of them young men who appeared briefly and were never seen again, such as Tink Turner, Joe Sherman, Jack Harper, and the immortal Squiz Pillion, who pitched in two games, was hit hard, and never appeared again.

The net result of all of the Athletics' efforts in 1915 was a record of 43 wins and 109 defeats. No other major league club has ever plunged from first place one year to last place the next in an eight-team league. The A's were 14 games behind the seventh-place Cleveland Indians, and home attendance fell to a pitiful 146,223.

The Athletics' problems in 1915 were compounded when their neighbors at Broad and Huntington, the National League Phillies, surprised most of baseball by winning their first-ever pennant. Under the leadership of new manager Pat Moran, with the sensational pitching of young Grover Cleveland Alexander and the slugging of Gavvy Cravath, the Phillies cruised to a seven-game triumph over Stallings and his Braves.

Ben Shibe offered Shibe Park to the Phillies for the World Series, but William Baker, the Phillies' owner, chose to play the games in his own smaller park. It was a decision he came to regret when the crowd spilled over into the outfield, necessitating the roping off of a part of the field, into which Red Sox batters hit home runs in the clinching fifth game. For the second year in succession it was Boston over Philadelphia in the Series, with Bill Carrigan's Red Sox grabbing the honors in 1915.

For Philadelphia baseball, the two seasons of 1914 and 1915, with the A's on top and plunging to the bottom, and the Phillies rising from sixth place to the league championship, truly represented a rollercoaster ride. There have never been two years like them in Philadelphia's baseball history.

CHAPTER 8

Rock Bottom

On December 22, 1915, a peace treaty was signed between the established leagues and the Federals. The outlaw league disappeared, but it was hard to say that the Americans and Nationals won the war. They paid a substantial sum of money to cover the debts of the Federal League clubs, the players who jumped were allowed to return without penalty, and two Federal owners were permitted to buy controlling interests in the Cubs and Browns respectively. The third-league experiment had been costly indeed, but the survivors looked to better days after the settlement.

In Philadelphia, however, those better days were not to be. Connie Mack's A's took up long-term occupancy of the American League cellar, and it was not long before their futility was matched by that of the senior circuit's Phillies.

There was a peculiar situation in the American League in 1916: almost everyone had a winning record. Even the seventh-place Senators finished only one game below the .500 level. The cause of this anomaly was Connie Mack's ball club which, with 117 defeats and only 36 victories, soaked up a huge number of losses which would normally have been spread around.

The 1916 Athletics may have been the worst team in the history of major league baseball. Their run production was 87 below the next lowest-scoring team, they yielded 155 more runs to their opponents than the next most generous team, they committed 66 more errors than any other club, their fielding average was far below anyone else's, they issued

137 more walks than any other team, and their pitching staff's earned run average was about a full run higher than any of their competitors. In one stretch the A's lost 20 games in a row. The Athletics finished 54½ games out of first place and 40 games behind their closest rivals in seventh place. Connie Mack had to sit in the dugout watching the 1916 edition of the A's and remember the club he managed just two years earlier.

Mack's big cleanout continued. In January 1916, he sold Jack Lapp to the White Sox and a month later peddled the disgruntled Frank Baker to New York for $37,500. Early in the season he sold Weldon Wyckoff to Boston, and the veteran Rube Oldring went off to the Yankees after 40 games.

Amazingly, there were still some of the former champions on the club. Dependable Stuffy McInnis held down first base, hit .295, and drove in 60 runs. Amos Strunk played 150 games and batted a sterling .316. Wally Schang, playing almost twice as much in the outfield as behind the plate, hit .266. At second base, the 40-year-old Lajoie hit .246, played his position ponderously, and, on August 22, appeared in the last game of his distinguished career, suffering an injury which mercifully kept him out the rest of the season.

Some of the numbers on the Athletics' 1916 pitching staff are hard to believe. Bullet Joe Bush was the workhorse at 15-24, with a respectable earned run average of 2.57. Bush had eight shutouts, almost a necessity to win as many games as he did. Rookie Elmer Myers, a tall, skinny righthander from York Springs, Pa., was 14-23; he led the league in walks. Then there was Jack Nabors, an Alabamian, who had been 0-5 in 1915. In 1916, given a chance to work regularly, Nabors compiled a record of one win and 20 losses. He started 30 games for Mack; he even completed 11 of them. Nabors pitched in two games in 1917 without a decision and then left the majors, his lifetime record at 1-25. Righthander Clancy Sheehan, in his second and last year with the club, won one and lost 16.[1]

It took a team effort to lose 117 games, and the 1916 A's were up to it. Only 184,471 people came out to see them do it, although the attendance was actually up slightly from 1915. If ever there were loyal supporters, the fans who paid to see the 1916 Athletics deserve the appellation.

Late in the season, an 18-year-old lefthanded batter from St. Louis appeared in a handful of games, hitting only .091. His name was Charlie Grimm, and he would have a long and productive big league career; unfortunately, it would not be in Philadelphia. The club had a 19-year-old third-string catcher named Val Picinich. He too would play in the majors for a long time, hitting .258 over 1048 games, but, except for two more A's games in 1917, following which he was traded to Atlanta of the Southern Association, his career would be spent elsewhere.

There were others who appeared briefly with the 1916 Athletics who would *not* have long stays in the big leagues—Ralph Mitterling, Mike Murphy, Les Lanning, Moose Brown, Minot "Cap" Crowell, Jack Richardson, a young Swede named Axel Lindstrom, Harland Rowe, Walt Whittaker, Marshall Williams, to name a few—young men who would never again show up in a big league box score.

It was to become a *modus operandi* for Connie Mack over the next few years, to bring in swarms of sandlotters and kids just out of school, put them in Athletics' uniforms, and let them play a few games. If he looked at enough young players, Mack reasoned, he would discover some bona fide big leaguers. Sadly, the ones he looked at were not future stars or, if they were, like Grimm, he did not recognize them as such.

The following year, in 1917, despite some early optimism by Mack ("I am convinced that I have at last found the proper combination, and it is only a question of a few weeks before this will be proved"[2]) the Athletics were last again, with a record of 55-98, but they were much better than the year before. The team finished 44½ games behind the champion White Sox but only a game and a half behind the seventh-place Browns.

McInnis, Strunk (who was suspended by Mack at the end of spring training for not hustling as well as for not speaking to the manager for ten days), and Schang all hit well, as did a chunky little righthanded-hitting outfielder named Francesco Pezzolo, who played ball under the name Ping Bodie. Bodie, a minor league legend, was a good-hitting, weak-fielding outfielder, a fan favorite who had trouble holding a steady job because of his bad glove. His one good year in Philadelphia enabled Mack to trade him to New York for first baseman George Burns before the 1918 season.[3]

The A's fielding, in spite of Ping Bodie, was much better in 1917, and even the pitching was improved. Bush was again the leader, suffering through an 11-17 season, and pitchers Win Noyes and Jing Johnson had moderately good years. The 1917 Athletics saw their attendance rise to 221,432 for the third consecutive last place club.

During 1917, the United States entered the World War. No one knew what the impact of the war on baseball would be in 1918, and the owners' reactions were haphazard. Some clubs offered free admission to servicemen in uniform, while others staged silly marching drills on the field, with their players carrying bats instead of rifles. The Athletics players had suffered through "military training" in Florida, and on Opening Day they were marched to the centerfield flag pole by an army sergeant, who then put them through some drills, allegedly "executed with the neatness and dispatch of regular soldiers," in front of the grandstand. The public noticed that there was no great rush of baseball players to enlist. Many players sought the sanctuary of shipyards and steel mills, where they played on company baseball teams to avoid military service. There were company teams which actively recruited big league ballplayers. Needless to say, the wages of these men did not depend on their ability as steamfitters.[4]

Nineteen-eighteen, of course, was the war year. A number of players had enlisted in the armed services, and more of them went to work in factories or shipyards. On July 19, the "work or fight" edict issued by Secretary of War Newton D. Baker made it apparent that the major league season was not going to be completed as scheduled. Most minor leagues ended their campaigns at that time, but the major league clubowners hoped to hang on for a while.

Ban Johnson and Cleveland owner James Dunn, without consulting their fellow moguls, announced after the games of July 21 that the American League season had just ended. There was an immediate howl from the other seven clubs; Connie Mack said Johnson and Dunn "acted entirely too hastily." He stated that "it is not necessary to close our parks in order to comply with Secretary Baker's order, and I, for one, am anxious to complete the season."[5]

Johnson immediately rescinded his order, and the campaign continued. On July 26, Baker stated play was allowed until September 1; he eventually permitted the season to run one day beyond, with the World Series starting promptly after that. With the curtailed season, Connie Mack saw ten scheduled home games wiped off the board.[6]

For the 1918 Athletics there was more improvement, although they remained in last place. The record of 52-76 left them only 24 games out of first place. Attendance was off, to 177,926, but that could be attributed in part to the shortened schedule.

Over the 1917-18 winter, Connie Mack had completed the dismantling of his old championship team, by now just a distant memory anyway. On December 14, he traded Strunk, Schang, and Bush to Boston, and on January 10, 1918, Stuffy McInnis went to the Red Sox in a separate deal.

Outfielder Clarence "Tilly" Walker, obtained in the McInnis trade, hit .295, and his 11 home runs tied him for the league title with Boston's Babe Ruth. Veteran Larry Gardner, also coming in the McInnis deal, batted .285 and played an impressive third base. George Burns hit .352, second to Cobb, leading the league in hits and total bases.

Joe Dugan, a young Irishman from upstate Mahanoy City, took over as the regular shortstop. A native Philadelphian named Jimmy Dykes came to the Athletics from the minors and played 56 games at second base before going into the service. Dykes had trouble hitting, but Mack liked what he saw of the roly-poly young infielder. Jimmy Dykes called himself "one of the many among the revolving-door, here-today-gone-tomorrow tailenders in camp."[7]

Ralph "Cy" Perkins, who caught 60 games in 1918, was a man who would stick with Connie Mack for a long time. Dykes, Perkins, and pitcher Eddie Rommel (who was to appear on the scene in 1920) were the three players Mack retained from these last-place teams to help build his future winners.

The Athletics' fans, long-suffering most of the time but occasionally obstreperous, disgraced themselves in the second game of a July 20 doubleheader with Cleveland when, with the Indians leading 9-1 in the ninth inning, a barrage of seat cushions poured out of the stands onto the field. Soon the spectators in the lower level seats ran onto the field to escape the cushions which were raining down on *them*. "The absence of police gave the fans free run of the field," a writer reported, "the few employees of the park being powerless to stop the throwing of missiles or to prevent the crowd surging on the field." Eventually the umpires awarded the game to Cleveland by forfeit.[8]

Mack and the Athletics were involved in 1918 in a dispute with broad implications for the governance of the game. Early in the season the club picked up a tall rookie righthander named Scott Perry, a Texan who won 21 games and lost 19 for the A's, with an earned run average of 1.98. After Perry started pitching well for Mack the Boston Braves claimed that he belonged to them. Perry had been sold on a 30-day trial basis from Atlanta to Boston in 1917, but after sitting on the bench for 17 days without pitching, and developing a strong aversion to Braves' manager George Stallings, Perry left the team. (Mack would soon learn that Scott Perry had wandering feet.) The Braves never paid Atlanta the $2000 they owed for Perry, they paid the $500 for the 30-day option only under duress, and they did not carry him on their reserve list after the 1917 season. In March 1918, Perry re-signed with Atlanta, and in April that club sold him to Connie Mack. After Perry put in four impressive performances in an Athletics' uniform, Stallings, on April 27, asserted the Braves' claim to him.

Syndicated writer Joe Vila expressed a widespread reaction when he wrote of Stallings's appeal to the National Commission: "If the commission sustains this unsportsmanlike move by the Braves' desperate manager, baseball fans doubtless will be surprised. Mack has at least a moral right to keep Perry and the commission should promptly dismiss the case in a spirit of fair play."[9]

Instead, when the National Commission, baseball's three-man governing body, augmented with two minor league representatives because the case also involved the Atlanta club, considered the matter of Stallings's appeal, it awarded Perry to Boston on June 12, 1918, by a 3-2 vote.[10]

Mack was outraged by the decision; "we will hold Perry," he announced, "and will pitch him in his turn. So far as we are concerned there is no change in his status." In a long statement, he reviewed both the legal and moral aspects of the case and found his own position sound in both respects. "Perry's record," he said scornfully, "is the thing that suddenly awakened the Boston Club to the injustice I was doing it." He sounded defiance to the establishment: "There will be no backdown from me.... I might as well close my park as to allow Perry to go to the National League under present conditions. I'd lose all my reputation as a manager fighting to protect the rights of his team and its fans." He recognized that "my attitude may force serious internal baseball trouble," but he welcomed the turmoil that might ensue, especially since there was widespread dissatisfaction with the National Commission system.[11]

The second shoe dropped on June 17, when attorneys for Mack went into court in Cleveland and obtained a preliminary restraining order against the National Commission and the Boston Braves, preventing them from changing Perry's status. Connie Mack, of course, was not alone; he was encouraged in his course by Ban Johnson, after a meeting of Johnson, Dunn of the Cleveland club, Harry Frazee of the Red Sox, Clark Griffith of Washington, and Mack.[12]

On the same day the injunction was obtained, Perry started for the Athletics in Cleveland, losing to the Indians and Stan Coveleskie, 6-3. In the meantime, however, Connie Mack, in his unaccustomed role as a rebel, was subjected to criticism for his course of action. An *Inquirer* columnist "censured" him for going into court and for "lack of loyalty to organized baseball," and Vila said Mack had "erred by resorting to legal proceedings." Nevertheless, both writers, and most other observers, had no doubt that an injustice had been done to the Athletics.[13]

When John K. Tener, president of the National League, declared on July 9 that he would have no more to do with Johnson and would not sit on the National Commission in any case involving the American League, as a result of the Perry matter, he ratcheted up the war fever a bit more. Many observers now predicted the end of the National Agreement and a renewed conflict between the two major leagues. One columnist, apparently writing *ex cathedra*, scoffed at rumors that Tener would quit: "Tener is not a man to resign under fire.... To fail to support President Tener in the premises would be to deal the senior league such a blow in public prestige that it could with difficulty recover from its effects.... President Tener has the solid support of his organization."[14]

Nevertheless, although Herrmann filed an answer in court on behalf of the National Commission, asserting that that body was to be the final arbiter of baseball disputes, it soon became evident that the National League owners did not want to go to war over the Perry decision. Boston's case was weak, except on narrow technical grounds, and the simultaneous problems with Newton Baker and the government demonstrated that organized baseball could ill afford to be divided.[15]

On August 6, John K. Tener resigned as president of the National League. The stand he had taken meant he had to go before the league owners could work out a quiet, face-saving settlement with Connie Mack and Ban Johnson. The equity action in the Cleveland court lay dormant until October 17, when the injunction was gently dismissed, "on statement of attorneys that the controversy had been settled out of court."[16]

The terms of the settlement soon made their way into the public press. The Braves gave up their claim to Scott Perry, and the A's paid them $2500, a very modest sum for a 20-game winner. "Both the Athletics and the Boston Club backed down a little," it was written, "and finally decided a matter that for a time bid fair to bring on a war in organized baseball."[17]

The year 1919 was a bad one in baseball, although it started out well as the game rebounded from the curtailed 1918 season and the public's perception that baseball had been a less-than-enthusiastic contributor to the fight against the Kaiser. But 1919 was the year seven members of the Chicago White Sox, including ex-Athletic Joe Jackson, conspired to lose the World Series, in exchange for bribes paid them by gamblers.

It was a bad year, too, in Philadelphia baseball. It was the year the Phillies dropped into the National League cellar, matching the last place finish of the Athletics. This double disaster had never happened in Philadelphia before, but it was to become all too familiar. In fact, in 1919, 1920, and 1921, the Phillies and A's both finished in last place. It was just five years away from Bender, Collins, Pete Alexander, and the $100,000 infield. It might as well have been a century.

The Athletics had another terrible team, finishing with a record of 36-104, 52 games out and 20 behind seventh-place Washington. On August 26 the club lost an exhibition game to Worcester, 6-5, and the next day's *Inquirer* headline read, "EVEN MINOR LEAGUERS CAN BEAT ATHLETICS." George Burns hit .296 and Tilly Walker .292, with ten home runs, and that was about it for offensive highlights.

Starting at first base for much of the 1919 season was a North Carolinian named Maurice "Dick" Burrus. He had been recommended so glowingly to Mack that the A's manager went to see him play in the minors. So impressed was Mack that he purchased Burrus for $10,000 and then called in the press. "I have bought the greatest young player in the country," he told his startled listeners. "Why, Burrus is no experiment. He would make good even if he didn't want to." Burrus in 1919 gave little evidence of whatever Mack saw in him; he hit .258 in 70 games with no home runs and only eight runs batted in.[18]

A couple of the old boys, Amos Strunk and Jack Barry, were obtained in a trade with Boston. Barry, with his college education, had no difficulty in seeing what he would be getting into with the A's, so he promptly retired. Strunk might as well have; he hit .211 for the Mackmen.

The Philadelphia pitching was awful. Jing Johnson and Walt Kinney led the staff with records of 9-15. Tom Rogers came from St. Louis, won four, lost 12, and departed. A Texan named Roleine Cecil "Rollie" Naylor had a 5-18 mark. Scott Perry, the 21-game winner of a year earlier, was 4-17. A couple of dozen other hurlers made appearances, and most were hit hard.

When the club's intention to release Rogers became known, he jumped the team, and Perry jumped with him, for the reason that "he and Rogers are chums." Perry soon returned, but it was not the last time that he would desert the Athletics.[19]

In 1920, the Athletics won 12 more games, but they finished last once again. It was becoming an unpleasant habit. They were not even close, ending up 13 games behind the next-to-last Tigers and an even 50 behind the pennant-winning Cleveland Indians.

Joe Dugan hit .322, playing all over the infield. Perkins had a good year behind the plate. Strunk batted .297 before Connie Mack sent him on his travels again, this time waiving him to Chicago in July. Tilly Walker hit 17 home runs and Jimmy Dykes eight. A tall, 23-year-old righthander from Baltimore by the name of Eddie Rommel made the A's staff, winning and losing seven with a good earned run average. Rommel threw a knuckleball, and he threw it well.

Philadelphia at the start of the 1920s was in some turmoil. With the war to end all wars, the great influenza epidemic of 1918, and several crippling strikes behind it, the city headed into the decade with a new charter, a new mayor in J. Hampton Moore, and two new amendments to the Federal Constitution, one giving women the right to vote, the other imposing Prohibition on the nation.

Mayor Moore, who had been nominated in opposition to the Vare machine, had an inadequate police force with which to handle the proliferation of automobile traffic, let alone the widespread defiance of Prohibition. He soon lost favor with the populace, which in Philadelphia was always ready to turn on any reformer or independent the moment he ran into trouble, and in short order the Republican machine was back in control.

The year 1920 was also when Babe Ruth was sold by the Red Sox to the New York Yankees for a huge pile of cash. Ruth, now a full-fledged outfielder, hit 54 home runs for the New Yorkers, and the game was changed forever. The Yankees' attendance more than doubled, to 1,289,000. It was the first time a franchise had drawn over a million customers in a season, and it marked the effective end of the dead-ball era. If home runs brought people to the ball parks, home runs there would be. The authorities made the ball itself more resilient, banned the spitball and other doctored pitches, and ordered umpires to change baseballs more frequently. The "lively ball" era was underway; home run production climbed from 448 in 1919 to 630 in 1920 and to 937 in 1921.[20]

In 1921, the two Philadelphia clubs finished last again, but at least they hit a lot of home runs. The A's hit 82 and the Phillies, with the ever-favoring Baker Bowl fences, hit 88. Still, they were bad ball clubs.

The 1921 Athletics improved some, but not enough to avoid their seventh consecutive cellar finish. From their spring training camp in Lake Charles, Louisiana, Mack let it be known that he was putting "his faith on the ability of the players used last year to show better development." This was unfortunately a faith not to be realized. By late June, *Inquirer* writer Jimmy Isaminger wrote that "the Macks have been shoved far into the cellar with little or no prospect of escaping from that thankless cavern." When the team started winning, however, Isaminger changed his tune and wrote in mid-July that "Mack's team is showing such consistent improvement … even a conservative supporter is justified in hoping it may wind up in the first division." It was all just a mirage, and last place was still the club's final resting place. Attendance increased, to 344,430, the highest since 1914, indicating perhaps that the fans had become accustomed to last place.[21]

The offense was up substantially, but the Athletics' major problem was pitching. Knuckleballer Eddie Rommel was 16-23, and his ERA of 3.95 was the only one on the staff under four. Slim Harriss, hailed by Isaminger in July as "one of the greatest pitchers in the country," wound up at 11-16. Righthander Bob Hasty was 5-16, and Rollie Naylor was 3-13.[22]

Scott Perry, who was fined $100 and suspended for ten days in early May for too much carousing and too little attention to training rules, won three and lost six before jumping the team again in July. It was his final jump, as he signed to pitch in an outlaw league in Franklin, Pa., thus ending a short but eventful big-league career with a record of 41-68.

Late in the season, Mack purchased the contract of first baseman Joe Hauser from the minors. Hauser, a lefthanded slugger known to the fans in his native Milwaukee as "Unser Choe," would become in later years one of the all-time minor league greats. Before then, however, he would give Connie Mack several creditable seasons in Philadelphia.

Mack needed all the help he could get. After seven years in the cellar, many Philadelphia fans grumbled that the game had passed the 59-year-old manager by and that a change to a younger man should be made. There can hardly be a doubt that with any other team Mack would have been fired long since, but a manager who owns 50 per cent of the club's stock is a hard manager to get rid of. So Connie Mack would persevere.

The acquisition of Hauser signalled a change in Mack's strategy for rebuilding his team. No longer would he try to find stars among the dozens of unheralded youngsters he tried out; that policy had clearly come up empty. He recognized that he would have to purchase up-and-coming ballplayers from the minor leagues or from other major league clubs, and Joe Hauser was just such a purchase.

On January 10, 1922, Mack traded Dugan to Washington for two players, the key man for the Athletics being outfielder Edmund "Bing" Miller, an Iowa farmboy who impressed Mack in his rookie season at Washington when he hit .288. Miller was a solid, consistent batter and a fine outfielder with good speed.

Bing Miller gave a big boost to the 1922 Athletics. He hit a healthy .336 with 21 home runs and 90 runs batted in. Tilly Walker drove in 99 runs and hit 37 home runs. Hauser, the rookie first sacker, hit .323 and banged nine home runs, and shortstop Chick Galloway averaged .324.

The heavy hitting—the A's led the league with 111 home runs—and a great season by Rommel pushed the Mackmen out of the basement for the first time in eight years. The Red Sox finished last, four games behind Philadelphia. Rommel won 27 and lost 13 and had an ERA of

3.28, leading the league in victories. The rest of the club's pitchers were as sad as ever, but Rommel's performance helped to boost the team's record to 65-89, easily its best since the 1914 champions. The fans started coming back, too; attendance exceeded 425,000, the club's highest since 1913.

For the Athletics, it was the beginning of a steady climb to the top of the league. Certainly they had a long way to go; but at least they were off rock bottom.

CHAPTER 9

On the Way Again

Over the next several seasons, the Athletics shook off the dust and ashes of their seven-year tenure in the cellar and transformed themselves, with the addition of several all-time greats, into strong contenders.

In 1923 Mr. Mack's team moved up a notch, finishing in sixth place, a game ahead of the White Sox. Home attendance climbed to 534,122. Joe Hauser banged out 16 home runs and Miller 12. Outfielder Frank Welch, rookie third baseman Sammy Hale, and Galloway had good years with the bat. Perkins batted .270 and did his usual excellent job behind the plate.

Rommel was 18-19 with a good ERA. Although his record looked a lot different from the year before, in fact he pitched just as well. Bob Hasty was 13-15, Rollie Naylor was 12-7 despite an injury, and Slim Harriss, still looking for that elusive greatness, was 10-16.

In April, the A's picked a 26-year-old lefthanded pitcher named George "Rube" Walberg off the waiver wire, from the Giants. A self-described "big, awkward farm kid" from Minnesota, Walberg had moved west to work in his brother's coalyard but given an opportunity by the Portland Beavers in 1919 he jumped at a chance to play baseball for a living. After four years in the minors, Rube made it to the Giants and then to Shibe Park, where he stayed a long time, despite a bad habit of tipping his curve. In his first season, however, he was 4-8 and had a high earned run average.[1]

Philadelphia's new mayor W. Freeland Kendrick started his term in

1924 by naming General Smedley D. Butler of the U.S. Marine Corps his director of public safety. Butler's vigorous and even-handed enforcement of the Prohibition laws brought him into conflict with influential Philadelphians, many of whom had investments in speakeasies, and after two stormy years Butler gladly went back to the Marines. The general was remembered for one other short-lived innovation, the ill-advised attempt to control all traffic on Broad Street, north and south, with one huge traffic signal mounted high on City Hall Tower.

The A's continued their rise in 1924, winning 71 games and finishing in fifth place. They started poorly but in the latter part of the season played as well as anyone in the league. In addition, Mack added a couple more pieces to what would become a championship lineup.

He paid $50,000 to Jack Dunn at Baltimore for a left-handed hitting second baseman named Max Bishop, whom Dykes called "a flashy fielder, smooth and sure." Bishop was nicknamed "Camera Eye" in tribute to his uncanny ability to work pitchers for bases on balls, an ability that made him one of the best leadoff hitters of the time.[2]

From Milwaukee Mack bought a slugging outfielder named Aloysius Harry Szymanski, more familiarly known as Al Simmons. Despite impressive minor league credentials, Simmons was regarded as a questionable performer because of his batting style, which had him pull his front (left) foot toward the third base line as he began his swing. Any good baseball man knew that a batter simply could not hit properly if he put his foot "in the bucket," as Simmons did. Simmons, however, did not know this; he kept doing it and the line shots kept ringing off his bat as he compiled a lifetime average of .334 over 20 big league seasons. As a bonus, Simmons was also an excellent outfielder. Mack once said, "Simmons has natural baseball instinct and, during his nine years with me, made only one bad play."[3]

In addition to purchasing Bishop and Simmons, Mack spent $100,000 for a 30-year-old Salt Lake City outfielder named Paul Strand. Strand, who began his career as a southpaw pitcher, first appeared in the big leagues as a teenaged lefthander with the 1913 Boston Braves. He was 6-2 for Stallings's 1914 champions, but arm trouble curtailed his pitching career and he was back in the minors by 1916. Strand made himself into an outfielder and in 1923 hit .395 in the Pacific Coast League, with 325 hits (in 194 games over the PCL's lengthy schedule).

Mighty Al Simmons (National Baseball Hall of Fame Library, Cooperstown, N.Y.).

The A's looked for great things from the righthanded-hitting Strand, but he never got started after a salary holdout, batting only .228 in 47 games before Mack returned him to the minors.

Mack had plenty of hitting even without Strand. Bing Miller batted .342, Simmons hit .308 and drove in 102 runs, and "Good Time

Bill" Lamar, whom Mack brought back from the minors after five earlier seasons in the National League, hit .330 in 87 games. Hauser drove in 115 runs and hit 27 homers, second in the league behind Ruth's 46. Sammy Hale hit .318, and Jimmy Dykes, playing all around the infield, hit .312.

The pitching was shaky, but Rommel was 18-15, and young southpaw Fred Heimach was 14-12. A surprise addition was lefty Stan Baumgartner, who had been a combined 7-11 in five earlier seasons with the Phillies. With the A's, he compiled a record of 13-6, with a good 2.88 ERA. The 1924 season was the high mark of Baumgartner's pitching career, but he went on to become a long-time baseball reporter for the *Philadelphia Inquirer*.

One other item of note for the Athletics' 1924 season was the purchase from the White Sox of good old Amos Strunk, now 34 years old, in August. Amos played in thirty games for the A's, hit only .143, and hung up his spikes for the last time.

After the 1924 season, Mack was approached by his old friend Jack Dunn of the International League Orioles. Dunn had a young lefthanded pitcher who had given him five good seasons, winning 109 Oriole games and losing just 36. From a small western Maryland town called Lonaconing and known as "Lefty," the 6 foot 3 inch Robert Moses Grove had a blazing fastball and a temper to match. One player wrote that Grove, on the day he was scheduled to pitch, "snarled at writers, ignored his teammates, seemed to hate humanity."[4]

Grove certainly could have pitched in the majors earlier, but Dunn had seen no need to let him go until now. He offered Grove to the Athletics, and Mack, who had been forced by his cash position to refuse Dunn's earlier offer of Babe Ruth, met the price this time, an astronomical $100,600, the extra $600 being added to top the amount of Ruth's sale to the Yankees by Boston. Mack gulped and made the deal; it was a good thing the A's attendance had been rising the last couple of seasons. But Lefty Grove was a great one. Sportswriter Bugs Baer once wrote that Grove "could throw a lamb chop past a wolf."

Another new acquisition was a round-faced, muscular, 17 year old from Maryland's Eastern Shore, named James Emory Foxx. Frank "Home Run" Baker, managing the Easton, Maryland, team, contacted his old boss about Jimmy Foxx. Mack signed the young catcher and got him into ten games in 1925; he appeared at the plate nine times and picked up a double and five singles for a tidy .667 batting average. Most of his season was spent in the minor leagues.

A third new face on the Philadelphia scene was that of Gordon Stanley "Mickey" Cochrane, a catcher born in Bridgewater, Massachusetts, whom the club purchased from Portland for $50,000. Indeed, so that he would be sure of getting the young man, Mack earlier bought a controlling interest in the Portland franchise. Mickey, a former football star at Boston University, was a fine hitter, but his catching skills were rudimentary. When Cochrane came to the A's spring camp, first-stringer Cy Perkins took him under his wing and taught him everything he could about the art and science of catching. Cochrane worked hard and caught two hours of batting practice every day during spring training. With the constant repetitions, the movements which Perkins taught became ingrained as reflexes.

On Opening Day in 1925, Perkins caught, but in the eighth inning, with the winning run in scoring position, Mack told Cochrane to bat for Cy. When Mickey singled home the game-winner, Cy turned to those around him in the dugout and said, "There goes Perkins' job on that base hit." And so it did; Cochrane caught 135 games, Perkins 58.[5]

In 1925, no longer was it said of the Athletics that they were coming back; in 1925 they were back. They led the league for a good stretch of the season, until they were knocked back to second place by an untimely 12-game losing streak in August.

Joe Hauser broke his leg and missed the entire season, so Mack dipped into the minors and came up with a 30-year-old Carolinian named Jim Poole, who played an acceptable first base and batted .298. Bishop, settling in now at second, hit a solid .280, and Hale averaged .345 at third base. Shortstop Chick Galloway hit only .241, but Jimmy Dykes, again playing all around the infield, racked up a .323 average in 465 times at bat. Simmons had a banner season, with numbers like .384, 24 home runs, and 129 RBIs. Lamar and Miller hit .356 and .319, respectively, and Cochrane exploded in his first year for a .331 batting average.

The pitching was respectable. Rommel had another excellent year, winning 21 and losing ten, as did Slim Harriss, with a 19-12 mark. Sad Sam Gray, a Texan in his second year, was 16-8. Grove started slowly, putting up a record of 10-12, and he led the league in both strikeouts and walks. Walberg was 8-14, and 41-year-old John Picus Quinn, picked up on waivers in July, won six games.

Despite the August losing streak, the A's fell no lower than second, finishing in that position, 8½ games behind Bucky Harris's Senators but 7½ games ahead of the third-place Browns. The Athletics were good, they were young, and they were getting better. They drew 869,703 fans, a mark which would stand as the club record until after World War II.

For the Athletics, 1926 was another relatively successful year. They won a few games less than a year earlier and slipped a notch to third place, but they were now solidly established as a first division club, and their young stars-to-be were maturing. They were only six games behind the first-place Yankees and in the race until just before the end.

Al Simmons led the way at bat, with his .343 average, 19 home runs, and 109 runs knocked in. Outfielder Walt French, a former West Point football star in his third season with the A's, hit .305, and Poole, Lamar, Cochrane, Hale, and Dykes did their part. Eighteen-year-old Jimmy Foxx, sitting on the bench or warming up pitchers in the bullpen, hit .313 in the 26 games he got into. Sportswriter Stoney McLinn predicted that the muscular young Foxx would "be a star at whatever job is assigned him," but that day was still down the road for the youngster.[6]

On June 15, Mack traded Bing Miller to the Browns for the elderly William "Baby Doll" Jacobson, who was then sent on to Boston with pitchers Slim Harriss and Fred Heimach for Howard Ehmke and outfielder Tom Jenkins. Jenkins did little, but the veteran Ehmke pitched for several more years. In the meantime, Mack waited to see how he could get Miller back.

The pitching staff had no big winners, but it was well-rounded and deep. Lefty Grove won and lost 13, but he led the league in earned run average (2.51) and strikeouts (194) and cut down his bases on balls considerably. He walked 101 in 1926, down from 131, and never again in his long career would he walk more than 83 in a season. All around the league, opposing hitters and managers knew that Grove was a star about to shine.

Ehmke was 12-4, Walberg 12-10, Rommel 11-11, Jack Quinn 10-11, and Sam Gray was 11-12. All of them except Gray had good earned run averages, and Gray's 3.64 would have looked awfully inviting six blocks away at Broad and Huntingdon, where the Phillies in Baker Bowl had a horrendous staff earned run average of 5.19. A 34-year-old lefty named Joe Pate came out of Alice, Texas, and won nine games, all in relief, without losing any; his ERA was 2.71.

The year 1926 was the Sesquicentennial, the nation's 150th birthday. Philadelphia planned an ambitious international exposition, located, thanks to the influence of political boss William S. Vare, in South Philadelphia. The Sesqui brought the city a new municipal stadium and the Dempsey-Tunney fight, but it also brought worldwide derision and a massive debt. Very little of the Sesqui was ready by the May 31 opening. Then poor attendance and rainy weather made Philadelphia's fair a fiasco. Afterward, the usual investigation turned up the usual graft and corruption. Fortunately, Philadelphia's political leaders were not running the city's American League team.

The man who was, Connie Mack, chose to add some seasoned veterans to his team for 1927. Eddie Collins and Ty Cobb were let go as managers by the White Sox and Tigers, respectively, and they both signed with Philadelphia. Cobb, along with Tris Speaker, had just been cleared by Landis of involvement in a conspiracy to throw a game back in 1919, but league president Ban Johnson announced that the two great stars could no longer play in the American League. In a rebuff to the fading Johnson, Speaker then signed with Washington and Cobb with the A's.[7]

When Mack introduced Cobb as a new member of the team at the February baseball writers' dinner, the old Tiger received a standing ovation and was touched by it, after "I'd battled and feuded with the A's and their fans most of my career, needed police protection at Shibe Park and received a good dozen anonymous death-threats there."[8]

Another newcomer was Zack Wheat, after an outstanding career of 18 years with Brooklyn. Collins and Cobb were 40, Wheat 41, but they were not added for ornamental purposes. Collins played in 95 games and hit .338, Wheat hit .324 in 88 games, and Cobb, playing as a regular outfielder, managed to run up a .357 average and led the team with 22 stolen bases.

But Mack did not need the 40 year olds to show his boys how to hit. The team average was .303, and the pacesetter again was Simmons with .392 (he still finished second, six points behind Detroit's Harry Heilmann). Al drove in 108 runs and hit 15 homers. Dykes, playing more first base than anywhere else after Joe Hauser broke his leg again, batted .324, and Sammy Hale hit .313. Mack bought 30-year-old Joe Boley from his friend Dunn at Baltimore, installed him at shortstop in place of Galloway, and watched with pleasure as the elderly rookie hit .311 and fielded impressively.

Cochrane averaged .338 with 12 home runs, and French hit over .300 again. Foxx, in 61 games this time, batted .323 and hit the first three home runs of his career. "Good Time Bill" Lamar, overdoing the good-time bit, got himself suspended and finally released by Mack, his big league career over at the age of 30, despite a lifetime batting average of .310.

Grove had his first 20-win season, with 20-13, and led the league in strikeouts as usual. Walberg, Quinn, Ehmke, and Rommel had good years as well, and the Athletics won 91 games. Where did it get them? It got them second place, 19 games behind the Yankees.

This was Babe Ruth's 60-home-run season, and this was the Yankee team known as "Murderers' Row." While New York's batting average was just four points higher than that of the A's, the Yankees scored 134 more runs. Ruth drove in 164 runs and did not even lead his team; Lou Gehrig drove home 175. Second place to this team was no disgrace. Connie Mack's problem was finding a way to cut down that 19-game differential.

CHAPTER 10

Top of the Mountain

One of the favorite pastimes of the history-minded baseball fan is arguing over which ball club can be considered the best of all time. There are, not surprisingly, a number of teams whose claims can be put forward for that honor.

One prime contender is the 1926-28 New York Yankee team. The claim is usually made for the 1927 Yankees, but the regular on-field unit for the Bronx Bombers was remarkably unchanged for the three-year period, with basic continuity on the pitching staff. Herb Pennock and Waite Hoyt served as mainstays through the period, with George Pipgras and Wilcy Moore supplanting Urban Shocker and Bob Shawkey.

Other teams for whom an argument can be made are the Cubs of 1906 (116 wins; too bad about the Series loss to the "Hitless Wonder" White Sox), the Joe McCarthy Yankees of 1936-39, the Brooklyn Dodgers of 1955 (Johnny Podres putting the "Boys of Summer" over the top), the Big Red Machine of Cincinnati in the early 1970s (except for shaky pitching), Billy Southworth's St. Louis Swifties of the early 1940s (but what about the war?), and the Indians of 1954 (no American League team had ever won more, but the World Series sweep by the Giants is an embarrassment).

The club which compares most readily with the Miller Huggins Yankees is the one which Connie Mack built in the 1920s for a championship run at the end of the decade. Mack started with Jimmy Dykes and Eddie Rommel, then added a Bing Miller here, a Cochrane there, a Grove or a Walberg on the mound. Throw in the slugging of Al Simmons and Jimmy Foxx and George Earnshaw's fireball, and the A's became an exciting and dynamic team.

Forgotten were the seven long years of last place. The Athletics were winners again. The second-place 1927 A's finished 19 games behind the Yankees, but that is one reason the 1927 New Yorkers are considered by many to be the best of all. For 1928 Mack planned a real run at the Bombers.

To strengthen his team, Mack purchased from the minors a 24-year-old outfielder named George "Mule" Haas, a hard-throwing righthanded pitcher named George Earnshaw, and Ossie Orwoll, who was supposedly both a pitcher and a first baseman. Wheat was let go, but the club signed Tris Speaker, who hit .327 as a 39 year old with Washington the year before.

Haas hit lefthanded and ran well, and he was projected as a spare outfielder. Earnshaw was a big man, 6'4" and 210 pounds, a Swarthmore College man with a sunny disposition and an excellent fastball. Jimmy Dykes said Earnshaw "had no nerves, a tireless arm, and could pitch with two days' rest, if necessary." His pitching style was to wind up and "let 'er fly," and he frequently gave up a lot of bases on balls. Nevertheless, he would be a big winner for Connie Mack's White Elephants.[1]

On December 13, 1927, Mack shipped Sad Sam Gray, winner of 44 games in four seasons with the Athletics, to the Browns for Bing Miller. Why Miller was traded away in the first place was none too clear, but now the A's had him back — at the cost of a good pitcher who would win 20 for the Browns.

The Yankees started 1928 as if they were going to repeat the easy procession of 1927. Through June, they piled up a big lead and looked ready to leave the rest of the league far behind. The A's were second, but they were 13 games back of Ruth, Gehrig, Lazzeri, et al., and matters looked glum. "The followers of baseball," wrote an *Inquirer* reporter, "were bemoaning the fates that caused a lopsided and unequal fight for two straight seasons in the American League."[2]

Then the Athletics caught fire with a sizzling 25-8 July record bringing them within range of New York. By August 11, after the A's had won 22 of their last 26 games, the Yanks' lead was down to 4½ games, and writers were speculating on the chances of Connie Mack winning his seventh pennant "in his advancing years."[3]

Lefty Grove, considered by some the best pitcher of all time (National Baseball Hall of Fame Library, Cooperstown, N.Y.).

The surge of the Athletics began when Mack made three changes in his everyday lineup: he replaced first baseman Joe Hauser with Ossie Orwoll, third baseman Sammy Hale with Jimmy Foxx, and centerfielder Ty Cobb, whose ancient legs were failing him, with Haas. Earlier, Mack had inserted Miller into the lineup in place of Speaker, whose average was dragging along in the .260s. The future of what was looking like a very good baseball team was placed in the hands of Connie Mack's young men.

On August 13, Lefty Grove won his ninth straight game and 17th of the season, a 7-1 gem over the Tigers. "Lefty Grove's pitching," the *Inquirer* said, "was a poem."[4]

Through the latter part of August, the Athletics crept closer to the Yankees. Simmons and Foxx led the A's batsmen, and everyone else chipped in. Boley starred in one game; in another Mule Haas homered in the 17th inning to win a game with the Indians. Grove kept pitching brilliantly and extending his long winning streak. Jack Quinn won several games, and Rommel and Earnshaw each contributed victories. Only Howard Ehmke was having trouble.

After Walberg beat the Red Sox on August 31 on a four-hitter, with Dykes making himself conspicuous both at bat and in the field, the Yankees' lead was pared to two games. The next day the Athletics played their final home game of the season, before a crowd of 25,000. Grove whipped the Red Sox and Red Ruffing, 14-2. Isaminger wrote that "the high pressure pitching of Lefty Grove has been the talk of baseball."[5] The Yanks kept pace by winning at Washington.

On September 2, the A's were idle but New York lost. On the 3rd, the Athletics lost two at Washington, Ehmke and Earnshaw taking their lumps, while the Yankees split with Boston, increasing their lead to 2½ games. On September 4, Walberg beat the Senators, 9-2, while New York did not play. The next day the A's were idle and the Yanks split a doubleheader with Washington, holding the Yankee lead at two.

After rainouts on September 6, both clubs played a doubleheader the next day. The Yankees lost both games at home to the Senators while Mack's team took two from the Red Sox, to move into a tie for first place. Grove struck out eleven and gave up four hits in a dazzling 1-0 win in the opener, again over Ruffing. Rommel won the nightcap in relief of Earnshaw.

On September 8, the Athletics won two more at Fenway, 7-6 in ten innings and 7-4, to take a half-game lead over the Yankees, who beat Washington behind Ruth's 48th home run. In the A's opener, Ossie Orwoll pitched the last three scoreless innings in relief of the luckless Ehmke, winning it on a sharp single by Max Bishop. Earnshaw won the second game.

Now in first place all alone, the club moved on to New York for a four-game showdown series with the Yankees. The September 9 doubleheader attracted a huge crowd, listed at 85,265 (81,622 paid), and the fans had quite a day with their Yankees.

Dapper Mayor Jimmy Walker was there, "looking like a cut from Vanity Fair," and so was every other notable who could get a ticket. A large delegation came up on the train from Philadelphia to support their White Elephants. There was a somber moment at the start, as the death of pitcher Urban Shocker from heart disease at the age of 38 was announced. Shocker had won 18 games for New York just the year before but had been able to pitch only two innings at the start of this season before yielding to his illness.[6]

After that sad beginning, the Yankees went out and "gave it to the Athletics with both barrels and shot them out of first place," as the *Inquirer* correspondent phrased it. George Pipgras of New York hurled a 5-0 shutout in the opener, beating Jack Quinn, and the Yanks went on to win the nightcap, 7-3, when Rommel served up an eighth inning grand slam to Bob Meusel. It was a black day for Connie Mack and his team.[7]

After an off-day, the Yankees won again on September 11, beating

Lefty Grove 5-3 behind Hank Johnson, ending Grove's streak at 14 victories. Dykes made a costly error in the eighth inning, fumbling Mark Koenig's double-play grounder and then throwing wildly past first. Given this opening, the Yanks quickly capitalized with Ruth's 49th home run to win the game.

The next day the A's salvaged one game of the series, winning 4-3 on Max Bishop's ninth-inning home run. Orwoll won in relief of Ehmke, whose knee injury put him out for the rest of the season. Walberg came in to get New York out in the ninth.

The Mackmen limped out of Gotham a game and a half behind and headed west. They spent the rest of the season hanging close, keeping the pressure on, but never quite catching the Yankees. On the 14th Quinn shut out Cleveland and cut the lead to a half game, but the Yanks kept winning. When Walberg lost to the Tribe on the 17th the New York lead was increased to two games. Back and forth they went, but the Yankees' lead never disappeared and the A's never caught them again. A couple of days before the end of the season, Huggins's team clinched the pennant, and the final margin turned out to be 2½ games.

The win total of 98 games was the fourth highest in Athletics history, and the mighty Yankees knew they had been in a fight all the way. Theirs was essentially the same squad as the great 1927 team. The major difference was in the A's. That 19-game gap had been closed in a hurry.

Grove's final tally was 24-8 and 2.58. He led again in strikeouts and was clearly established as the best pitcher in the league. Jack Quinn, at the age of 44, was 18-7 and 2.90. Walberg was 17-12, Rommel 13-5, Ehmke 9-8, and Earnshaw 7-7.

Al Simmons hit .351 with 15 home runs and 107 RBIs. Hauser hit 16 homers in part-time play, and Miller batted .329, Bishop .316, and Foxx .328, with 13 home runs. Fiery Mickey Cochrane batted .293 and was described as "the motor who keeps the entire team on its toes."[8] Even Ty Cobb, who announced on September 16 that he was retiring at the end of the season, hit .323 at the age of 41.

For 1929, Connie Mack made no changes in his basic roster. There was some shuffling of second-line pitchers and utility players, but his regular lineup was fixed. Jimmy Foxx was the full-time first baseman, with Hauser sold to Cleveland. Bishop played second and Boley shortstop. Sammy Hale played more games at third than anyone else, but

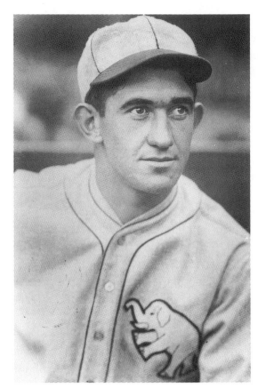

The fiery catcher and team leader Mickey Cochrane (National Baseball Hall of Fame Library, Cooperstown, N.Y.).

Jimmy Dykes, who played all over the infield, was the regular there by the end of the year.

The outfield was set, with Miller, Haas, and Simmons, and Cochrane was the regular catcher, with Cy Perkins filling in occasionally. Grove, Earnshaw, and Walberg started the great majority of games, with Quinn and rookie Bill Shores trailing behind. Howard Ehmke got a few calls. Rommel did most of the relief work, although Mack had no hesitation in calling on a starter for a stint out of the bullpen.

Everything worked. Jimmy Foxx, given a chance to play every day, hit .354 with 33 home runs and 117 runs batted in. For his first couple of years with the A's, Foxx had been a man without a position. He was still learning to play big league ball, and he was considered variously as a catcher, a first baseman, a third baseman, and even as an outfielder. Mack said of him, "He is the easiest boy on the team to handle—does whatever I ask—plays any position and never complains." Foxx spent his time listening to his elders: he said that Ty Cobb "gave me a lot of tips on running the bases and some tricks on sliding."[9]

Foxx was too much of a hitter not to be in the lineup on a steady basis. Writer Fred Lieb said, "The boy is only twenty-one, but I venture to say he will take his place with the great right-handed hitters of all time." Hauser on first gave way for the Maryland strongboy. It was a smart move on Mack's part, though it did not take a genius to make it.[10]

Simmons, still putting his foot in the bucket, still leveling a malevolent glare at all pitchers, whom he regarded as personal enemies, hit .365; *his* power totals were 34 homers and a league-best 157 RBIs. Tommy Henrich once recalled Simmons as "the most vicious man I ever saw at home plate.... He hated that pitcher with a vengeance, and showed it." Bing Miller hit .335 and drove home 93. Dykes hit .327, with 13 home runs and 79 runs batted in.[11]

For those managers who decided to throw righthanded pitching at the Athletics, Cochrane and Haas posed problems. These southpaw swingers had excellent years, too. "Black Mike" averaged .331 with 95 RBIs, and Haas hit .313, driving in 82 runs with the help of his 16 home runs. The Athletics threw a tough batting order at the opposition.

The A's pitching was superb. Earnshaw, using what the *Philadelphia Record* called "his scorchball,"[12] won 24 and lost eight. Grove was 20-6 and led the league with his 2.82 earned run average. Rube Walberg was 18-11, Quinn 11-9, Eddie Rommel 12-2 with his knuckleball working to perfection, Bill Shores 11-6. Even Ehmke was 7-2 in limited action.

The result of all this superior work was that the A's ran away from the league. By July 30, they had a 9½ game lead over the Yankees. On August 1, Mack cautioned, "I always regard the Yankees as dangerous." The next day the A's spotted the Detroit Tigers eight runs but came roaring back to win, 11-10.[13]

By August 20, when they led New York by 12 games, a *Record* columnist complained that they were not colorful enough and that was why they were not filling Shibe Park. (Not "colorful enough"? Foxx and Grove and Simmons and Cochrane? Talk about a tough press!) All possible doubt as to the outcome of the pennant race ended when the A's took three in a row from the faltering Yankees at Shibe Park on Labor Day and the day following.[14]

On September 10, Jimmy Foxx hit a Wes Ferrell fastball over the Shibe Park left field roof. It was his third ball over that lofty roof for the season but easily the longest of the three. An awestruck reporter wrote, "The ball cleared the stands by at least fifty feet and seemed to rise as it traveled."[15]

On September 14, Earnshaw shut out the White Sox, 5-0, to clinch the pennant. Columnist S.O. Grauley wrote, "The Athletics are back in the baseball sun which shunned them for the last fourteen years."[16] The A's won 104 games, more than any other team in the club's history, and their final margin over the Yankees was an impressive 18 games.

Still ahead for Mack and his Athletics was the World Series against Joe McCarthy's powerful Chicago Cubs, featuring Rogers Hornsby, Hack Wilson, Riggs Stephenson, Kiki Cuyler, Charlie Grimm, and pitchers Pat Malone, Charlie Root, and Guy Bush. The Chicagoans were confident. Scouting the A's for McCarthy had been former shortstop Joe Tinker who announced, "If we can stop Simmons and Foxx, the series is ours. They are the only men we are afraid of." Asked about the Athletic pitching, Tinker replied, "The Cubs will murder Grove and Walberg. Our players eat up southpaws."[17]

Back on September 8, Jimmy Isaminger wrote in the *Inquirer*, "Ehmke is not used much, but in a crisis he ever proves helpful and a lot of Philadelphia fans believe that he will deal a coup for the Macks in the series with the Cubs.... The sage of Lehigh Avenue has never breathed a word about his pitching plans, but he has an ace in the hole in Ehmke."[18]

Aside from the fact that most Philadelphia fans had probably forgotten Ehmke was still on the roster, Isaminger was on to something. Mack sent Ehmke off to scout the Cubs, and he made Ehmke his surprise starter in the Series opener at Chicago.

Mack said nothing about his pitching plans, and his players had no inkling of what was going on when Ehmke started to warm up before the game. But Mack knew that the Cubs' lineup was loaded with righthanded hitters, and he figured that Ehmke's sidearm delivery, coming out of the background of white shirts in Wrigley Field's jammed center field bleachers, would be just the thing to neutralize Chicago's power.

Ehmke and Charlie Root of the Cubs matched scoreless innings until Foxx powered a home run in the seventh inning. Ehmke was tossing up one slow strike after another, and the Cubs' hitters were flailing away in vain. In the ninth, Chicago shortstop Woody English made a couple of errors that led to two more Athletic runs, and Ehmke sailed through despite giving up one unearned run. He struck out 13 Cubs, for a new World Series record, in his 3-1 victory.

Grantland Rice wrote, "The long, lazy right arm of Howard Ehmke ... sounded the drum beat of woe to 51,000 Chicago rooters this afternoon as it fell across the back of the Cubs like a whip." Hornsby said, "Ehmke had us crazy with that slow motion and slow hook. I never saw a pitcher with such perfect control." Hack Wilson said simply, "That guy Ehmke had me cuckoo." [19]

For Game Two, it was George Earnshaw against Pat Malone, the Cubs' 22-game winner. In the third inning, Foxx smashed a three-run homer, and the A's scored three more in the next inning. Chicago came back to tally three in the fifth, but Mack brought in Grove to replace Earnshaw, and that was that. Grove was not at his physical best, as he was having trouble with the tips of his fingers. Cochrane later said, "Even when he pitched in the relief roles they bothered him. At times they bled, but Lefty's courage pulled him through."[20]

Grove set the Cubs down without a run the rest of the way, Simmons hit one out for the White Elephants, and the visitors coasted to a 9-3 victory. Joe McCarthy looked at his team's two-game deficit and said, sourly, "We just didn't get the breaks, but we'll get them yet."[21]

Two days later, the World Series returned to Shibe Park for the first time since 1914. Before the series began, there was legal skirmishing between the Athletics and the Twentieth Street Householders Association, as the ball club tried unsuccessfully to stymie the neighbors and their rooftop bleachers. Public opinion was with the homeowners, since many regular fans were sore because they had been shut out by the manner in which the Shibes had allotted World Series tickets.[22]

When the game got under way, before a capacity crowd of 29,921, and hundreds more on the 20th Street rooftops, Guy Bush opposed Earnshaw. Each starter went all the way in a 3-1 Cubs win. Earnshaw fanned ten, but he was done in by a three-run sixth inning, with the deciding runs coming across on a hit by Cuyler after a costly error by Dykes. Bush scattered nine hits for the Cubs' victory. A confident Rogers Hornsby said, "We'll go out and beat 'em tomorrow and then they'll fold up.... We'll run 'em right off the field now."[23]

The Athletics held a two-to-one lead in games, but that lead looked very precarious the next day, October 12, as the Cubs touched Jack Quinn for two runs in the fourth and picked up five more against Quinn and Walberg in the sixth. When they got another run off of Rommel in the next inning, Chicago led by 8-0. The game appeared over, and Root "held the mightiest of Mack sluggers in a grip of iron."[24]

But the Cubs were up against one of the greatest teams of all time. Al Simmons led off the bottom half of the seventh with a home run, to spoil Root's shutout. Foxx and Miller hit safely, and Dykes singled home the second run. The inning was becoming an annoyance to manager Joe McCarthy, and he started some bullpen activity. Joe Boley singled, but pinch-hitter George Burns hit a pop fly for the first out. Max Bishop then singled in two more runs to make the score 8-4.

McCarthy lifted Root, replacing him with veteran lefty Art Nehf, who came in to a two-on one-out situation. Mule Haas hit a liner toward center fielder Hack Wilson, who lost it in the sun. Wilson flailed futilely at the ball, and by the time Stephenson tracked it down, Haas had an inside-the-park home run and the score was 8-7.

When Nehf walked Cochrane, righthander Sheriff Blake was brought in to pitch for Chicago. Simmons singled, and Foxx followed with another hit to score Cochrane and tie the game.

A disgusted McCarthy took Blake out and brought in his ace, Pat Malone. No matter. After Miller was hit by a pitch to load the bases (McCarthy had to love that!), Dykes doubled to left, off Stephenson's glove, and two more runs scored, numbers nine and ten of the inning. Malone then fanned Boley and Burns to bring things to a close. "Never in all world's series history," wrote one reporter truthfully, "was there such an inning."[25]

Shocked as they were by the sudden turnaround in the game, the Cubs had to be more disheartened by the sight of Lefty Grove strolling in from the Philadelphia bullpen. Lefty got all six hitters he faced in his two innings of work, striking out four, to wrap up the victory. With the extraordinary triumph, the A's had a 3-1 lead in games and a stranglehold on the Series. A fine Chicago Cubs team was gasping for air.

For the fifth game, two days later, Mack sent Howard Ehmke to the mound once again, against the Cubs' Malone. President Herbert Hoover showed up to watch Game Five. When he was escorted across the field to the box he would share with Mayor Harry Mackey, "the stands roared a greeting," as the *Bulletin* said. "It was a great reception," wrote Thomas Healey in the *Public Ledger*, "and the President and Mrs. Hoover appreciated it."[26]

When the game started, Malone was extremely sharp, and Ehmke did not have the elements of surprise, unfamiliarity, and a bright bleacher background going for him. Chicago got two runs in the third. Walberg in relief held the Cubs scoreless the rest of the way. Still, the Athletics had only two hits against Malone and trailed 2-0 as they came to bat in the ninth. Cubs shortstop Woody English later recalled, sadly, "All we needed was three more outs and we were back in Chicago for the last two games. It looked like we had it salted away."[27]

Malone got the first of those three outs when he struck out pinch hitter Walter French. He got two strikes on Bishop before Max singled sharply to left. With the hometown crowd hoping for another miracle finish Mule Haas hit the first pitch, lofting a drive over the right field fence and onto 20th Street. Just like that, the score was tied. Cochrane grounded out, but Simmons brought the fans to their feet again with a shot high off the scoreboard in right, pulling in to second with a double. Malone, seeing his game slip away, walked Foxx intentionally to pitch to Bing Miller.

Miller, a great curveball hitter, took two fastballs for strikes, then laced another Malone heater over second baseman Rogers Hornsby's head, a line drive double to right-center between Wilson and Cuyler. Simmons romped home with the run that ended the World Series, stomping on the plate with glee as Dykes greeted him, followed by the rest of the team. It was a stunning ending. Mayor Mackey abandoned the President and climbed onto the field to congratulate Miller and join in the team's celebration.

After 16 years, the Athletics of Connie Mack were again champions of the baseball world. Mack, Ed Pollock wrote, "had waited through weary years for that moment when his ball club would again be ruler of the game."[28]

The 1929 A's team was one of the best ever, with excellent pitching, the infield of Foxx, Bishop, Boley, and Dykes, the stellar outfield combine of Miller, Haas, and Simmons, and the mighty Cochrane behind the plate. Mack called it "the gamest that ever played baseball." A measure of the greatness of Mack's 1929 team was its being able to go through the World Series against a dangerous opponent using Lefty Grove, in the prime of his career, only in relief.[29]

In February 1930, the prestigious Philadelphia Award, honoring the person who, during the preceding year, had most furthered "the best interests of the community of which Philadelphia is the center," was presented to the 66-year-old Connie Mack. The people of the city reacted with delight to this accolade to the leader of their world champions. They were accustomed to the sight of the lean, quiet manager of the Athletics, sitting in dignified elegance on the dugout bench, waving his scorecard to position his outfielders, occasionally summoning an umpire over to help straighten out some complexity into which a game had unexpectedly fallen, maintaining a splendid composure in both victory and defeat. They had come to think of Connie Mack as one of the first men of the city. For some time Mack and the Athletics had been a significant part of Philadelphia's economic and cultural mix, a fact now truly recognized by the award.

CHAPTER 11

Another Dynasty

The accomplishments of the 1929 team were tough to follow, but the 1930 Athletics were equal to the task. There was little change from one team to the next. In December, Sammy Hale was traded to St. Louis for 40-year-old Wally Schang, returning to the scene of his early feats. (Mack always had a weakness for bringing back his old stars late in their careers.) A 27-year-old rookie pitcher named Roy "Popeye" Mahaffey came up from the minors, as did 20-year-old infielder Dibrell Williams. Two players who had seen action in only two games the year before, infielder Eric McNair and outfielder Roger "Doc" Cramer, made the 1930 roster, although they saw limited action and Cramer spent part of the season at Portland.

The year 1930 has a special meaning to baseball historians: it was the season that the swing to the offense went to its extreme. A more tightly wound ball, restrictions on pitchers, more frequent changes of baseballs—these factors produced a season in which the entire National League, including pitchers, compiled a .303 batting average and the American League hit .288. Home run totals rose from 1349 in 1929 to 1565 in 1930. The barrage was unremitting, and the pitching fraternity was shell-shocked by the time it was over.

The Athletics shared in the hitting bonanza, with Simmons leading the league at .381, the club's first batting champion since Lajoie in 1901. Although he missed all of spring training in a salary holdout Simmons still hit 36 homers and drove in 165 runs, in a showing which might have killed the whole institution of spring training. Foxx was close behind, with .335, 37 home runs, and 156 RBIs. Cochrane batted .357, Miller and Dykes hit over .300, and Mule Haas was just a point under at .299.

Lefty Grove gave the club a spectacular pitching performance. In the midst of all the offensive fireworks, he won 28 and lost five and took his sixth straight strikeout title with a career-high 209 (it doesn't matter how lively the ball is if a batter can't hit it). He was the only pitcher in the league with an earned run average of less than three. His ERA of 2.54 was far ahead of runner-up Wes Ferrell's 3.31. Grove and Earnshaw (22-13) were the only pair of pitchers on one club to win 20, but Grove was the only pitcher on the A's staff with an ERA under four. Walberg, Rommel, Shores, Mahaffey, and Quinn won their share of games, but all had high earned run averages. So did everyone else that year—except Lefty Grove.

The Athletics had trouble early with the Senators, losing seven in a row to the team now managed by Walter Johnson, but they swept a doubleheader from Washington on Memorial Day. In the opener the A's trailed by three runs with two out in the ninth, when Al Simmons slugged a three-run home run. They won in the 13th inning when Simmons doubled, Dykes followed with an infield single, and Eric McNair singled to drive in the tie-breaker. Simmons, his knee hurting from a baserunning mishap and confined to pinch-hitting duties in the nightcap, went to the plate with the bases loaded in the fourth inning and responded with a grand slam that helped mightily in the 14-11 victory.

The sweep of Washington set the Mackmen on the right track. They overtook the Senators and then turned it up a notch to take charge of the race. The pennant was clinched on September 14, and the team's eventual margin over second-place Washington was eight games.

Grantland Rice looked at the accomplishments of the Athletics and gave the credit to Mack. "The wonder is," Rice wrote, "that Connie Mack was able to engineer his present ball club into another pennant." Grove and Earnshaw, he said, were the "only two dependable pitchers" and Mack had to "jockey these in the most skillful fashion."[1] The A's won 102 games but, ominously, attendance declined to 721,663 as the nation and the area settled into the Depression.

World Series opponents were the St. Louis Cardinals, managed by Gabby Street. Led by the bats of Sunny Jim Bottomley, Frankie Frisch,

Sparky Adams, Chick Hafey, and Taylor Douthit, and the hurling arms of Burleigh Grimes, Wild Bill Hallahan, Jesse Haines, and Flint Rhem, they edged the Cubs in a tight National League race. The Redbirds piled up a .314 team batting average during the regular season, and the Athletics knew they would be no pushovers in the Series.

The first game took place on October 1, with an expanded-capacity crowd of 32,295 filling every seat in Shibe Park. There was no repeat of an Ehmke-like surprise: Mack started his ace, the best pitcher in baseball, Robert Moses Grove, against the stubble-bearded spitballer, Burleigh Grimes. President Hoover threw out the first ball, and Grove and his teammates took it from there.

Lefty scattered nine Cardinal hits and held the Redbirds to two runs. The Athletics collected only five safeties against Grimes, but each was for extra bases and each produced a run. Cochrane and Simmons hit home runs, Foxx and Haas blasted triples, and Jimmy Dykes chipped in a two-base hit. The result was a satisfying 5-2 Philadelphia victory.

The next day the colorful, hard-drinking Flint Rhem took the mound for St. Louis, against Earnshaw, and the result was about the same. Cochrane homered in the first inning as the A's took control with two runs, George Watkins hit a roundtripper for St. Louis in the second, and it was all Athletics after that. Earnshaw's fastball was buzzing with authority, and the Cards could get only six hits. The A's made good use of their seven, for a 6-1 win, and Walter Cahall in the *Inquirer* wrote that "once more the House of Mack tumbled the House of Cards." [2]

The Series moved to St. Louis for Game Three, and the Cardinals seemed more comfortable in their home surroundings. In the fourth inning, Taylor Douthit led off with a home run against Walberg, and his mates added another run in the fifth, two in the seventh off reliever Bill Shores, and another in the eighth against Quinn. The Mackmen were unable to solve the slants of southpaw Hallahan, who held them to seven hits (three by Bishop) and no runs. Final score: St. Louis 5, Philadelphia 0.

The next game was a matchup of two future Hall of Famers before a crowd of just under 40,000 at Sportsman's Park. Grove faced the veteran Jesse Haines, and the A's scored first on a single by Simmons in the opening inning. In the third, shortstop Charley Gelbert tripled and was brought home by Haines. In the fourth, two runs scored after Dykes threw

109

Ray Blades's ground ball away. Grove gave up nothing after that, but the A's were unable to do anything with the knuckleballing Haines and the 3-1 score stood up for the Cardinals. The Series was tied, 2-2.

Game Five was a classic pitchers' duel between Earnshaw and Grimes through seven innings, and neither team was able to score. The tension mounted as the innings rolled by, because everyone knew that the winner of the fifth game would have a major advantage in the Series.

In the top of the eighth, the A's filled the bases with one out but could not get the run home as both Bishop and Dykes grounded out. Earnshaw left for a pinch-hitter and Grove came in to pitch in relief. Lefty set the Cards down in the eighth, and, in the ninth, Jimmy Foxx belted a decisive two-run homer. Grove squelched the home team in the bottom of the inning, and the Athletics headed back to Philadelphia with a 2-0 victory and the Series lead in games. Foxx's home run looked huge.

After a travel day, George Earnshaw took the mound again on October 8, before 32,295 at Shibe Park. Hallahan opposed him for the National Leaguers. In the opening inning, Dykes walked and scored on a Cochrane double. After Hallahan fanned Al Simmons, he walked Foxx and gave up a two-base hit to Bing Miller for a second run. In the third, Simmons homered, and an inning later Dykes hit one out with a man on to make it 5-0.

The A's tacked on single runs in the fifth and sixth, while Earnshaw moved steadily through the St. Louis lineup, blanking the Cards inning after inning. The White Elephants smelled victory and there was no stopping them. The Cards' lone run in the ninth was far too late. The Athletics won it, 7-1, to wrap up another world's championship.

Earnshaw had simply overpowered the Cardinals. As Isaminger wrote in his wrapup, "Pitching twenty-five innings in three games in the series, the Swarthmore Hercules held the Street ensemble to two skimpy runs." Jimmy Wilson, the Cardinal catcher, said, "I thought Earnshaw might be a little worn out today but he had more stuff than in either of the other games he pitched. He's an iron man if there ever was one."[3]

Earnshaw, Dykes, Simmons, Foxx, Grove and the rest: if one test of a great team is to repeat as champions, these Athletics had proven they were a great team.

For 1931, Connie Mack's aim was simple: do it again. He told reporter Bill Dooly that his team "proved it was a great ball club last season. It will be better this year.... I think we have an excellent chance of finishing on top again."[4] Mack's chief concern was to come up with a dependable third starting pitcher, to go along with Grove and Earnshaw. He hoped that Walberg would rebound from his disappointing 13-12 record.

The Mackmen started slowly by splitting their first ten games, but Mack said his team looked as good as ever and would start winning steadily as soon as its hitting picked up. In May, the A's won 17 in a row, and by June 11 they had a five-game lead over Washington. At that point it was apparent that Mack's pitching worries were needless; Grove's record stood at 10-2, Walberg was 9-1, and Earnshaw was 8-2.

The club suffered several injuries—to Dykes, Boley, and Cochrane —but subs Eric McNair, Dib Williams, and Johnny Heving did well and the A's kept winning. Later Mack had to shift Foxx to third and put Phil Todt, picked up during the offseason from Boston, on first. The A's kept on winning. Early in July the team obtained 31-year-old Waite Hoyt, the former Yankee star, from Detroit as hoped-for pitching insurance.

The Athletics then ran off a 13-game winning streak. By the end of July they had an 11-game lead and the inside track on another pennant. In August, attention centered on Grove, who was having an incredible season, winning every time out. When he recorded a victory on August 19 it was his 16th straight, to tie the league record. However, he lost in his next outing, 1-0 to the Browns, when substitute outfielder Jimmy Moore lost a fly ball in the sun. The mercurial Grove, who had been known in the past to throw a tantrum or two, went on a rampage in the clubhouse, his anger directed not at the hapless Moore but at Al Simmons, who had taken the day off and made Moore's misplay possible.

On September 15, the Athletics sewed up the 1931 pennant with a 14-3 victory over the Indians at Shibe Park. Despite the injuries, which continued to strike throughout the season, the Mackmen won 107 games, a franchise record to this day, and outdistanced the second-place Yankees by 13½ games. Attendance for the year, reflecting the scarcity of money in a Depression-wracked economy, was off once again, falling to 627,464, a drop of 94,000 from 1930.

Grove rang up an astonishing mark of 31 wins and four defeats, with a league-leading earned run average of 2.06. As usual, he led the league in strikeouts. He even had five saves out of the bullpen (based on the modern definition of "saves"). No pitcher in the game was even close to the Athletics' sensational southpaw.

Grove had substantial help in 1931, from Earnshaw, who was 21-7; from Walberg, who came back to post a career best record of 20-12; from Roy Mahaffey at 15-4; from Hoyt, who was 10-5 with the A's; and from Rommel, who was 7-5 and pitched well, mostly in relief.

Simmons won another batting title, with his .390 mark, and he drove in 128 runs. Foxx had 30 home runs and 120 RBIs. Cochrane hit .349 and drove in 89, and Haas hit .323 despite breaking his wrist in July. Bishop, Miller, Dykes, and Dib Williams, now the regular short-stop, all contributed their share to the Mack attack.

The Athletics were strong favorites to win the World Series, despite the fact that the Cardinals had run away with the race in the National League. Gabby Street's Redbirds were basically the same team as the 1930 winner, except for the addition of a rookie righthander named Paul Derringer, who won 18 games, and the replacement of Taylor Douthit in center by a young Oklahoman named John "Pepper" Martin, playing his first full year in the league. The hustling, free-spirited Martin had a good season, hitting .300.

Grove opened in Sportsman's Park against young Derringer, and although Lefty was not at his best he went the route and defeated the Redbirds, 6-2. He yielded an uncharacteristic 12 hits, but he was suffering from a blister on the second finger of his pitching hand. For the last five innings the finger was dripping blood. Simmons hit a two-run roundtrip-per as the Athletics came back from a first inning Cardinal two-spot, provided by Jim Bottomley and Martin.

Game Two went to the Cardinals, as Wild Bill Hallahan outpitched Earnshaw by a 2-0 score. Both St. Louis runs were generated by Mar-tin's base running; Pepper stole two bases and had Mickey Cochrane looking puzzled. Hallahan held the Athletics to three hits for his shutout win.

After two days off for travel, the teams met at Shibe Park for the third game on October 5. Grove squared off against Burleigh Grimes, and it was a St. Louis day. The blister was still troubling the lefthander, and he was forced to rely primarily on his curve ball, without his normal fast ball. He gave up four runs in eight innings, with Pepper Martin again in the midst of both two-run outbursts. Grimes held the Athletics hitless until Bing Miller singled in the eighth. In the ninth inning, the Redbirds added another run off Mahaffey, and the A's only response was a two-run homer by Simmons, just their second hit. St. Louis won, 5-2, and took the Series lead. *The Sporting News*, taking note of Martin's 7-for-11, three stolen bases, and four runs scored in the first three games, said that Pepper "was well on his way to a niche in the hall of fame as a World Series hero."[5] The Cardinals' confidence was soaring now that they had beaten both Grove and Earnshaw.

In the fourth game, however, Earnshaw was at his best and held the visitors to just two hits, both by the irrepressible Martin, who also stole another base. The A's picked up an early run on a Bishop single and Simmons double, and they scored two more in the sixth when Foxx slammed one over the left field roof and Dykes singled home Miller. These runs were plenty for Earnshaw, who waltzed to a 3-0 win.

For Game Five, Mack pulled another surprise when he started Waite Hoyt rather than his twenty-game winner Rube Walberg. It was a case of Mack being a little too cute; Hoyt, who had never really gotten in shape, was not the man for the job. Hallahan took the mound for St. Louis and had little trouble posting a 5-1 victory. The Cards scored a run in the first inning, driven in by Martin on a sacrifice fly, and two more in the sixth, on Pepper's two-run home run.

After the game it was reported that "Connie Mack was considerably peeved" at Hoyt's "failure to take his job seriously and will give him his walking papers this winter." And so he did. Still, no one forced the A's manager to start Hoyt in this critical game.[6]

After the train ride back to St. Louis, the two teams met in the sixth game at Sportsman's Park. Grove faced Derringer, and with his blister gone he had it all. He held the Cardinals to five hits and one run while striking out seven. He even held Pepper Martin hitless, and the A's were starting to think that impossible, at least in this series. The Athletics put together two four-run innings on their way to an easy 8-1 win.

So it all boiled down to one game, the last World Series game, though no one suspected it at the time, that the Philadelphia Athletics would ever play. It was Earnshaw against Grimes, winner take all, before a surprisingly small crowd of only 20,805 at Sportsman's Park.

The Cardinals broke the ice with two first-inning runs. After singles by Andy High and George Watkins and a sacrifice bunt, High scored on Earnshaw's wild pitch. Martin walked and stole second. When Ernie Orsatti struck out, the third strike got away from Cochrane. Mickey threw to first, and Watkins broke for the plate, scoring ahead of Foxx's off-line throw. In the third inning, Watkins hit a two-run home run.

Grimes carried his 4-0 lead into the ninth, when Simmons led with a walk. Foxx fouled out to the catcher and Miller forced Simmons at second base. Down to their last out, the Athletics demonstrated they would not go meekly. Jimmy Dykes waited out a walk, and Dib Williams singled to left to load the bases. Pinchhitter Doc Cramer dropped a single into short center field to score two runs. Down 4-2 the Mackmen were still alive. With the tying runs on base, Street lifted the tiring Grimes and brought in Hallahan to pitch to Max Bishop. Bishop flied to center field, and Pepper Martin, quite appropriately, pulled it in to win.

It was a hard-fought, well-played World Series, and the Cardinals deserved their victory. Along with the outstanding hurling of Grimes and Hallahan, the Redbirds had the superb play of Martin, and that was decisive. New York writer Bill Corum wrote that Martin "stole everything but the elephants' trunks and at the finish he had catcher Mickey Cochrane searching himself to find out if he still had his shoes."[7]

Although they followed the Cardinals the last month of the season Connie Mack's scouts had turned in no report on Martin. Cochrane said it would have made no difference; "they tried everything on Pepper, but he hit 'em just the same."[8] Martin was 12-for-24 in the Series for a .500 average, with four doubles, a home run, five runs batted in, and five stolen bases. Sometimes, in a short series, a player simply explodes. It was the A's ill fortune to have it happen to them.

The remarkable three-year run of Connie Mack's Athletics was over, but quite a run it was: three pennants, two world championships and a near-miss, 313 regular season wins, and the multi-faceted heroics of Grove, Simmons, Foxx, Earnshaw, Cochrane, Dykes, and the rest of Mack's talented crew. If the failure to win the third World Series in a row somehow tarnishes the A's as a team for the ages, it should be remembered that two years after their 1927 championship the Yankees were 18 games out of first place. Mack's team, two years after the 1929 club, went to the seventh game of the World Series.

CHAPTER 12

Back to the Basement

Philadelphia's long-suffering baseball fans, who had been subjected to a string of last-place clubs at the end of the teen years and into the 1920s, discovered to their dismay that the middle and late '30s were to be more of the same. Both the Athletics and their National League colleagues in Baker Bowl fell to the bottom of their leagues—and stayed there. At least this time the collapse of the Athletics was more measured.

The team's failure in the World Series of 1931, disappointing as it was for Mack, his players, and their fans, was nothing like the blowout to which his overconfident 1914 squad had been subjected. A couple more hits and three more A's runs in Game Seven would have stretched the run of world championships to three, and the 1932 team would have been looking to make it four in a row. Losing to the Cardinals, though, took the sheen off Mack's machine, and 1932 looked different as a result.

The Athletics' nucleus remained intact, although Boley, no longer a regular, was released early in the season, Eddie Rommel pitched in only 17 games, and Bing Miller, going on 38, played fewer games in the outfield than did Doc Cramer. Mack's team, aging in some areas but boasting several great players in the heart of their careers, won 94 games, a very creditable showing, but the powerful Yankees under Joe McCarthy won 107.

Attendance fell off substantially for the third year in a row, to 405,500, a major worry to Mack and the Shibes. The Depression was cutting harshly into the area's economy, but Connie Mack got into his head the fixed idea that Philadelphia would not support a winning team.

He first suspected this with the attendance drop his pennant-winning 1914 team had suffered, and the steady decline from 1929 to 1932 confirmed this truism in his mind. The fans would come out to watch a team on the way up, but, at least in Philadelphia, he theorized, they became bored with a steady diet of victories. That there might be other extraneous factors contributing to a faltering gate was something he refused to concede. This idea was a strong factor in his management practices over the years.[1]

Still, with 94 victories and some shining individual performances, there was much in the 1932 season to savor. The biggest story in Philadelphia was Jimmy Foxx, who had a tremendous season and was voted the most valuable player in the American League. Muscular Jimmy, called "the Beast" for his imposing physique and the ferocity of his long drives, compiled an average of .364, three points behind the league-leading Dale Alexander, even though Alexander's 392 times at bat would not in later years have qualified for a batting title.

Foxx hit 58 home runs and drove in 169 runs, both totals tops in the league. No right-handed hitter in the major leagues had ever hit more home runs in a season than did Jimmy Foxx in 1932. But that's not all: he hit two more home runs in games at Detroit that were washed out because they did not go the required five innings. Another thing: Jimmy hit the screen atop the right-field wall in Sportsman's Park, keeping the ball in play, five times in 1932—a screen which was not there in 1927 when Ruth hit his sixty home runs.

Simmons too had an outstanding season. Al batted .322, with 35 roundtrippers and 151 runs batted in. Cramer hit .336, Mule Haas hit .305, and Cochrane batted .293, with 23 homers and 112 RBIs, showing that Pepper Martin had not damaged his psyche much. Grove had another fine year, going 25-10 with a league-leading 2.84 ERA. For the first time Lefty failed to lead the circuit in strikeouts, although his 188 were just two behind Red Ruffing's total.

Earnshaw, Walberg and Mahaffey won a lot of games, though their earned run averages were high, and rookie lefthander Tony Freitas was 12-5. There can be few disappointments for a team that wins 94 games, and not much could be done about the Yankee steamroller which flattened the rest of the league.

There was, unfortunately, the matter of money. In 1932, Simmons

Jimmy Foxx: so strong they called him "Beast" (Brace Photo).

was paid more than $33,000, Foxx made over $16,000, and the other A's stars were paid similar figures. Mack himself drew a salary of $50,000. There were debts from a recent renovation of Shibe Park and rumors that Connie Mack had lost heavily in the stock market crash. Declining attendance put the club in the red, and unlike some other clubowners the Macks and Shibes did not have a cushion of wealth with which to absorb losses.

At the end of the 1932 season Mack began what several sportswriters had been predicting, the dismantling of his great team. He sold Al Simmons, Mule Haas, and Jimmy Dykes to the White Sox for $100,000, on September 28, telling the press that it was a "spur of the moment" transaction, certainly an odd comment. "Under no circumstances do I intend to break up the club," Mack went on. "We are going to rebuild some portions, that's all."[2]

With three regulars gone and the aging Bing Miller's playing time reduced further, the 1933 Athletics were still a good team, but clearly on the downgrade. They won only 79 games as they finished third, 19½ games behind Washington's pennant winners. The fans were unhappy with Mack's changes and home attendance dropped off again, to 297,138.

The fans still had some bright spots to talk about. Jimmy Foxx won all three of the major offensive titles. He led the league in batting, with .356, in home runs with 48, and in RBIs with 163. Foxx's Triple Crown led to his second consecutive MVP award. Mickey Cochrane had another splendid season; he hit .322, with 15 home runs, and did his usual fine work behind the plate. Bishop hit .294 at second base, and shortstop Dib Williams batted .289.

The club introduced two fine youngsters from the Portland farm. Replacing Dykes at third was a rookie from the University of Texas, a tough Irish kid named Mike Higgins, who carried the nickname "Pinky." Higgins hit .314, with 14 homers and 99 runs batted in. He was a little rough around the edges at third base, leading the league with 24 errors, but his hitting offset a lot of fielding mistakes. The other productive rookie was a husky righthanded outfielder named Bob Johnson. Johnson, one-quarter Cherokee from Oklahoma, was soon called "Indian Bob." Under any name, Bob Johnson was a hitter. In 1933 he batted .290, hit 21 home runs, and drove in 93 runs. A third rookie from Portland, coming up with Higgins and Johnson, was outfielder Lou Finney, who disappointed with a .267 average and only three home runs.

Lefty Grove won 24 and lost eight, leading the league in wins, percentage, and complete games, although his strikeout total was down as his fastball faded at age 33. In late May, curiously, Mack used Grove in relief in five straight games; in this stretch Lefty pitched 18 innings and yielded one run. Mahaffey and Merritt "Sugar" Cain each won 13 games, but with high earned run averages. Walberg and Earnshaw struggled. In September, a young righthander named Johnny Marcum, purchased from Louisville for $30,000, began his big league career by shutting out Cleveland and Chicago in successive starts.

A midseason diversion, originally planned as a one-time adjunct to Chicago's Century of Progress Exposition, caught the fancy of the public and became a fixture. In the first All-Star Game, played July 6, 1933, at Comiskey Park, Connie Mack managed the American League team against a National League squad run by his old adversary, John McGraw. The players from the junior circuit won, 4-2, as Grove finished off the National Leaguers with three scoreless innings.

Baseball in Philadelphia received one big boost during 1933. Professional baseball clubs had for many years suffered from the Pennsylvania "blue laws" which barred professional sports on Sundays. There had long been pressure to ease this restriction; as far back as 1918 Dennis J. Dougherty, Archbishop of Philadelphia, said, "I am heartily in favor of Sunday baseball, providing it is played after church hours and in no way interferes with religious duties. I can see no sin in it if it is properly conducted." But the Roman Catholics of the big cities carried little weight in the Pennsylvania General Assembly, where small-town Protestants held sway.[3]

The Athletics played a Sunday game in 1926 as a test case, but the state Supreme Court upheld the law. By 1933, though, seven years later, baseball people were hopeful that the Sunday ban would go the way of Prohibition.[4]

Late in 1932, Connie Mack blamed the blue laws for the A's finish in the red that year. He said that if Philadelphia had enjoyed Sunday baseball in 1932 he would not have been forced to sell Simmons, Haas, and Dykes. He hoped that the legislators in Harrisburg would vote to permit local option on the question so that, as sportswriter Bill Dooly quaintly put it, "the benighting influence of the holier-than-thou element will be properly disposed of at the polls."[5] In early 1933, the legislature finally passed the necessary measure, which was signed with reluctance by Governor Gifford Pinchot.

On November 7, 1933, Philadelphia's electorate voted to permit the playing of professional baseball on Sundays from 2 p.m. to 6 p.m. It was often impossible to squeeze a Sunday doubleheader into four hours, and over the years there were some weird-looking performances as teams struggled to get four-and-a-half innings in, or prevent the opposition from doing so, before the curfew struck: batters trying to make outs, and pitchers trying to keep them from doing so, for example—but it certainly beat an outright ban.

Five weeks later, on December 12, almost as a thank-you to the voters of Philadelphia who had removed the Sunday ban from his team's back, Mack made a series of startling trades.

He sent Lefty Grove, Rube Walberg, and Max Bishop to the Red Sox, in exchange for two second-line players and $125,000 cash. The same day, Mack shipped the fiery heart of his club, Mickey Cochrane, off to Detroit, where he was to become player-manager, for catcher Johnny Pasek and $100,000. And for good measure, he immediately traded Pasek and George Earnshaw to the White Sox for $20,000 more and catcher Charlie Berry.

Thus, almost casually, Connie Mack discarded the man whom some experts consider the best pitcher of all time and the catcher who is still rated as the best at his position by many students of the game. Grove, Walberg, and Bishop, it could be said, were all getting along in years, but Mickey Cochrane was only 29 and at the peak of his game. In announcing these transactions, Mack told the press, apparently with a straight face, "I am not breaking up my ball club."

The fans could see that the A's still had Jimmy Foxx, player-coach Bing Miller, and a few lesser lights from the championship team. They could be thankful that Connie Mack had not plunged them from first place to last in one year as he had in 1915. The letdown had been more gradual this time—and now they could come to see the A's, or what was left of them, play on Sundays.

In 1934, with Sunday baseball, the A's attendance increased by some 8000, moving up to 305,847, though the club slid back into the second division, finishing a distant fifth with a losing record of 68-82.

For the followers of Connie Mack's Athletics, it was the start of a long sojourn in the American League's nether regions. Fans could have been excused for feelings of *déjà vu*, but the uncritical local baseball writers printed every spring Mack's hope for "just one more pennant," which kept the aging leader at the club's helm for many more years, into his dotage. The next pennant for the Athletics would fly in Oakland.

For the 1934 A's, there were a number of impressive offensive performances. Foxx hit .334, with 44 home runs and 130 runs batted in.

This came on the heels of Mack's abortive attempt to subject him to a substantial salary cut. Higgins, Cramer, and Johnson hit well over .300, and Bob Johnson banged 34 home runs. Eric McNair at shortstop hit 17 roundtrippers and posted a good .280 average.

The pitching staff, though, had passed from Grove-Earnshaw-Walberg-and-Rommel to Marcum-Cascarella-Dietrich-and-Cain. It wasn't the same. Connie Mack was often quoted as saying that pitching was 75 per cent of the game, but 1934's Athletics seemed to emphasize the other 25 per cent. Marcum was 14-11, Joe Cascarella 12-15, local product Bill "Bullfrog" Dietrich 11-12, and Sugar Cain was 9-17; all four had earned run averages in the middle fours. The good hitting covered up a lot of poor pitching, at least enough to win 68 games.

After the 1934 season, the Shibes sponsored a goodwill tour to Japan of a picked team of American Leaguers, many of them Athletics, including Foxx, Miller, Rabbit Warstler, Frankie Hayes, Joe Cascarella, and Eric McNair, under the leadership of Connie Mack. The interest of the Shibes in the trip was to open up Japan as a market for their sporting equipment. The Japanese were baseball enthusiasts who were eager to see the stars like Ruth whom they had been following from such a distance. After a two-week cruise across the Pacific, the ballplayers traveled around Japan for 17 games in 12 cities, before crowds that sometimes exceeded 50,000. The games were played against an all-star team of Japanese high school and college stars called the Tokyo Giants. While the Americans won every game, including a 1-0 squeaker, each appearance was an event in itself, with much ceremony and ritual taking place before the first pitch. The U.S. ambassador said that Babe Ruth was worth a hundred ambassadors. Leaving Japan the tourists played one game in Shanghai and two in Manila before sailing back to the United States.[6]

When the Athletics returned, rumors were afoot that Ruth was to become manager of the club. Mack squelched them, saying, "As I shall continue to manage the Athletics, we can't have two managers, can we?" He said he felt great and "I know as much baseball as I ever did."[7]

Back from the Far East, as Mack prepared for the '35 season, he turned down the Yankees' proposal to swap Tony Lazzeri, Newark first baseman George McQuinn, and $50,000 for third baseman Higgins. "I regard Higgins as the greatest third baseman in the major leagues," said

Mack, and if New York would not increase the cash to $100,000 there was no deal.[8]

Mack decided to switch Jimmy Foxx to catcher, putting rookie Alex Hooks, from Tulsa in the Texas League, on first base. Foxx, newly appointed club captain, was dubious about the change; "Connie and I talked hours over this catching proposition," the young slugger said. "I told him I liked first base best of all, but he convinced me I could do the club more good by going behind the bat again, so I finally agreed." He asked for more money, which Mack gave him, and he said he would catch for only one year. "Jimmy will make a first class catcher," Mister Mack said. He later predicted that "it's an open race this year and our chances must be considered as good as the others."[9]

It did not take long for cold reality to set in. Shortstop Dib Williams was bitten by "Rags," the club's mascot dog, Higgins sprained his ankle, Hooks did not hit, and the A's lost ten of their first 12 games. On May 2, Williams, booed by the Shibe Park fans for three years, was waived to the Red Sox, Eric McNair was moved from third to short, Foxx was put on third base, and Lou Finney replaced Hooks at first. When Higgins returned, Foxx went reluctantly back behind the plate again.[10]

Near the end of May, the A's sent Hooks, hitting .227 with no home runs, back to Atlanta. Jimmy Foxx went to first base, Finney moved to right field, and light-hitting Paul Richards was purchased from the Giants to catch. It made little difference.

For the 1935 A's, the hitting was not good enough, and the pitching was worse. The team scored 54 fewer runs than in 1934, won ten fewer games, and fell into last place with a resounding thud, 34 games from the top. Home attendance fell way off, to 233,173. A 12-game losing streak in late August and early September dropped the team behind Washington and St. Louis, for its first last-place finish since 1921. "Financially and artistically," said one writer, "the season of 1935 will be regarded as a nightmare by Athletic owners."[11]

Foxx hit .346 with 36 homers (tied for the title with Detroit's Hank Greenberg) and 115 runs batted in. Cramer batted .332, while a rookie from Uvalde, Georgia, named Wally Moses hit .325 in 85 games, before he broke his arm. The writers found Moses a good source of copy (example: "a young Moses has been discovered by Connie Mack ... to lead the A's out of the wilderness"), and he proved to be a good player, a solid hitter, fine outfielder, and topnotch baserunner. *The Sporting News* called Moses "the major league outfield find of 1935."[12]

Indian Bob Johnson hit .299 with 28 home runs, while Higgins was at .296 with 23 fourbaggers. The team's pitching, aside from Marcum's 17-12, was nondescript. Cain and Cascarella departed for other venues, and Dietrich and Al Benton did very badly. Cascarella's separation from the team was particularly messy. The pitcher came into a May 29 game in Boston, walked the two men he faced, both with the bases loaded, and was lifted. When he returned to the dugout, Mack said angrily to him, "Take that uniform off and don't ever put it on again." Cascarella was soon on his way to Syracuse.[13]

The Athletics clashed with their neighbors on 20th Street when, after the 1934 season, John Shibe had a 38-foot addition built on top of the 12-foot-high right field fence. The new green corrugated-iron fence destroyed the once-thriving trade in roof-top seats overlooking the ball park. No bones were made about the fence's purpose: "This was done to defeat the outlaw stands built on roof tops on an adjoining street."[14] At one point, the neighbors tried litigation to have what they called the "spite fence" removed, but the club, represented by a young attorney and future mayor named Richardson Dilworth, was successful in defending the case.

Another annoyance to the customers kicked in on July 22, when a new state tax on admissions went into effect. Admission prices at Shibe Park went to 57 cents for the covered bleachers, $1.14 for the grandstand, and $2.28 for box seats. The new tax made baseball admissions in Pennsylvania higher than anywhere else in the majors. It irritated the ticket sellers, who had to make change in pennies for nearly every customer. "No doubt there would be a far greater storm of protest," one writer said, "if the turnstiles were clicking, as they do when the team is winning."[15]

On December 10, 1935, the last great star of the last great A's team was disposed of. Mack traded Jimmy Foxx, along with pitcher Johnny Marcum, to the Boston Red Sox for two players and $150,000 cash. This time, there was no pretense by Mack that the deal was for any other reason than "hard times." A month later, Mack got together again with Boston owner Tom Yawkey and sent the Red Sox outfielder Doc Cramer and infielder Eric McNair, receiving in return two players and cash reported to be $75,000.

Shortly after that, on February 16, 1936, Tom Shibe, who had been club president since the death of his father in 1922, passed away. His brother John succeeded Tom, but John's tenure was brief, ending with his death on July 11, 1937.

With the departure of Foxx and Cramer, the nucleus of the A's offense was now Johnson, Higgins, Moses, and Frankie Hayes, a young catcher. Moses hit .345 and Johnson drove in 121 runs. These were the team's offensive highlights. The mound crew compiled a collective 6.08 earned run average, as the club dropped further into the basement, winning only 53 games. A little righthander named Harry Kelley, back in the majors ten years after being dropped by Washington, was 15-12 with a 3.87 ERA. After Kelley, though, there was chaos.

The team lost 100 games, but attendance rose, to 285,173. It certainly wasn't the ball club which caused that increase; the waning of the Depression made more spendable dollars available. Another contribution to the gate may have been the inception in 1936 of regular live radio broadcasts of the home games of the A's and Phillies. An announcer named Bill Dyer was the pioneer of play-by-play descriptions to the ever-increasing number of radio owners in the Philadelphia area.

The years between the breakup of the Grove-Dykes-Simmons A's and the Second World War were not happy ones for Philadelphia baseball. Fans in the area and around the country became accustomed to thinking of "Philadelphia" and "last place" as synonymous. Both the A's and Phillies carried on their business in a penurious, hand-to-mouth fashion, and the third largest city in the nation became a

Indian Bob Johnson, who carried the team through lean years (Brace Photo).

baseball joke. After a few seasons of this, one columnist wrote: "Like thousands of other rooters in Philadelphia, we're sick and tired of try-ing to cheer from baseball's coal bin."[16]

In the summer of 1936 the city hosted the Democratic National Convention, at Convention Hall in West Philadelphia. The Democratic ticket of Franklin Roosevelt and John Nance Garner carried the city in the fall by more than 200,000 votes. Philadelphia would continue vot-ing Republican in local elections a few more times, but it was fast becoming a two-party town. What effect this change would have on Philadelphia's baseball teams was problematic; there was a theory in Philadelphia that Republicans were A's fans, while the more plebeian Democrats supported the Phillies, at least up to World War II. Whether this was so is obviously a matter of conjecture; the theory was not tested in the late '30s, despite the growth of Democratic strength in the city, because of the sheer awfulness of Gerald Nugent's Phillies.[17]

In 1937, Mack took the Athletics to Mexico for spring training, although it was reported that "the high altitude bothered some of Con-nie's athletes." The excursion may have done some good, because the A's rose to the heights of seventh place. They won only one more game than in '36 (54), but the Browns had a really bad ball club, won but 46, and let the A's escape the basement rather easily.[18]

Curiously, the Athletics' seventh-place team increased its home attendance from 285,173 to 430,733, while a similar improvement by the Phillies was accompanied by an attendance decline from 249,219 to 212,790. Philadelphia was still the Athletics' town. Sam Breadon, owner of the Cardinals, said, "If I finished last twice in succession in my town, I would be through. Mack can finish last season after season and still have the fans piling up in front of his turnstiles."[19]

Moses and Johnson were the big guns for the club, each of them hitting 25 home runs and batting over .300. Billy Werber, a veteran infielder who had been obtained from Boston for Higgins during the off-season, hit .292, led the league with 35 stolen bases, and played an indifferent third base.

Harry Kelley won the most games among the pitchers, with 13, but he also lost 21 and sported a 5.36 earned run average. George Caster, rookie lefthander Edgar Smith, and Cubs castoff Lynn Nelson had sad-looking records. Nelson, a righthander with a herky-jerky delivery, was so ineffective in Chicago that he picked up the nickname "Line Drive." One Cub infielder said, "If he lives to be a thousand years he'll never be a pitcher."[20] Years before, Nelson had toured the northwest with a carnival as the "Masked Marvel," fighting all comers. He never lost a fight, so it was said, but gave it all up for baseball.

The year 1938 saw both Philadelphia teams drop back into last place, the A's with 53-99. The most newsworthy event of the year in Philadelphia baseball was the Phillies' final abandonment of Baker Bowl. On June 25, sportswriter Walter "Red" Smith wrote in the *Record* that "after more than forty years in the fusty, cobwebby House of Horrors known as Baker Bowl, the Phillies are preparing to pull up stakes." Arrangements with the Athletics to share Shibe Park were almost completed. "Surroundings in Shibe Park may not lend the comic relief which often has provided a large share of the entertainment for Baker Bowl patrons," Smith wrote. In the years since the Phillies' 1915 pennant, he went on, "the only genuine, spontaneous excitement in Baker Bowl has been inspired by the occasional collapse of a section of stands."[21]

On July 1, the lawyers for the Charles W. Murphy Estate, the actual owner of Baker Bowl, announced in Chicago that an agreement had been reached permitting the Phillies to vacate. Phillies president Gerald P. Nugent and Mack then signed the Shibe Park lease at the Phillies offices in the Packard Building. Connie Mack commented grandly that "I think the change will benefit both clubs and will make for better baseball in Philadelphia. I am sure the Phils will play better at Shibe Park." (He was wrong, of course; the Phillies' woes continued, as it became clear that they could play very bad baseball anywhere.) Even playing half the season in the more refined surroundings of Shibe Park, the Phillies drew only 166,111 fans, far under the 385,357 who paid to see the Athletics.[22]

For the A's in 1938, Bob Johnson had an outstanding season, batting .313 and driving in 113 runs with 30 home runs. Moses hit .307, and catcher Frankie Hayes batted .291 with 11 home runs. Werber hit only .259 and was called a "protect-yourself-at-all-times third baseman"; it was now clear that the trade of Higgins for Werber was a major mistake.[23]

A former All-American halfback from the University of California, Sam Chapman, showed up on the recommendation of Ty Cobb and was signed. Chapman passed up two better offers, signing with the A's because Cobb told the young man that Connie Mack knew more about the game than anyone else. When Chapman reported, expecting to be farmed out, he was startled to be told that he was starting in center field. (Apparently no one told Mack that Chapman was an infielder, and Sam never broke the news to the old man.) Chapman hit .259 with 17 home runs in 114 games that first year, all in the outfield.[24]

Another noteworthy addition to the Athletics' scene in 1938 was a young Texan named Byrum Saam. Hired from a station in Minneapolis to broadcast the A's home games, Saam stayed around to do most of the A's games until they left town, Phillies' games to 1949, and the Phillies again from 1955 to 1975.

By Saam's smooth and mellow voice was the sound of baseball to several generations of Philadelphians. He called the game straight, with no frills and no gimmicks. What humor there was in his broadcasts was unintentional, such as in the late night game from the West Coast when he tried to explain a complicated play by starting, "For you guys scoring in bed..." In his years of describing Philadelphia baseball, Byrum Saam broadcast, with style and grace, more losing games than any other man in history.[25]

Connie Mack's 1939 A's finished seventh, 13 games ahead of the Browns, and they outdrew their new tenants by about 120,000 admissions. The Athletics became the first American League club to add light towers to its ballpark, eight of them, each 146 feet high. Both the A's and Phillies played seven night games in Shibe Park in 1939, to the dismay of their neighbors. A major renovation was done to the interior of the park as well, and "the former dark and forbidding causeway on the ground floor" was transformed into a restaurant serving such items as hot soup, roast beef, and lamb stew. A reporter pointed out that with the late, ultra-conservative John Shibe in charge "Shibe Park was the last park in the majors to be so rash as to offer a hot dog to its supporters." Shibe, he thought, would roll over in his grave if he could see the new setup, but "Connie Mack and his lieutenants are different.... Their policy is to keep pace with the times."[26]

Bob Johnson, with .338, 23 roundtrippers, and 114 RBIs, was a legitimate attraction. Moses hit .307, first baseman Dick Siebert batted .294, and Hayes hit 20 home runs. Outfielder Wilson Daniel "Dee"

Miles was purchased from Chattanooga for $25,000, "an upper bracket purchase," Isaminger called him, and he hit .300 in 106 games, but he had no power at all.[27] The pitching was a problem, with Lynn Nelson the big winner at 10-13. Mack himself, taken seriously ill on June 28, was hospitalized and missed most of the balance of the season, with his son Earle running the Athletics on the field.

In 1940 the Mackmen joined the Phillies in last place with a 54-100 record. Johnson's batting average fell, but he banged 31 home runs and drove in 103. Young Sam Chapman had 23 fourbaggers, and Moses and Frank Hayes each hit over .300. Moses had been traded to Detroit in December 1939, in exchange for a hotshot second baseman named Benny McCoy, but the next month McCoy was one of 91 Tiger farmhands made free agents by Judge Landis because of cover-ups by the Detroit front office. The deal was canceled and Moses returned to the Athletics. Mack outbid several other clubs to sign McCoy for $45,000. Benny hit .257 and .271 in two years with the A's before entering the service.[28]

The Republicans came to town in the summer of 1940. It was at Convention Hall that the chants of "We Want Willkie!" helped to win the day for Wendell Willkie, the Hoosier utilities executive, who came from nowhere to seize the Republican nomination. In the campaign that followed, local Willkie manager Robert T. McCracken made the unfortunate remark that "only paupers will vote for Roosevelt" and then watched as FDR carried Philadelphia by 178,000 votes.[29]

In the last peacetime season, 1941, the Athletics improved but again finished in last place. The attendance figures for Gerry Nugent's sad-sack Phillies were again down near the 230,000 mark, while the A's drew over 528,000. While Nugent and his club were in desperate financial straits, Connie Mack in December 1940 was able to purchase the stock of the late John Shibe for $42,000 to attain majority control of the Athletics franchise. Although his ball club was not very good, the old man seemed to be in a healthy economic situation.

The '41 A's put together a record of 64-90, with splendid hitting by Siebert, Johnson, Moses, Chapman, and Hayes. Siebert's .334 was fifth in the league, Chapman and Johnson each exceeded 100 runs batted in, and Chapman and Moses were both over the .300 mark. Chapman, the erstwhile infielder, led all American League outfielders in putouts, assists, and errors, covering a lot of ground in center field. Veteran pitcher Jack Knott led the staff with 13-11 and 4.40. A likely looking 27-year-old rookie named Phil Marchildon, a French-Canadian righthander, was 10-15 with a good ERA of 3.57. The rest of Mack's pitching, except for that of righthander Tom Ferrick, was shabby.

After the '41 season ended the Japanese bombed Pearl Harbor and the United States entered the Second World War. It would prove to be an interesting if arduous time for Connie Mack and his White Elephants.

CHAPTER 13

The War Years

The four years of World War II were tough times for Organized Baseball. Players were drafted, materials used for making baseball equipment were in short supply, spring training was held in strange and chilly places, even the time of playing games was altered, with many more games played at night or even at twilight. The hardest part of all for the men running baseball was the sheer uncertainty whether the game would continue or shut down for the duration.

But baseball persevered and in fact did better than anyone expected. Many top players continued to perform for all or part of the war, while the vacancies on major league rosters gave deserving but hitherto unlucky minor leaguers the chance to shine. New stars developed, many of whom would continue to play well after the war. Some clubs, however, suffered greatly during the war, on the field, in the front office, and at the counting-house. No baseball teams were hit harder by the privations of war than were those in Philadelphia.[1]

After Pearl Harbor was bombed, Connie Mack told the press, "I don't know what the future holds for us, but whatever we can do to help the Government in this war, we are going to do it."[2]

What could not be foreseen at the time was that in the four years of the Second World War Philadelphia would furnish six of the eight last place teams and that several of these would be ranked among the worst of all time. While a leveling of talent might be expected to benefit Philadelphia's chronic tailenders, for some reason it did not work that way. For the Phillies and Athletics, the woes of the prewar seasons continued.

It was the A's who found an outfielder named Joe Cicero, who had played 28 games for the 1929-30 Boston Red Sox, and brought him back to the majors 15 years after his last appearance. (Cicero hit .158 for the 1945 Athletics, not too startling since he hit .167 for the 1930 Red Sox.) It was the A's who found a 39-year-old pitcher named Jonas Arthur Berry, nicknamed "Jittery Joe," and made him their top reliever. It was the A's who brought back a retread catcher named Greek George who ended his big league career with a kayo punch of a homeplate umpire, after the ump made a bad call *in the A's favor*! It was the A's who made 16-year-old Carl Scheib the youngest player in major league history, at least until a younger one came along the next season. The fans at Shibe Park were introduced to such personalities as Orie Arntzen, Edgar Busch, Luther Knerr, Charlie Gassaway, and Talmadge Abernathy.

Nevertheless, with all its problems, baseball, thanks in part to those just mentioned and others like them, survived in Philadelphia and around the country. Indeed, the game was positioned at the end of the war in 1945 for the great boom which followed.

Early in 1942, Organized Baseball received word that it would be permitted to continue. President Franklin D. Roosevelt wrote a letter to Landis on January 15, in answer to an inquiry from the commissioner, stating "that it would be best for the country to keep baseball going." This was FDR's famous "green light" letter, and it relieved the game's officials of the fear that the sport might be closed down as it had been in 1918. Roosevelt's letter promised no special treatment for the game, but at least there was semi-official encouragement for it.[3]

The citizens of the Philadelphia area were preoccupied with the war and their places in it. Many men volunteered for military service, and others worked in defense-related industries. Within months after Pearl Harbor, a Stage Door Canteen was in operation in the basement of the Academy of Music. Air-raid drills became commonplace in the early months of the war, and a rash of oil-tanker sinkings by German U-boats necessitated after-dark blackouts along the Jersey shore and dim-outs farther inland. Shortages and rationing soon became a way of life for civilians, as more and more of the nation's resources were devoted to the war effort.

There was no way of knowing whether the customers would come out in 1942, with all the uncertainties of the war. Mack pushed for permission to schedule a doubleheader every Sunday the A's were at home, because that was the club's big attendance day. It had been determined that the Athletics drew heavily from upstate areas—about 40 percent of their crowds—and a Sunday twinbill was a major inducement for these fans to drive down to make a day of it at the ballpark. Conversely, few upstate fans came to night games because they could not get home in time to get to work the next day. Unfortunately, gasoline rationing would soon upset these calculations and pull attendance down.[4]

With everything so much up in the air, Mack indicated that his players would have to take what he offered in the way of salaries, perhaps with attendance bonuses in case of a good year. "There'll have to be a limit on our financial commitments," he said. "...It doesn't seem right that the club owner should have to take all the risk."[5]

What this meant became clear when the club mailed out its 1942 contract offers, with pay cuts across the board. "I'm advising all of them," Mack said, "to look for jobs in defense work if they don't think we're being fair with them."[6] First baseman Dick Siebert, after hitting .334 at a salary of $9500, was offered a $1000 cut. He and Bob Johnson staged long holdouts, although they eventually signed, mollified by bonuses based on attendance. The bonus gimmick backfired in the case of Johnson, when Indian Bob, furious that Mack refused to pay the bonus simply because attendance did not reach the stipulated figure, forced a trade before the 1943 season.

The Athletics traded Wally Moses to the White Sox and sent pitcher Johnny Babich to the Yankees' farm at Kansas City for a sore-kneed third baseman named Buddy Blair. They lost Chapman, pitcher Porter Vaughn, and infielders Al Brancato, Benny McCoy, and Don Richmond to the military. They then proceeded to finish last, with a record of 55-99.

Mack got decent pitching from two Canadians, Marchildon and Dick Fowler, from a 31-year-old rookie knuckleballer named Roger Wolff, and from second-year man Lum Harris. Jack Knott was hit hard, posting a record of 2-10 and 5.59 before joining the service. Russ Christopher, a tall, skinny righthander with a leaky heart, pitched in hard luck, winning four and losing 13 but putting together a good ERA. Overall, the A's pitching was serviceable.

The team's hitting, though, was bad. Johnson hit .279 with 13 home runs, and his 80 RBIs led the team. Siebert fell off to .260, and Hal Wagner, who took over the catching after Frank Hayes was traded to the Browns, batted only .236 with one home run.

The club's attendance fell to 423,487, but the Athletics, with the rest of the teams, completed their season, in the face of many experts who predicted the baseball clubs would fold up their tents on Memorial Day, or the Fourth of July, or Labor Day, or sometime before they played out their schedule. Rosters were rather fluid, as the decisions of local draft boards took their toll on available manpower.

One of the most visible effects of World War II on baseball was the restriction of big league teams to the north for spring training in 1943, 1944, and 1945. Judge Landis had been asked by the director of War Defense Transportation to curtail baseball's use of the nation's railroad facilities. Some clubs were already looking for more northerly sites for their camps when, on January 4, 1943, Landis decreed that all clubs except the Browns and Cardinals must find spring training sites north of the Potomac and Ohio Rivers; the two St. Louis clubs could train anywhere in Missouri. This edict resulted in ball clubs doing their conditioning in exotic northern locales.

The Athletics held their spring training in Wilmington, Delaware, and a spartan camp it was in 1943. The A's had but 13 pitchers in camp, and only three of these, Harris, Wolff the knuckleballer, and Christopher, called "a tall tower of bones with a fast ball" by a reporter, had any real major league experience, although Jesse Flores, a Mexican screwballer, had enjoyed a cup of coffee with the Cubs in '42. There were hopes for young Don Black, a chunky righthander out of Iowa with "an agreeable-looking hard one" and a serious drinking problem, but Connie Mack told the press, "Along with our pitching, there'll be a big question about our hitting."[7] Mack's 1943 team, as he feared, was very bad. Its record of 49-105 fixed it securely in last place, 20 games out of seventh, and in one particularly awful stretch the club lost 20 games in a row to tie American League and 20th-century records. Attendance dropped to 376,735, even behind the Phillies, and no one could criticize Athletics' fans for staying away. After the season, Mack said that Dick Siebert and veteran outfielder Jo Jo White "were the only two men on my club who I would consider major leaguers."[8]

Over the 1942-43 offseason, Mack had drafted Eddie Mayo, an infielder with a couple of years in the National League behind him, to play third base. Shortly before the end of spring training, Mayo and catcher Bob Swift had a man caught in a rundown between third and home. A throw by Swift glanced off the runner's head and hit Mayo in the eye, causing a retinal hemorrhage. Mayo had a blind spot in the eye all year, affecting his hitting, and he wound up batting only .219. The condition cleared up on its own after the season ended, but by that time the A's had let him go. Picked up by the Tigers, Eddie Mayo put together several outstanding seasons in Detroit.[9]

On September 6, young Scheib, a pitcher from Gratz in the Pennsylvania Dutch country, appeared on the mound for the Macks, at the age of 16 years, eight months, five days, the youngest player ever to appear in a big league game. This record was broken in 1944 by Cincinnati's Joe Nuxhall, who was under 16, but Scheib is still the youngest American Leaguer ever.

The annual major league All-Star Game was played in Philadelphia for the first time on July 13. The A's were the hosts, although the local clubs had but one player each on their respective teams, Siebert and the Phillies' Babe Dahlgren. It was the first "midsummer classic" played at night, and it drew a crowd of 31,938. The American League, as it did so often in those early years of the game, won, 5-3, as pitchers Dutch Leonard of Washington, Hal Newhouser of Detroit, and Tex Hughson of the Red Sox stifled the National Leaguers.

After the 1943 season, Commissioner Kenesaw M. Landis booted Phillies' owner William Cox from the game for betting on his team. Cox had purchased the franchise in March 1943 after an almost-bankrupt Gerry Nugent sold it back to the league. With Cox forced to sell, Robert R.M. Carpenter, vice president of E.I. DuPont de Nemours, Inc., the giant chemical company, and married to a DuPont, purchased the club for his son, Robert R.M. Carpenter, Jr., for a reported $400,000. For the first time in many years the Phillies had real money behind them.[10]

One unforeseen effect of the Phillies purchase was that in a postwar baseball world in which two-team cities became on the whole economically impractical, the Phillies were now in a position to outspend the frugal Athletics by a wide margin. Over time Philadelphia, which had for so long been the Athletics' town, gradually swung over to the Phillies.

In the meantime, though, there was a war on, and more wartime seasons to play. The Athletics trained in Frederick, Maryland, in 1944 and 1945. They had had a lucky break with decent weather in Wilmington in 1943, but the next two northern camps were very cold, with a number of exhibition games canceled by snow.

The A's climbed to a tie with Cleveland for fifth place in 1944, with a mark of 72-82. The Phillies' attendance dropped with their won-lost record, to 369,586, while that of the Athletics jumped substantially, to 505,322. At the end of the season, the A's were 17 games behind the pennant-winning St. Louis Browns, the closest they had been to the top since finishing second in 1932.

A labor dispute in August 1944 between the Philadelphia Transportation Company and its workers over the hiring of blacks brought the city to a standstill. On August 1, all PTC trolleys, buses, and subways shut down. When the strikers refused to work despite a War Labor Board order, Franklin Roosevelt dispatched an army unit to the city to run the system. The strike collapsed, and by August 6 the PTC was again in operation.

In the midst of the strike, on August 4, with no functioning public transportation, 29,166 fans turned out at Shibe Park nevertheless for a tribute to Connie Mack, "the Grand Old Man of Baseball." FDR sent a message—"May your scorecard continue to wave"—Bud Abbott and Lou Costello did their famous "Who's on First?" routine, Mack was presented a $5000 check, and Chief Bender, Ira Thomas, Rube Oldring, Bullet Joe Bush, Joe Boley, and Howard Ehmke showed up to honor their old manager. Mack then introduced his all-time team, with stars like Sisler, Wagner, Ruth, and Johnson emerging from the dugout to join him. It was a great evening, marred only by the A's 1-0 loss to the Yankees, as Hank Borowy outpitched Bobo Newsom.[11]

The old man was beginning to have trouble keeping things together by that time, and coach Al Simmons really ran the club on the field. Woody Wheaton, who came up in 1944 as an outfielder but was soon converted into a pitcher, remembers Connie Mack as "a great man and a good manager, but he was in his eighties and had trouble remembering things." At one point, Wheaton was sitting in a hotel lobby in Cleveland when Mack came over to him and said, "Young man, you look familiar. Do I know you?" George Staller, who played for the A's the year before, said that Mr. Mack "was sharp and had the respect of everyone.... [I]n 1943 he was fine," and Charlie Metro, a 1945 outfielder, said, "he was real sharp." Sam Lowry, though, who pitched briefly for Philadelphia in 1943, said, "Mack was getting senile by that time." George Kell, who really admired the old man, said Connie Mack was "more or less a figure head" when he was with the club in 1944 and 1945; "he made so many mistakes," Kell said.[12]

Siebert hit .306, Bobby Estalella, an ageless Cuban outfielder, batted .298, and catcher Frank Hayes, reclaimed from the Browns, belted 13 home runs. Edgar Busch, "the best beer drinker on the club," played shortstop and hit .271. "He was a nice guy," said pitcher Luther Knerr, "but we once made him so mad he didn't talk to anyone for a week" when they bribed the public address announcer at Sportsman's Park in St. Louis to introduce him as "Strictly" Busch.[13]

The club's biggest improvement was on the mound, where good work was done by Christopher, Black, Harris, Flores, Newsom, and the slight "Jittery Joe" Berry, "pound for pound ... the best relief pitcher I've ever seen," according to Knerr. (He weighed only about 145 pounds, of course.)[14] Christopher was 14-14, and Newsom and Hayes served on the American League All-Star team. The A's had a rookie third baseman named George Kell, up from Lancaster in the Interstate League, where he had led all of Organized Baseball with his .396 average in 1943. Kell, a personable Arkansan, hit just .268 as the Athletics' third sacker, but he clearly had the goods.[15]

When the 1945 baseball season opened, Nazi Germany was out of the war, but no one could predict how long the fighting in the Far East would last. The manpower needs of the military were greater than ever, and Selective Service relaxed its standards in order to get more men into uniform. This change resulted in some ballplayers being drafted who had previously been rejected. At the same time, there was a trickle of players coming back after being discharged from the service, a trickle which increased as the 1945 season progressed.

All baseball could do was grit its collective teeth, hang on, and hope to make it. In addition to the players drafted since the end of the '44 season, there was another great void. On November 25, 1944, the cantan-

Connie Mack and Mrs. Ben Shibe in spring training (The Falvey Collection, courtesy Philadelphia A's Historical Society Archives).

kerous old commissioner, Kenesaw Mountain Landis, a contemporary and good friend of Connie Mack, had passed away in Chicago at the age of 78, and the owners were looking for a new commissioner. Judge Landis had his faults—he was often arbitrary and high-handed, and his opposition to blacks in Organized Baseball was notorious. But he watched out for the players' interests, and his severe attitude toward gambling after the Black Sox scandal was instrumental in redeeming the game.

Both Philadelphia clubs were terrible in 1945. Each finished a distant last, and they had awful records. The Phillies were 46-108, 52 games out. The Athletics were a trace better, at 52-98, but they trailed the seventh-place Red Sox by 17 games. A local serviceman, Lieutenant Jim Skardon from West Chester, wrote home plaintively from the Philippines that even on Luzon he heard the troops roar with laughter at the records of the A's and Phillies: "Can't something be done about Philadelphia baseball after all these years?"[16]

There was clearly no relief in 1945. Home attendance for the Mackmen dropped to 462,631, while the Phillies, temporarily rechristened the Blue Jays, fell to 285,057. The A's won six of their first eight games, so their ultimate descent to the bottom was delayed until May 23. From that time on, there was no dislodging the Athletics. Mack's pitching was not so bad, but his team was dead last in hitting and managed only 33 home runs. Russ Christopher, the skinny submarine-ball pitcher with the bad heart, was 11-2 for the A's at midseason, winning more than half the team's victories, but his teammates stopped hitting for him after that and he finished with a record of 13-13, though he continued pitching well.

Not much can be said about the 1945 A's. Bobby Estalella batted .299, Kell hit .272, and catcher Buddy Rosar, obtained from Cleveland for Hayes, hit .210. The A's had a couple of colorful veterans, one of them the entertaining Bobo Newsom, who won eight games and lost 20. Old Bobo was always interesting, he always gave a good effort, and people came out to Shibe Park to see him.

Charley "Greek" George, the hot-tempered catcher, who had been around with Cleveland, Brooklyn, the Cubs, and a lot of bush league teams, was a minor legend for some of his zany antics. For the A's, Greek hit only .174, and his season (and big league career) came to a premature end when he was suspended for punching umpire Joe Rue in the face. He had been going back and forth with Rue all day, and when the umpire called a Yankee batter out on a pitch that was clearly a ball outside, George hooted, "There, do you see what I mean?" As George was walking away, Rue called him "a name I won't repeat," according to the catcher. "I started back toward him and said, 'What did you call me?' When he said I'd heard right the first time, I punched him."[17]

The Athletics played a game at Shibe Park on the afternoon of July 21, with the Tigers, before 4325 fans. Each team scored an early run, and the score stayed even as the innings rolled along. Christopher pitched 13 innings, and then reliever Joe Berry took over for the next 11, opposing a returned veteran named Les Mueller for Detroit. Mueller pitched 19⅔ innings before giving way to Paul "Dizzy" Trout. The game went on for 24 innings, matching the American League record, before umpire Bill Summers called it on account of darkness, still tied at 1-1. Summers said he could not see Dizzy Trout's fastball, and "I don't think any one else could."[18]

Philadelphia second baseman Irv Hall played the whole game on no sleep and an empty stomach. Scheduled to take his pre-induction physical that day, Hall had stayed out partying the night before and then took a cab to the army induction center in West Philadelphia without stopping for breakfast. After a couple of hours at the center, Hall was told that he had failed the physical. He took another cab to 21st and Lehigh, arriving just before gametime, and a surprised Connie Mack wrote him into the lineup. Batting out of the leadoff position, Hall went 2-for-11 and handled 14 fielding chances without a miscue. He slept well that night.[19]

The Athletics' press box attendant, Otto Susnek, was required, after the eighth inning of each home game, to bring the tower elevator to the ground floor and hold it there until Mack appeared from the dugout. On this day, poor Otto stood from the ninth to the 24th inning, holding the elevator door open for Connie Mack. When Mack finally appeared, Susnek said, according to a reporter, "Gee, that was a long ninth inning, Mr. Mack." Without cracking a smile, Mack agreed, "Yes, it was," and strode into the elevator.[20]

Several weeks after the Japanese surrender which ended World War II, Dick Fowler, just out of the Canadian army, rejoined the Athletics and threw a 1-0 no-hitter against the Browns. Fowler had pitched for Mack before going into the service, and the gem he hurled upon his return was encouraging. It was a nice way to end the war, and hopes were high for the future. Perhaps something could be done for Lieutenant Skardon after all.

CHAPTER 14

New Day Coming

The spring training camps in 1946 were crowded. With the war over and a rapid dismantling of the great American military machine underway, most of the baseball players who had been in the service were back. More players reported while spring training continued, as their discharges were processed. In addition to the returnees, there were many fine players, like Hal Newhouser, Phil Cavarretta, Bob Elliott, Marty Marion, and Eddie Stanky, who had played through the war and were anxious to continue their careers against the veterans coming back. With all the players available, there was fierce competition for the precious roster spots. A Federal law requiring that returning veterans be given their old jobs back for at least 30 days made for further complications.[1]

The game had a new commissioner in former U.S. Senator Albert B. "Happy" Chandler of Kentucky, but the owners who appointed him carefully trimmed away some of the unrestricted powers Landis had enjoyed. Baseball men looked forward eagerly to the new season, when the fans would pour into the ball parks with money in hand to see their old favorites once again.

Some sour notes were heard during the spring, when Jorge and Bernardo Pasquel, two brothers who ran what was called the Mexican League, invaded the American camps and lured players away with salary offers far in excess of what the big league owners were paying. Mickey Owen, the Brooklyn catcher, and Browns shortstop Vernon Stephens were the biggest names to go for the Pasquels' money, although Stephens was unhappy with what he found in Mexico and quickly returned. Seven New York Giants jumped, including pitching prospect Sal Maglie, as did infielder Murray Franklin of Detroit, and outfielders Luis Olmo of the Dodgers and Bobby Estalella of the A's. The most serious defection came after the season started, on May 24, when three Cardinals, southpaw Max Lanier (6-0 at the time), pitcher Fred Martin, and infielder Lou Klein, headed south of the border.

The most important impact of the Pasquels on the game was to foster a sudden change in bargaining positions, as clubowners had to offer far more than they were accustomed to in order to keep players who would otherwise have listened with interest to the Pasquels. Several of the biggest stars in the game, like the Cardinals' Stan Musial and Detroit's Newhouser, let it be known quite pointedly that they had turned down substantial offers from the Pasquels and that they did not intend to suffer for it.

During the season, the Pittsburgh players affiliated with a labor union called the American Baseball Guild, although they fell short of voting to strike when the chips were down. As a result, owners and players met to discuss ways in which the players' lot could be improved. Changes were made in the basic contract, and the players learned that unionization, or its threat, could have a decided effect upon the hitherto obdurate clubowners.

In July there were reports that Robert Murphy, the lawyer who conceived the American Baseball Guild, was looking into rumors that the Athletics, along with the Browns, were the lowest paid players in the majors. Shortstop Jack Wallaesa, it was noted, had an A's contract for $2000. When the Macks offered a similar salary to pitcher Les McCrabb, purchased from Lancaster, he told them, "I can make more than that just by pitching on weekends near my home," and stayed with Lancaster. Pitcher Lew Carpenter, drafted by the A's from Atlanta, for whom he had a record of 22-2, chose to stay in the minor leagues rather than to accept the A's offer. Philadelphians were hardly shocked at these revelations of Mackian frugality.[2]

Connie Mack, of course, had little alternative. Unlike many of his colleagues in the big leagues, he had no personal wealth on which to draw in the operation of his club, and he and his family depended upon the baseball team for their livelihoods. The fans of Philadelphia had not exactly been breaking down the doors of Shibe Park to shower cash upon the Macks. In better times, though, when he could afford it, Connie Mack had given sizable contracts to players like Simmons and Foxx. In addition, many of his players offered examples of Mack's personal acts of generosity.[3]

The Mexican League imbroglio had little effect on the A's, since the Mackmen had few players in whom the Pasquels were interested, other than Estalella, a colorful Latin. The season, even without Mexican League inroads, however, was not very enjoyable. It started with an embarrassing episode, when, on April 22, with the team already off to a stumbling 2-4 start, Mrs. Cornelius McGillicuddy announced that she was separated from her husband of 36 years, distressed at his action in distributing more than half of his controlling stock in the franchise to his three sons, Earle, Roy, and Connie, Jr. "[T]here are nine persons to be considered in this," she said, "his eight children and me." Mack said he had no comment; he hoped people would recognize this as a private matter "and keep out of it." The newspapers played up the split for a couple of days, then let it drop, as a reconciliation was discreetly worked out. It would prove to be the first public manifestation of what became a nasty family division, one which would ultimately work to the detriment of the franchise.[4]

Over the winter Mack traded first baseman Dick Siebert to St. Louis for his opposite number with the Browns, George McQuinn, but when the Browns tried to cut Siebert's salary, he retired. On April 19, Commissioner Chandler turned down the Browns' plea for the return of McQuinn. It looked like a great triumph for Connie Mack, but by the end of the year, McQuinn's feeble .226 average, three home runs, and 36 runs batted in made that judgment questionable. In July, the disappointed Mack said of McQuinn: "The boy has played a year too long."[5]

Another major disappointment for the Athletics was second baseman Benny McCoy. McCoy, the recipient of a substantial amount of Connie Mack's cash back in 1940, had given the Athletics two modestly good seasons before entering the service. When he came back from the war, however, McCoy had nothing left, and he never even made it out of spring training with the A's. Mack let him go, and he never appeared in another big league game.

On April 16, 1946, the largest Opening Day crowd in Shibe Park's history, 37,472, came out to see the dawn of postwar baseball. The lineup that trotted on the field for the Athletics featured an infield of McQuinn, Gene Handley, Jack Wallaesa, and Kell, with Ford Garrison, Chapman, and Hal Peck across the outfield, Rosar behind the plate, and Russ Christopher on the mound. Unfortunately, these players picked up only five hits as they lost to the Yankees and Spud Chandler, 5-0. Bobo Newsom won for the A's the next day, but they then lost three in a row before Newsom beat Boston, 3-0, on Easter Sunday. Six more losses followed before the club won a couple from St. Louis, and it was clear that the A's were not going to have a successful 1946 season. By Memorial Day, they were 22 games out of first place and 7½ behind seventh-place Chicago. The Mackmen did not win their tenth game of the season until June 1, when Christopher beat the Indians, 10-4.

On June 3, the A's released Newsom, at his own request, so he could look for a job with a winning team. "I figure I'm still a good pitcher," the big righthander said, "and Mr. Mack didn't want to let me go, but I think a change will do me good. Mr. Mack probably could have sold me and gotten some money.... It was mighty wonderful of him."[6]

On June 6, Mack denied rumors that he might step down, saying there would be no other manager of the A's "as long as I live." He admitted the 1946 club was not much good but stated, defiantly, "We'll have a good club before long and a great one again. And I'll manage it. Put that down once and for always." For many A's followers, the statement did not have quite the reassuring ring that Mack intended.[7]

After moderate success during June and July, losing only four more games than they won each month, the Athletics crashed in August and September, with records of 4-19 and 7-18 for those two months. It all added up to another dismal season in the cellar.

Sam Chapman hit 20 home runs for the A's, half the team's total. Elmer Valo, a 25-year old outfielder born in Czechoslovakia, batted .307, although he hit but one home run and drove in only 31. Valo, who had played with the A's before going into the service, looked like a ballplayer. The fans loved his aggressive, wall-banging style of outfield play. "Elmer Valo," one of his teammates said, "put out 100 percent every day, running, catching, throwing."[8]

Outfielder Barney McCosky hit .354 after coming over from the

Tigers, but he had a shadow hanging over him. On May 18, the A's traded third baseman George Kell to Detroit for McCosky, who was hitting only .196 at the time but had been a consistent prewar hitter for the Tigers. Mack called young Kell to his hotel room in Detroit to tell him of the trade. "You're going to be a great one," Mack told Kell, who was chagrined at being traded so early in his baseball life, "but I'm trading you because I won't be able to afford to pay your salary."[9]

Kell hit .327 over the balance of the season in Detroit and went on to have a career, with a .306 lifetime average, which landed him in the Hall of Fame. Poor Barney McCosky always hit well (though with no power), but he was not a good outfielder and he had increasing problems with a bad back, missing the 1949 season altogether and declining rapidly thereafter. No matter what McCosky did, Kell did more, usually much more, and Philadelphia fans had a hard time forgetting this. (In 1949, the year McCosky missed, Kell won the American League batting crown.) On top of everything else, George Kell was four years younger than McCosky.

The 1946 A's got good pitching from Marchildon, Fowler, and Jesse Flores, although their won-loss records did not reflect the fact. Marchildon, with a good fastball and a knuckle-curve that was hard to hit, had excellent stuff on the mound. The club got a lot of innings, high earned run averages, and bad percentage records out of Lum Harris (3-14), Bob Savage (3-15), and Luther Knerr (3-16), and all of it added up to a club record of 49-105, 55 games out of first and 17 out of seventh. 621,793 people paid to watch the Athletics at home, but this number was far below what every other team in the majors except the Browns drew in that booming postwar year. The Phillies, with new uniforms, new stars, and a new attitude, surged to fifth place and drew over a million, the first time ever for a Philadelphia ball club.

The A's had a stellar performance from catcher Buddy Rosar. Rosar, in 117 games, made not one error, an unprecedented feat for a catcher. Rosar made 532 putouts and had 73 assists, and his tally of 605 errorless chances in a season was a new record as well. With nine errorless games left over from 1945, he tacked on another 21 games at the start of the 1947 season to run his errorless string to 147 games, handling 755 chances. The consecutive errorless games and chances records have since been broken, but no catcher save Buddy Rosar has gone through a whole season as he did without a single error. Of course, it was not the kind of feat that packed fans into the ball park.

The Athletics by this time had finally put together what could be called a "farm system," consisting of 12 teams, the highest of which was Birmingham in the Double-A Southern Association. Early in 1947 they appointed Arthur H. Ehlers head of the minor league operation. "Money is no object with Mr. Mack," Ehlers enthused (to the astonishment of the reporters present). "We're going into this thing for keeps. Mr. Mack told me he realized that he couldn't go on forever—and that he didn't want the whole thing to go 'boom' when he decided to relax a little." Mack, he said, had declined to put together a farm system in the past because of the opposition of Landis and his reluctance to cross the commissioner.[10]

For years, Mack had relied on an informal network of old ballplayers, old friends, and college coaches to turn up new recruits. The A's never had a roster of scouts out beating the bushes for prospects. Ira Thomas, his old catcher, did most of Mack's scouting—"the ablest scout I have ever known," Mack called him in his book. Jack Coombs, coaching at Duke, sent his onetime boss a steady stream of players like Ace Parker, Chubby Dean, Eric Tipton, Wayne Ambler, Hal Wagner, and Bill McCahan. Home Run Baker sent along Jimmy Foxx, and Cobb recommended Sam Chapman. As far back as 1911, the Athletics signed a young slugger named Herman Warner at the suggestion of Ralph "Socks" Seybold.[11]

Mack's system worked fairly well in the early years, when player procurement and development for all clubs were on a catch-as-catch-can basis. When Branch Rickey and those who followed him rationalized scouting and farm systems, the A's fell behind because they clung to an outmoded process. They would find it hard to catch up in the post-war years.

They tried, though, in the somewhat bumbling way that had become characteristic of the Athletics. They even signed a "bonus baby," an untried youngster signed under a complex, ever-changing rule. Under the rule then in effect, the player had to be brought up to the major league club after not more than one year in the minors. The tyro, signed on June 16, 1948, was a catcher named Earle Brucker, Jr., nicknamed "Gidge," who happened to be the son of the A's bullpen coach. Ehlers, who outbid six other clubs for young Brucker, said, "We were glad to pay a $30,000 bonus to land this boy."[12] Gidge Brucker, a solidly built lefthanded hitter, made it to the majors for two games with the Athletics in 1948. He picked up one hit in six at bats and then disappeared from the scene, back into the minors. His $30,000 hit was a double.[13]

1947 was a watershed season in baseball, the year that Brooklyn's general manager Branch Rickey and Jackie Robinson overcame the unwritten but quite effective ban against black players. Robinson led the way, but before the season was out he was followed by teammate Dan Bankhead, Cleveland's Larry Doby, and Henry Thompson and Willard Brown of the St. Louis Browns.

There was no encouragement for integration coming from Philadelphia. Ben Chapman, manager of the Phillies, was notorious for his racial baiting of Robinson. Connie Mack was also dismayed at Robinson's arrival in the majors, though he received no publicity about it. He responded to a reporter's question about Robinson's possible appearance in a Dodger-Athletics spring training game by "blowing his stack," according to Red Smith, saying, "I have no respect for Rickey. I have no respect for him now." Don Donaghey of the *Bulletin* convinced Mack to take his remarks "off the record," so the old man received no publicity for his feelings, much to the chagrin of the *Inquirer*'s Stan Baumgartner, who wanted to write the story.[14]

In Philadelphia, 1947 saw a reversal of what appeared to be happening the year before. The A's surged upward in the standings while the Phillies slid back into a tie for last place. The Mackmen wound up fifth, two games out of the first division, as they posted their first winning record, 78-76, since 1933. The fans who came to A's games at Shibe Park numbered 911,566—a new club record—and they were rewarded with a surprisingly good and exciting team.

McQuinn, the bust of 1946, was released, but Connie Mack plucked a prize in the minor league draft to fill the hole at first base. From the San Francisco Seals, he drafted a lefthanded fighter named Ferris Fain, nicknamed "Burrhead" from his appearance, and a joy to watch.

Fain hit the ball hard, although he did not have a home run swing, and he piled up a great many doubles and triples. He played an aggressive game at first base, going after everything near him flat out. When a sacrifice bunt was in order, Fain charged in until he was within a few feet of the batter, so he could grab the bunt and throw out the lead runner at second or third. In effect, he dared the hitter to swing away and try to get the ball past him, and sometimes the hitter did, occasionally bouncing a ball off some part of Fain's anatomy. More often than not, however, Fain would mess up the opponents' sacrifice and with it the potential for scoring a run or so. Ferris Fain developed a reputation over the years as a heavy drinker—one teammate said, "No one drank as much"—but he always played hard on the baseball field.[15]

Another key acquisition by Mack was shortstop Eddie Joost. Shortstop was a disaster area for the A's in 1946, with Pete Suder, Jack Wallaesa, Jack Caulfield, Irv Hall, Oscar Grimes, and Gene Handley all taking shots at the position. During the offseason, Mack decided to take a flyer on Joost, who had played well at Rochester in the International League in 1946.

Joost was a gamble on two counts: first, because he had put in eight years with Cincinnati and the Braves and proven to be a rather weak hitter; second, because he had a reputation as a troublemaker, arising out of problems he had had with Bill McKechnie, Casey Stengel, and John Quinn in the National League. Mack checked out Joost's conduct and satisfied himself that the reputation was overblown, and he felt that Eddie had shown at Rochester that he could hit well enough. What he really wanted Joost to do was to play the key position in a manner sufficient to solidify the A's infield. Jack Barry, he remembered, was not the most highly-publicized member of the "$100,000 infield"; he simply tied it all together. Eddie Joost, it turned out, produced a huge return on Connie Mack's modest investment in him. He was probably the best shortstop ever to play for the Philadelphia Athletics.

Mack had been using Pete Suder, a slender young man of Serbian ancestry from Aliquippa, Pa., all over the infield for several years. For 1947, he stuck Suder at second base, and he suddenly found himself with the league's fielding leader at the position. In addition, Suder was a more than adequate hitter.

In June 1946, the A's had picked up a stocky third baseman named Hank Majeski from the Yankees' surplus of ballplayers. In 1947 Majeski came into his own. He was not the most graceful of third basemen; his style of play was to knock a ball down with his chest, then pick it up and throw the batter out, but he was effective doing it that way. Joost called Majeski "a great third baseman, as good as I ever saw defensively." Majeski had some power at bat, and he drove in a lot of runs.[16]

The outfield was Valo, Chapman, and McCosky, and it was a good one, even though Sam Chapman, after the war, never quite fulfilled his prewar promise as a hitter. As a center fielder, he was one of the best. Rosar behind the plate was spelled on occasion by Fermin "Mike" Guerra, a Cuban obtained from the Senators. On the mound, the Athletics had Marchildon, Fowler, Flores, Christopher, and Savage, as well as a pair of good-looking rookies, Bill McCahan and Joe Coleman.

The A's started the season poorly, languishing in last place until the second week of May. They put together a winning record in May and June—on Memorial Day they shut out the Yankees twice, behind Fowler and Coleman—and rose as high as third place in the fourth week of June. They stayed in fourth place until well into September, when they fell to fifth, where they finished.

Marchildon had a fine season, winning 19 and losing 9, with a 3.22 ERA. Fowler was 12-11 and 2.81, and McCahan and relief pitcher Christopher each won ten games. On September 3, McCahan pitched a no-hit, no-run game against Washington, the only baserunner reaching on an error by Ferris Fain.

Fain led the league's first basemen in errors, as he would in all but one of the years he played for Philadelphia, but this was a by-product of his aggressive style. He hit .291 and drove in 71 runs, so no one complained. Joost had a low batting average, but he hit a surprising 13 home runs, drove in 64 runs, and walked 114 times as a leadoff hitter. His hitting picked up late in the season when he started wearing glasses to overcome astigmatism. Better yet, he gave Connie Mack the shortstop play the A's needed. Majeski hit .280 and drove in 72 runs, while Valo hit .300, McCosky hit .328, and Chapman slugged 14 homers to lead the team. Rosar batted .259 and made only two errors, again leading the league's catchers in fielding. It was a surprising A's team, and entertaining to watch.

Philadelphia began in 1947 the final stages of its conversion from a rock-solid Republican town to a Democratic bastion. A prominent young lawyer and ex-Marine named Richardson Dilworth, wealthy, Yale-educated, and fearless, ran a street-corner campaign as the Democratic candidate for mayor, against the colorless Republican incumbent, Bernard

The postwar A's outfield: Elmer Valo, Sam Chapman, and Barney McCosky (The Falvey Collection, courtesy Philadelphia A's Historical Society Archives).

Samuel. Dilworth was not well thought of on North 20th Street, where the citizens remembered him as the lawyer who defended John Shibe's "spite fence," but he captivated much of the rest of the city.

Despite Dilworth's hard-hitting campaign, spelling out the graft and corruption of the long-entrenched organization, the machine roused itself for one more victory. Barney Samuel defeated his young challenger to retain the mayoralty, but it was hardly worth it. Dilworth's charges were investigated and most were proven. The tired old Republican organization broke down in a rash of suicides by exposed city officials. There was indeed a new day coming in Philadelphia, and it looked very much as if the Athletics, behind the Grand Old Man of Baseball, would be a part of it.

CHAPTER 15

A Surprising
Pennant Race

The year 1948 saw the first Philadelphia involvement in a pennant race since the distant second-place finish of the 1932 Athletics. It appeared for several magical months as if this might actually be that "just one more" that Connie Mack had been using for so long to justify his continuing tenure as manager of the A's.

Everyone connected with the club was aware that the 85-year-old Mack was becoming senile and that while he continued to sit on the dugout bench and wave his famous scorecard at his outfielders his coaches ran the team. For so long, however, had Philadelphia gloried in its possession of the "Grand Old Man of Baseball," "Mister Baseball," "The Tall Tactician," "the Spindly Strategist," and so forth, that no one had the heart to say publicly what so many knew privately. He still gave statements to the press, but the reporters straightened them out so they made sense. Both the local and the national press corps went along.

Few even pointed out the other fact that accompanied Mack's growing and obvious incapacity, that the Philadelphia American League franchise was operated in a uniquely peculiar, penny-pinching and inefficient way, by a coalition of Macks, Shibes and McFarlands (the McFarlands were married to Shibes, and Ben McFarland was the club's traveling secretary), none of whom seemed to have any aptitude for running a baseball team in the postwar world.

For example, in 1951 the club hired as a scout William "Judy" Johnson, one of the greats of Negro baseball, but when Johnson recommended signing young black prospects like Henry Aaron he was ignored. "I could have gotten Hank Aaron for them for $3,500 when he was playing with the Indianapolis Clowns [in the Negro American League in 1952]," Johnson said. "I got my boss out of bed ... but he cussed me out for waking him at one o'clock in the morning. He said, 'Thirty-five hundred! That's too much money.' Too much for a man like that!"[1]

The club's longtime physician, Doctor Ilarion I. Gopadze, was a Russian refugee. A member of the Czarist diplomatic service, Gopadze was on a mission in Turkey when the Russian Revolution began in 1917. "When I heard the news," Gopadze said, "I kept right on going until I wound up in America." It was not unlike the way many others associated with the Athletics showed up.[2]

Yet, in 1948, with a ball club put together in the usual haphazard Athletic way, the A's made a strong run at first place. Fain had come to the A's in the minor league draft, Majeski was sold off by the Yankees, Joost was a National League castoff, Suder had been drafted out of the Yanks' farm system before the war, McCosky came over in the Kell trade, and the three catchers were all picked up from other teams. Somehow they blended together. It was a lovely team and, for those in and around Philadelphia and elsewhere who were A's fans in spite of all logic, a lovely season. It just lasted a few weeks too long. Looking back on it from a perspective of years it may appear that A's fans got too excited, too early, over too little, but at the time it looked like a real pennant race, with Mack's White Elephants right in the midst of it.

The 1948 A's had a solid starting lineup, a good starting rotation, no bench, and no bullpen. The infield of Fain, Suder, Joost, and Majeski was as good as any in the league. The outfield of Valo, Chapman, and McCosky was strong, if a little shy on power, although Chapman's hitting picked up early in June when, to correct a minor visual defect, he started wearing glasses. Rosar, Guerra, and veteran Herman Franks gave the A's competent catching, though Guerra's batting continued to be weak.

The pitcher the A's counted on most before the season began was a major disappointment. Phil Marchildon had arm miseries which reduced his record to 9-15 (with his arm shot, Marchildon never won another big league game after 1948). Despite his big year in 1947, it was evident that Marchildon was not the same pitcher he had been before the war. He was extremely fidgety and nervous on the mound, and clearly his extended stay in a German prisoner-of-war camp had affected him. George Kell said that Marchildon "had a funny look in his eye that hinted his thoughts were about the war and not baseball," and Joost described periods when Marchildon "would wander behind the mound, fool around with the resin bag, and hit his palm with his glove for maybe thirty seconds. You'd know something was wrong." And the next pitch could wind up anywhere, once even hitting a spectator in the stands.[3]

With Marchildon's woes and McCahan's sore arm limiting his usefulness, Fowler, Coleman, Carl Scheib, and Lou Brissie picked up the slack. Interestingly, none of the pitchers had come from other organizations. Fowler worked 205 innings and put together a 15-8 log. Hard-throwing Joe Coleman was 14-13 and pitched in the All-Star game; he credited his improvement to the catching and pitch-calling of Herman Franks. Scheib, still just 21 in his fifth season with the club, won 14 and lost 8.

Brissie, a tall southpaw from South Carolina, was a story in himself. He was signed by the Athletics out of Presbyterian College, where he had been coached by Chick Galloway, the old A's shortstop. Entering the army in late 1942, Brissie was severely wounded by a German artillery shell in northern Italy in December 1944. "My leg had been split open like a ripe watermelon," he said later, but he convinced an army surgeon not to amputate it because he was a ballplayer. With the help of a new wonder drug called penicillin, 23 operations, and a metal plate that covered his misshapen left leg, Lou Brissie returned to civilian life and talked Mack into giving him a 1947 trial at Savannah in the Sally League.

Brissie won 23 games for Savannah and was promoted to the A's. He could not run normally or without pain, but he could pitch and he had guts. In the young lefty's first start, Ted Williams hit a line drive off Brissie's left leg. It "made a noise that sounded like a drum," the Boston slugger said. "Boom! and there he is lying on the ground in pain." "I got up and we beat them," Brissie said, and he went on to win fourteen games in 1948. He had a difficult time with players like New

York's Phil Rizzuto, who frequently bunted on the immobile lefty, but Brissie developed a method to cope with would-be bunters: "It's called retaliation," he said. "That translates to: 'You bunt on me; I stick it in your ear.'"[4]

Beyond the starters the pitching staff was thin. Russ Christopher, who had pitched dependably in relief in 1947, had been sold to Cleveland, and the bullpen was in the hands of Bob Savage and Charlie "Bubba" Harris, two tall righthanders. Harris was an untried rookie while Savage was a disappointment after showing prewar promise. "Bullfrog Bill" Dietrich, a veteran whose best years had been with the White Sox, was back, but his aging right arm had seen its best days.

The 1948 race originally involved the A's, the Yankees of Bucky Harris, and Lou Boudreau's Cleveland Indians, but a surge in June and July by the Red Sox under Joe McCarthy made it a four-way struggle. The Mackmen opened the season with three straight victories at Fenway Park, and this sent them off on a pace to which Philadelphia fans were not accustomed. The A's went 21-7 in May to take over the league lead at the end of that month. They slipped a little in June, going only 14-15 for the month, although this still kept them close to the top.

On June 13, an Athletics homestand came to an end with a Sunday doubleheader against the lowly St. Louis Browns. In the clubhouse before the day's activities, Bill Dietrich complained to Connie Mack about the few chances he had had to pitch, just four games, with a 1-2 record. "If I can't do my regular turn," said the 38-year-old righthander, he would rather have his release.

Mack turned on the startled pitcher and snapped, "All right, you have it!" With that Dietrich's long major league career, which began with three years for the Athletics in the early 1930s, came to a sudden close. Dietrich left for his home in nearby Frankford. The A's took the field for their twinbill.

In the eighth inning of the first game, Brissie held a 5-2 lead when he loaded the bases with no outs and was relieved by Nelson Potter. Potter was a strong-armed righthander who had been picked up from the Browns on May 15. Potter had pitched earlier for the A's, from 1938 to 1941, with little success, and when Mack sold him to the Red Sox on June 30, 1941, he said, "I never did think he could pitch." During the war, though, Nelson Potter became a star for the Browns, winning 19 games for the 1944 champions. Mack acquired him in 1948 to strengthen the A's bullpen, and Potter had done just that. In seven games, he had a 2-1 record, with three saves and a 3.18 earned run average. June 13th, though, was not his day.

Potter walked Joe Schultz, the first batter he faced, to force in a run. Paul Lehner singled to center, and when outfielder Ray Coleman threw wildly, all three runners scored. The old man on the bench, already agitated after the confrontation with Dietrich, seethed. Potter got Roy Partee to foul out, but when George Binks and Ed Pellagrini followed with hits, another run scored and Charlie Harris was brought in to pitch.

As Nelson Potter reached the dugout, Mack exploded: "Young fellow, were you doing your best out there? You have pitched your last game for this club!" He also said, according to Mack later, "I paid $20,000 for you and that was my mistake. I don't care how good any player ever was, has been, or could be—all I care about is how much good is he for me?" Potter said he was doing the best he could but otherwise took the tongue-lashing in silence, out of "respect," he said, "for age."

Earle Mack tried to cool things off, and Connie Mack, Jr., flew out to see his father the next day, but there was no turning back. Fan reaction in Philadelphia was sympathetic toward the pitcher, but the old man was adamant. Potter returned to his home in Illinois, Mack put him on waivers, and the A's started a key western swing with only eight pitchers. On June 21, Potter signed with the Boston Braves, for whom he did an excellent job as the top reliever on Billy Southworth's pennant-winning staff. The Athletics' bullpen, reduced once again to Bob Savage and Bubba Harris, continued as the weakest part of the ballclub. Lou Brissie, years later, felt that the loss of Nelson Potter may have been even more instrumental in the team's ultimate failure than the late-season injury to Eddie Joost.[5]

The A's came on strong in July, with a mark of 18-13, to move back into first place. On the last day of the month, Brissie relieved McCahan in the third inning at Detroit and pitched brilliantly the rest of the way for an 8-3 win, with big hits by Chapman and Joost. As July ended, the A's were sitting one-half game behind Boston, with Cleveland and the Yankees another game and a half back.

The next day Marchildon beat the Tigers 4-2, giving up only five hits but allowing seven walks and a hit batsman. Charlie Harris had to

Shibe Park: pennant fever in July 1948 (Urban Archives, Temple University, Philadelphia).

come in to get the last out. Fain had four hits including a home run. The Red Sox lost two to the Indians, so Connie Mack's men were in first place, one game ahead of each of the other three contenders. It was in this game that an errant Marchildon pitch conked a fan who was sitting in the third base stands lighting a cigar at the moment of impact.

The A's moved on to Chicago, where the Yankees had been battling the White Sox, and when they checked into the Del Prado Hotel Mack found a note on his bureau: "Dear Mr. Mack: Congratulations on taking first place. Please keep the race close. /s/ Bucky Harris." Mack told a reporter, "I believe this is the closest American League race we've ever had." He compared it to the 1908 struggle but thought this was closer because there were now four teams involved rather than three.[6]

When the A's lost to the White Sox the next day, 2-1 in ten innings, the other three leaders all won, so the four teams were in a four-way tie for first place. The loss to Chicago was a tough one, because Dick

Fowler had a one-hit 1-0 game going into the ninth. The Sox tied it on a couple of hits, an intentional walk, and a Pat Seerey fly ball, and they won it in the tenth on two walks and a single by Jack Wallaesa, an A's castoff.

After a rainout, "those meteoric Macks," as Art Morrow called them in his *Inquirer* report, won two at Comiskey Park to take a half-game lead over Cleveland. Coleman won the opener, 3-0, and Scheib won the second, 7-4 in relief of McCahan. The A's broke a 4-4 tie in the ninth when, with one out, Eddie Joost walked and scored on McCosky's double. Chapman then hit the next pitch into the stands for his eighth home run.[7]

On August 6, Marchildon lost 2-1 to the Browns, although his effort was his best performance of recent weeks. Ferris Fain had to leave the game in the fourth inning and was replaced by oldtimer Rudy York. In the eighth inning the slow-moving York was thrown out at the plate to cut off a potential rally.

The next night, August 7, Brissie beat the Browns, 7-1, behind batting power supplied by Herman Franks, Suder, Fain, and Joost. The A's, Indians, and Yankees were tied for the lead, although Cleveland technically led by a few percentage points. This turned out to be a disastrous game for the A's, even with their victory. Eddie Joost jammed his thumb sliding into a base, and he missed the next game because his hand had swollen up. What the Mackian players and supporters did not realize at first was that Joost would be in and out of the lineup—and Graduate Hospital—over the next several weeks with his hand injury, and his absence would help knock the A's out of the race.

Joost was the inspirational leader of the squad, a fine shortstop and a leadoff hitter who was among the league leaders in bases on balls and had 16 home runs besides. The A's had no one to take his place. They tried to replace Joost with young Billy DeMars, who hit only .172, with 38-year-old Jim "Skeeter" Webb, who hit .148, and even with Majeski, which resulted in weakening two positions when they stuck a light-hitting outfielder named Don White on third base.

The slippage was gradual. In the first game Joost missed, on August 9, Fowler beat the Browns, 7-5, winning his 11th of the year and even hitting his first big league home run. On the tenth the Athletics split a twi-nite doubleheader with Washington, playing DeMars at short in the opener, Majeski in the nightcap. When Ted Gray of the Tigers beat Cleveland's Bob Feller, the A's and Indians were effectively tied for first once more.

By now more than a thousand applications for World Series tickets, some with blank signed checks enclosed, were pouring in on the startled Athletic front office. The A's management returned them all with a form letter.

On August 11 the A's beat the Senators 8-3 in a game delayed by rain. When play resumed Scheib replaced Marchildon and went the rest of the way for the win, also banging a key two-run double. The next day the A's had a respite from American League play, as they journeyed to Albany to beat the local Eastern League club in an exhibition. The Indians lost to the Browns, 8-4, before crushing them in a second game, 26-3. The A's were in first place by a half game and two percentage points.

Mack took the opportunity to ruminate on his team. "This is it," he was quoted as saying. "This is my greatest team. Maybe I have had better teams in respect to ability … But this is the best team I have ever had in regard to effort…. [W]hether this team wins or loses, it is great." Road secretary Benny McFarland added, "By golly, when we hired these fellows, we weren't hiring ball players. We were hiring hearts."[8]

On the 13th, with Joost back in the lineup, the A's had a 5-0 lead at Yankee Stadium when New York rose up to score eight runs in the eighth inning against Brissie and Harris. It was obvious that Joost was having trouble handling the ball in the field. The 8-5 loss, combined with Cleveland's 5-0 win over Chicago, behind the ageless Satchel Paige, moved the Indians a half game ahead of the A's. Another eight-spot the next day, this time in the second inning, gave the Yankees a 14-3 victory, Vic Raschi beating Fowler.

On August 15, the biggest crowd of the year at Yankee Stadium, 72,468, was shocked to see the A's take two from the Bronx Bombers, by identical 5-3 scores. In the first game Marchildon took a 2-0 lead into the ninth but walked the leadoff hitter in front of a Joe DiMaggio game-tying home run. In the visiting tenth, Chapman singled with one out, went to third on a hit by Fain, and scored on Majeski's safety. Valo moved the runners up with a ground ball, and both scored on Pete Suder's hit. The Yankees got one run back in the bottom of the inning on a DiMaggio triple, but Brissie came in to retire Yogi Berra and end the game. McCahan won the second game after Mike Guerra tripled with the bases loaded.

The next day, August 16, was a sad day for baseball, for it saw the death of the great Bambino, Babe Ruth. Fittingly, there were no games scheduled in the American League, so Cleveland maintained its game and a half lead over the Athletics. Mack announced that his pitchers would no longer be able to designate whom they wanted to catch them: "From now on, Rosar will do all of our catching when he is able."[9]

After a rainout, the A's lost to the Red Sox at Boston, 10-2, as Denny Galehouse beat Carl Scheib. Birdie Tebbetts and Ted Williams had three hits apiece for Boston, and Joost left the game in the third inning because of his aching hand. He was sent back to Philadelphia for treatment and X-rays.

On August 20, the papers reported the Athletics' win of the day before, 10-3 over Boston behind Dick Fowler, as well as the results of the X-rays of Joost's hand: "the pictures show that no bones were broken and that he could play again when he desired."[10]

The return of the A's to Shibe Park was greeted by a crowd of 21,460, which saw the Yankees behind Eddie Lopat squelch the home team and Phil Marchildon, 6-2. Joost did not play, as the A's fell 3½ games back. Hopes were starting to fade as the gap between the A's and first place slowly widened.

On August 22, a capacity-plus crowd of 33,306 saw the A's lose to the Yankees, 10-0, in the first game of a scheduled twinbill; the second game was rained out. "The rain was all that was needed to complete the disappointment of the onlookers, many of whom had come 100 miles or more," the *Inquirer* noted. People had started arriving at Shibe Park as early as 4 a.m., and by 6 a.m. there were long lines at the ticket windows. "Every seat was occupied by 11:30, two hours before game time," a writer said, "and still fans continued pouring in."[11]

Eddie Joost tried to play in that Sunday game with the Yankees, but it was clear that the damaged hand was affecting both his batting and fielding. "I guess I'll just have to wait," the shortstop said; "it's a question of time." He added, "The hand's a lot better than it was— maybe it will recover completely overnight."[12]

On the 25th, with Joost back in Graduate Hospital, the A's lost to

Detroit, 7-4, the crucial play being an error by Don White, the outfielder playing third because Hank Majeski was at shortstop. After another loss, 10-4 to the Tigers, the A's ended their losing streak at five games on the 26th, beating the great Detroit lefthander Hal Newhouser, 4-3.

The Mackmen were barely hanging in the race. On the 27th they beat the St. Louis Browns twice, 6-0 and 9-1, behind Fowler and McCahan. Majeski had seven hits in the doubleheader, including six doubles. Skeeter Webb played the two games at shortstop, and Mack was pleased to hear that Joost had been released from the hospital and it was "only a matter of days until he returns to the lineup." The A's were still three games behind Boston, in fourth place.[13]

The next day, in the midst of a record-setting heat wave, the team beat the Browns again, 5-4 in ten innings, on a triple by Don White and a single off the wall by Chapman. On the 29th, the A's split a pair with the White Sox; each of the other contenders split as well, so there was no change in the standings.

The Athletics then lost their next seven games, one to Chicago, two to Cleveland, three to the Red Sox, and one to New York, before Joe Coleman stopped the losing streak at eight with a 6-2 win in the second game of a doubleheader at Yankee Stadium. The A's were now 9½ games back, and for all practical purposes their run at the pennant was over. Even a five-game winning streak early in September gained no ground for them, and they scrambled through the rest of the month trying to maintain their position. Eddie Joost got back into the lineup, but his hand still hurt and the magic was gone. The Athletics, with their 84-70 mark, finished in fourth place, 12 games behind the Indians and Red Sox, whose tie produced the league's first sudden-death playoff, won by Cleveland.

It was a fine year for the Athletics, who drew a club-record attendance of 945,076. (It was the last time the A's would ever outdraw the Phillies.) McCosky, Majeski, and Valo all hit over .300, and little Hank drove in 120 runs. Fain hit .281 and drove home 88 runs. There was little help coming off the bench, and the bullpen was mainly in the unsure hands of Savage and Bubba Harris, who each won five games but had high earned run averages. The departed Nelson Potter would have been useful to the thin mound staff. For serious relief work, they often called on one of their starters like Brissie or Scheib. The staff easily outpaced the league with 74 complete games, but it was a matter of necessity.

The 1948 A's were unlikely pennant contenders. They scrapped and hustled and waited out bases on balls, and they made lots of double plays. No team in the league had fewer errors. They had no superstars, their bench was thin, and their best pitcher suffered through a poor season. Compared with the teams they were battling—Cleveland with Boudreau, Keltner, Gordon, Feller, and Lemon; the Red Sox of Williams, Doerr, Vern Stephens, and Dominic DiMaggio; and the Yankees with Raschi, Joe DiMaggio, Rizzuto, and Yogi Berra—the A's hardly figured to be in contention at all. Only Rosar and Coleman were named to play in the All-Star Game in 1948. All the A's did was play well enough to win.

There was extra excitement in Philadelphia in the summer of 1948, as three major political conventions were held in the city. The Republicans nominated New York Governor Tom Dewey, the Democrats reluctantly picked President Harry S Truman, and the Progressive Party named Henry A. Wallace as its candidate. It was the last year in which the conventions were covered primarily on the radio, so while listeners across the country heard some of the sounds of Philadelphia they did not get to see the city. Philadelphia Congressman Hugh Scott, as chairman of the Republican National Committee, grandly predicted a Dewey "landslide of history-making proportions," a landslide which disappeared with Truman's stunning comeback triumph.[14]

The Athletics slipped in 1949. Their 81-73 record was identical to that of the Phillies, and their attendance of 816,514 was just 3000 below the Phils' draw. But the A's finished fifth and were no factor in the pennant race. They were second, 5½ games behind the front-running Yankees, at the end of June, but after the first week of July they faded, holding fourth or fifth the rest of the way.

Marchildon was virtually useless, with a sore arm which restricted him to only 16 innings all season. Barney McCosky played not a game, with his bad back. All was not bleak, however, as Sam Chapman put together a good year, with 24 homers and 108 RBIs, Joost banged out 23 home runs, and the club's total of 217 double plays set a single-season record which still stands. The infield of Fain, Suder, Joost, and Majeski was a joy to watch.

A rookie lefthander from Arizona named Alex Kellner won 20 games, losing 12, a record blemished only slightly by the fact that he was a combined 12-1 against the last two clubs in the standings, the dismal Browns and Senators. Brissie had another good campaign, at 16-11, and Fowler, who developed bursitis in his right shoulder, was 15-11, even though the act of throwing the ball had become painful to him.

The A's had a second rookie southpaw, a young man from the sandlots of nearby Pottstown named Robert Clayton Shantz. Shantz was making 73 cents an hour working in a sawmill when the Athletics signed him, after a Phillies scout turned him down as "too small." Bobby Shantz was listed at 5'6" and 139 pounds, but no one ever questioned the size of his heart.

In April 1949, Shantz, who had had a bone spur removed from his shoulder blade during spring training, came north with the club, pitched two-thirds of an inning in relief on May 1, and was then optioned to Buffalo. While driving to western New York, he was recalled by the A's, although he didn't find out until he arrived in Buffalo. He drove on to Detroit and got into the game the day he arrived, May 6, relieving Scheib in the third inning. He worked inning after inning against the Tigers, as the A's tied the game, and no one got a base hit against the lefthander. In the top of the 13th, Wally Moses hit a two-run homer for the A's. George Kell's single in the bottom of the inning was the first hit off Shantz, and the Tigers finally scored a meaningless run. In his second big league game, Bobby Shantz pitched nine innings of no-hit ball and picked up the win. Shantz quickly became a fan favorite.

The A's spelled Suder at second base with a young infielder named Nelson Fox. Fox hit .255 in 1949, but the A's braintrust somehow got the idea that the youngster was a bit lackadaisical. "For some unknown reason," Joost said, "Mack wasn't impressed with him." After the season they traded Fox to the White Sox for journeyman catcher Joe Tipton. Mark the date, October 19, 1949, for it may fairly be said that the day the A's traded Nellie Fox for Joe Tipton they took the first steps on the road to Kansas City.[15]

In 1949, the Democrats began to take over the city. On July 12, Dilworth demolished Sheriff Austin Meehan in a debate on municipal corruption at the Academy of Music before a packed house and a huge radio audience. Dilworth announced that he would run for city treasurer and his colleague Joseph Sill Clark, Jr., for controller in the upcoming municipal election. With the continuing revelations of scandals and corruption, the Democratic ticket won in November to seize the two fiscal offices. The Dilworth-Clark team was on its way; two years later, Clark was elected mayor and Dilworth district attorney. It was the dawn of a new era in the City of Brotherly Love.

The baseball teams had high hopes for 1950. The Phillies, loaded with young stars like Robin Roberts, Richie Ashburn, Granny Hamner, and Del Ennis, were buoyed by a fast finish in 1949, while the Athletics, still with the nucleus of the 1948 pennant contender, looked forward to celebrating Connie Mack's 50th year as manager of the club. It would be a fitting time for that "just one more" he had been awaiting so long. While the Fox-for-Tipton trade was in the works, the A's swapped Rosar to Boston for a well-traveled but competent infielder named Billy Hitchcock. With a couple more deals, they felt, the A's could contend for the 1950 pennant.

CHAPTER 16

Jubilee

To the outside world, 1950 was the year Senator Joseph R. McCarthy took off on his skyrocket to notoriety and the year North Korea invaded South Korea, but in Philadelphia baseball 1950 was the year of jubilee. The 50th season of Connie Mack's tenure as manager of the Athletics had been designated his Golden Jubilee, the culmination of his remarkable career, though he was 87 years old and obviously failing.

For both local clubs, expectations were high as preparations for the season went forward. The Phillies were confident they could pick up where they left off in 1949, and the A's hoped to offer a strong challenge for the American League pennant. The Mack Jubilee might provide an added psychological impetus to carry them to the top.

In preparation for the Jubilee, the A's surrounded Mack with some of his greatest players from the past. Coming in as coaches were three mainstays of the last pennant-winner, Jimmy Dykes, Mickey Cochrane, and Bing Miller, although this meant letting Simmons and Brucker go. Dykes, who had served as manager of the White Sox for 12 years after Mack traded him away, had returned to the A's in 1949. Miller and Cochrane were brought back for 1950. Mack's son Earle, whose title was coach and assistant manager, remained on the staff.[1]

In October the A's made the deals which brought them Billy Hitchcock and Joe Tipton in exchange for Rosar and Nelson Fox. In December, the club pulled off its big trade, the deal it hoped would win the pennant. The A's brass bundled together four marginal players, sweetened the package with $100,000 cash, and shipped it to St. Louis for the Browns' Bob Dillinger and Paul Lehner.

The deal was primarily for Dillinger, a highly rated third baseman who had, in each of his four seasons with the Browns, increased his batting average and RBI total. He led the American League in stolen bases the three prior seasons and hit .324 in 1949. Dillinger, a bespectacled, blond Californian, was to lead the A's in their assault upon the American League heights.

Lehner, the throw-in, was a small outfielder who had played with the Browns for four years without creating any particular excitement. None of the four men the A's gave up had played in Philadelphia the year before, so they were considered no loss.

The key to the deal was the cash, for Bill DeWitt's faltering St. Louis franchise was resorting to the old expedient of selling its better players for what cash they would bring. The odd part of the transaction is that Connie Mack had often been on the other end of such sales and was not that flush financially himself. Clearly, the Dillinger deal was the result of a decision on the part of the Macks to shoot the works for a pennant in the Golden Jubilee year.

The day after the Dillinger trade, the A's swapped Hank Majeski, now clearly a surplus third baseman, to the White Sox for a relief pitcher named Ed Klieman. In the euphoria of the trade with St. Louis, no one took the trouble to try to obtain fair value for Majeski; certainly Klieman did not represent it.

Having reinforced the team for the run at the pennant, management spent $80,000 on improvements to the ball park and worked out new means of getting the A's message to their fans.

For many years, Byrum Saam and Claude Haring, the gravel-throated second banana on the broadcast team, had been describing home games over the air to both Athletics and Phillies fans. Road games were broadcast only when not in competition with a home game, and then only by telegraphic reconstruction, what was known as a "ticker tape game." As of 1950, however, ticker tape games would be a thing of the past in the Quaker City.

The Athletics and Phillies decided to broadcast all their games live, both home and away. Radio station WIBG, which had long been the town's baseball station, would carry the A's, while nearby WPEN signed on to broadcast the Phillies. Saam and Haring stayed with the A's, and the Phillies hired a tall, colorful West Virginian named Gene Kelly to cover their games.

Spring training gave concern to the Athletics. The A's had an unhappy camp at West Palm Beach. There had been contract difficulties with Dillinger, who knew he was supposed to be a savior and wanted to be paid like one. Large salaries, however, were anathema to Connie Mack and his sons, and in their opinion "large salaries" started at about $17,500. Dillinger eventually signed, but bad feelings persisted. After he showed up, it became evident that Dillinger's interest did not go much further than his personal statistics, and some of the other players resented him. This showed in the team's performance. The elder Mack was quoted as saying the team looked "dead on its feet."[2]

Management was particularly concerned about the pitching, which was supposed to be the A's strong point. Coleman and Fowler had sore shoulders, and Kellner and Brissie, who were healthy, could not get anybody out. "I just can't figure Kellner," said Mack. "He hasn't shown anything to me."[3]

Still, when the team arrived home on April 12, Mack was quoted as predicting a close race of five clubs; "we have a good chance to win the pennant." Sticking to the winter's optimism, a few sportswriters like the *Bulletin*'s Ray Kelly picked the A's for first place, and season ticket and Opening Day sales were reported to be at a new club high.

As the teams prepared to open the season, the local entertainment scene featured Billie Holliday and George Shearing onstage at the Earle, Jane Russell and her cantilevered bra in "The Outlaw" at the Pix, Orson Welles and Joseph Cotten in the Viennese thriller, "The Third Man," at the Stanley, and Doug Arthur, the best disc jockey in town, filling three hours of air time every day with his "Danceland" on station WIBG. But on Opening Day attention swung over to the ball clubs.

The A's opened the Golden Jubilee season in Washington. Harry Truman threw out the first ball lefthanded, threw another righthanded, and then settled back to enjoy the game. Carl Scheib was chosen to start for the A's, and the fate of that move may have tipped off what was in store for the year. The Senators pummeled Scheib for five runs in the first inning, frustrated the A's with a couple of great catches by outfielder Gil Coan, and outlasted the visitors to win, 8-7.

Over the next couple of weeks, with Ferris Fain hitting well, the A's won a few games, though they lost more than they won and did not look good. Then, at the end of April, they went to Boston and lost three straight at Fenway Park, including a horror of a Sunday doubleheader.

In the first game, Fowler, rookie Harry Byrd, Coleman, and Shantz all pitched, trying vainly to stem the powerful Red Sox. Ted Williams had two homers and a single for seven runs batted in, and Bobby Doerr and Vern Stephens homered as well. Boston won, 19-0, and the extent of the A's pitching problem began to be seen. Fowler, his shoulder painful with bursitis, was throwing up big, fat pitches, and Joe Coleman looked as if everything was at half speed. The second game went to Boston, 6-5, when pitchers Hank Wyse (twice) and Scheib butchered bunt plays.

Mercifully, Monday's game was rained out and the team escaped from Boston with a 4-8 record, in last place. Earle Mack, arriving home, moaned, "We can't possibly be as bad as we've looked so far."[4] After 12 games, though, Bob Dillinger had a 12-game hitting streak. Although he wore the same uniform (some gold trim for the Golden Jubilee added to the usual royal blue) as the rest of the A's, he did not appear to be functioning in any meaningful association with his teammates.

Two games at Shibe Park with the Tigers were rained out, and then one was played. Detroit's Art Houtteman won, and Dillinger parted company with his hitting streak. On May 6, Earle Mack issued the first denial of dissension on the team; he and his father were having almost daily closed-door team meetings, trying to generate some spark, some drive.

At this point the St. Louis Browns came to town, and Kellner beat them, 12-4, behind the strong hitting of Fain and Paul Lehner. The win moved the A's out of the cellar, and a couple of days later they moved into fifth place when Fain, Valo, and Joost hit homers in a 9-8 victory over Cleveland.

But the surge was short-lived. On May 11, Sam Chapman hit his first home run of the season, but the Indians won 4-3 in ten innings. Two A's runners were picked off base in the ninth inning with the score tied. Home attendance was off 50 per cent from the year before, and the slide now began in earnest. It was at this point, too, that the Phillies climbed into first place in the other league.

The success of the Phillies, Eddie Joost noted, "certainly didn't do anything to bolster our attendance, but there really wasn't much of a rivalry between the Athletics and Phillies.... I'm sure some of their fans would come out every once in a while and root like crazy against us—but it may have been our fans who were booing."[5]

The problems of the A's continued. On May 12, Connie Mack was quoted as saying, "If we ever get ourselves straightened out, we'll give them all a run for their money," but the words rang increasingly hollow. On the 19th, in Detroit, Mack benched Chapman and Valo. He called his team "a happy family," but the inordinate number of team meetings was clearly an effort to manufacture some enthusiasm and dash in a team that looked dead.[6]

Paul Lehner, the throw-in in the Dillinger trade, was hitting .400 and leading the league (he wound up hitting .309, one of the club's few bright spots), but the much-touted pitching was terrible. Brissie was 0-6, Fowler's shoulder was sore, Joe Coleman could hardly throw a baseball, and Kellner was being pounded. Only the unheralded Bobby Shantz gave the mound staff any respectability. On May 23, pitching coach Cochrane announced a definite starting rotation, with starters no longer to double in relief efforts. The next day, Bob Hooper, one of those supposed to be in the new rotation, appeared in relief and blew a 7-5 lead in Chicago. So much for the new rotation. The woeful White Sox, one of the few teams below the A's in the standings, scored five runs in the eighth to win, 10-7. On the 25th Shantz beat the Pale Hose, 6-1, to stave off last place, but it was a faltering team which returned to Philadelphia.

On the night of May 26, the A's board of directors met and made some startling changes in the direction of the club. For years Earle Mack had been assistant manager and heir-apparent to the manager's job when his father should step aside; there was no discernible reason why this should be, except that Connie Mack had decreed it, perhaps for reasons of primogeniture. The Athletics players did not respect him. "You wouldn't listen to him," Metro said, and Barney McCosky commented that, "Earle, I don't think he knew too much baseball."[7] Suddenly Earle was transferred to chief scout, and Dykes was named assistant manager. Cochrane was removed as pitching coach and installed instead as general manager.

The impetus for these changes came from Connie Mack, Jr. The young man, backed by the Shibe and McFarland interests, which still held minority shares, was asserting new-found authority in the operation of the family business. The split between Connie, Jr., and his two older half-brothers, Earle and Roy, was now out in the open.

Clearly, Dykes, a veteran manager in both the major and minor leagues, was taking over the day-to-day direction of the team, with Connie Mack receding into the background. "Any order that comes from Dykes is the same as coming from me," Mack told his players. "He has full authority."[8]

The case of Cochrane was curious. He was being assessed at least some of the blame for the pitching failures, and it was unclear what was expected of him as general manager, other than to represent the interests of Connie, Jr. It was soon announced that the reassignments were only for the balance of the Golden Jubilee season, which seemed odd as well. But seasoned observers of the Philadelphia baseball scene were accustomed to these strange and byzantine goings-on in the Athletics' front office.

Early in June, Coleman and Fowler were dispatched to Johns Hopkins Hospital in Baltimore for examination, to see what could be done for their achy arms. In the meantime, on June 7, Shantz pitched the first A's shutout of the year, beating the White Sox before a sparse crowd of 2,536 diehards.

On June 8, local trucking magnate and Democratic fundraiser James P. Clark announced the formation of a syndicate to make an offer for the Athletics franchise, which, in addition to the right to play in the American League, owned contracts with a total payroll (including administrative personnel) of about $400,000, eight minor league clubs, all Class A or lower, which passed for the Athletics' farm system, and an old ball park. "To me," said Clark, "it appears that Mr. Mack is the most valuable asset the club has." Which gives an idea of what the A's had become. Mack was quoted as saying, "I would like to stay in baseball. But you always have a price, and if they meet that we'll sell." Soon four more groups were reported interested. Just as hopes were rising for the injection of new money and new life into the franchise, however, the A's management announced on June 12 that the club would not be sold in 1950.[9]

The next day, with some bad baserunning and a costly error by Dillinger, the A's lost to Detroit 6-5 and fell into the cellar. By the 20th, when Brissie lost to Ned Garver of the Browns by a 1-0 score, they were three games out of seventh. Connie Mack called a clubhouse meeting before the game but walked out in disgust, leaving Dykes to blister the players for their lack of effort. A couple of days later, pitcher Hank Wyse was fined $250 and sent back to Philadelphia for not being in his room when a bed check was made.

The Browns were not giving up the cellar without a struggle. They kept losing, and when the A's won a doubleheader on June 30 in Washington, the Browns sank below them. On the 4th of July, the A's were still one game ahead. On the 5th, though, the A's lost to the Yankees, 12-8, and Eddie Joost went to the hospital with pulled knee ligaments. The next day Yogi Berra doubled in the winning run in the ninth, and Ferris Fain hurt his back. By the All-Star break, after Dick Fowler won his first game of the year, the A's and St. Louis were tied.

On July 14, 3,000 curious people showed up to watch the two teams play a doubleheader. After their split they were still tied. Through July and August the struggle continued. At one point the Athletics lost five in a row at Boston, but the Browns lost five to the Indians to keep pace. On the last day of August, the two teams played another doubleheader, a twi-niter this time, and attracted 1,161 paying customers. Again they split, although it may have been the fastest doubleheader of the postwar era, the two games being played in 1:37 and 1:39.

As September wore on, though, the A's inexorably fell further and further behind, until it was clear that last place was theirs beyond question. After that, they faded from view, except on the day that young catcher Joe Astroth drove in six runs in one inning and the game in which Chapman's ninth-inning home run delayed the Yankees' pennant-clinching by one day.

Off the field, however, the A's did make news during that dismal summer. On July 15, publicity director Dick Armstrong denied a rumor that the club was planning to acquire a black player in order to boost attendance. Pitcher Sam Jones of Wilkes-Barre was the man they were thought to be after. They should have bought Jones, if he was available, since he was much better than what they had.[10]

Four days later, Bob Dillinger was sold to the Pittsburgh Pirates, just after making another error in a crucial spot. The third baseman was still batting .310, but he had gone hitless in his last 14 plate appearances and had only five stolen bases for the season. Dillinger's comment was, "I am not surprised and not unhappy." The highest paid player on the squad, at $22,500, his salary negotiations in the spring had left both Dillinger and the front office disenchanted. John Webster of the *Inquirer* wrote of him as "one whose enthusiasm is not pronounced and whose worth to the team's effort is less than sensational." Dillinger, a "good-hit, no-field third sacker," he wrote, "didn't figure to be missed either by the loyal rooters or by the struggling Athletics." The Macks were cutting their losses.[11]

On August 28, the controlling interest in the club was sold—to Earle and Roy Mack, who exercised an option to buy out the Shibe-McFarland interests, Mrs. Mack, and Connie, Jr. To do it, they mortgaged the club to the Connecticut General Life Insurance Company for $1,750,000, and they borrowed additional cash from local builder John McShain.

This transaction insured that the franchise would continue to be run on a shoestring, cash-poor and never knowing how the next payroll would be met, but Earle and Roy had finally gotten rid of their half-brother and their stepmother and taken full control of what they regarded as their inheritance. A few days later, the old man officially ended his historic tenure as manager, and Dykes was named in his place. Mickey Cochrane, who had been installed in the front office by Connie, Jr., saw what was coming, resigned, and went home.

The Golden Jubilee was over, although few Philadelphians were paying attention by now, enthralled as they were—except for die-hard A's fans—with the Phillies. The despised, downtrodden Phillies won their first pennant since 1915, only the second in their lackluster history.

CHAPTER 17

The Road to
Kansas City

The ancient Connie Mack, 88 years old on December 22, 1950, retained the title of president of the Athletics after he stepped down as manager, but the club was no longer his. The Philadelphia American League club had always been a unique institution, almost an extension of Connie Mack's personality. This had set the A's apart from other teams, and the singularity of the situation had been enhanced by Mack's own distinctive attributes. Now that was over. He was still the club president in name, but he had a manager just like everyone else, and he even had a general manager, his former farm director, Arthur Ehlers. And his sons Earle and Roy were running the front office.

The year after the disastrous Golden Jubilee season was not so bad. The club under Jimmy Dykes climbed a couple of notches to sixth place, moving ahead of the Senators and Browns on the strength of a late-season surge. There were several excellent individual performances and some inspired trading by the new general manager.

Still, home attendance picked up only to 465,469, and this was not really adequate. The Phillies flopped in 1951, but they were now clearly the darlings of the Philadelphia fans. There just were not enough loyalists who would stick with the Athletics no matter what. The Macks had to make annual payments of $200,000 on their mortgage with Connecticut General, and their gate was not generating anything like that. The Athletics' financial situation looked precarious.

On the field, though, things did look up. At the end of April, Ehlers engineered a complicated three-way deal with the White Sox and Indians. The Sox shipped outfielders Dave Philley and Gus Zernial to the A's and Cleveland kicked in pitcher Sam Zoldak and catcher Ray Murray, while all the A's gave up was Paul Lehner to the White Sox and Lou Brissie to the Indians. The other part of the trade sent Orestes "Minnie" Minoso from Cleveland to Chicago, a very good acquisition for the Sox.

The trade was a steal for the Athletics. Philley and Zernial had played together for some time, and they became stars in Philadelphia. Philley, Zernial said, "was a hard-nosed all-around player, a switch-hitting outfielder with some power and good speed." Joost said the Texan "played hard every day. He'd challenge everyone."[1]

Dykes also got some serviceable work from Murray and Zoldak. On the other hand, Lehner did nothing for the White Sox and soon moved on, while Brissie, the key man in the transaction for Cleveland, won only seven games in three seasons with the Tribe.

Zernial, in fact, claimed both the home run and RBI crowns for the A's in 1951, both titles which no Athletic had won since Jimmy Foxx in 1933. Zernial was a big, handsome blond from Texas with an open face and a free swing. He did not run very well, and his play in the outfield left a lot to be desired, but he could rip the ball and he liked the inviting target of the Shibe Park left field bleachers. Zernial went on a slugging binge shortly after joining the A's and for the season hit 33 fourbaggers and drove in 129 runs. The fans liked big Gus, although they rode him hard for his fielding deficiencies and the strikeouts which accompanied his slugging feats.

Ferris Fain came into his own as a hitter in 1951. He had always been a productive swinger, but his highest previous average had been .291. In 1951, he seized the batting leadership early in the season and won the title with a mark of .344. An aggressive hitter, Ferris sprayed base hits all over the field. He did not swing for home runs (ten in 1950 was his career high) and his RBI total fell off as his average rose, but he stung the ball and piled up a lot of doubles. His own fiery temper almost kept him from winning the title. In mid-July, after hitting a popup, Fain fractured his foot when he angrily kicked the first base bag. He missed 37 games but came back in late August to add ten points to

Ferris Fain, two-time batting champion in 1951 and 1952 (Urban Archives, Temple University, Philadelphia).

his average. *The Sporting News* named Fain the top player in the American League in 1951.

Elmer Valo and Billy Hitchcock both hit over .300, and Joost had a good year. Philley was a valuable acquisition, batting .262 with 61 runs driven in, and Hank Majeski, reclaimed from Chicago for infielder Kermit Wahl, hit .285 to help out. A couple of old friends departed: Sam Chapman was sold to Cleveland, and Barney McCosky took his bad back to Cincinnati and ultimately to Cleveland. Both of them were just about at the end of the line.

The big pitching story for the A's was Bobby Shantz. The little lefty, a great favorite of the fans, won 18 games and lost ten for Dykes. Shantz stood up to the big hitters without giving an inch, made the fielding plays with his great agility off the mound, hit in the clutch, and laid down well-placed bunts when needed.

Dykes got good pitching from Kellner, from Bob Hooper, and from a southpaw drafted out of the Brooklyn organization, a chunky Missourian named Morrie Martin. Martin went 11-4 to tie for the best percentage in the league. Some of the other hurlers fared not so well. Fowler's bursitis made throwing more and more painful, and his record of 5-11 showed it. Joe Coleman's arm was still bad, and his record was 1-6. Carl Scheib also won one game and lost 12 times. It was a mixed bag of a season.

The next year, 1952, was much better. The A's were 79-75; Fain won another batting championship with a .327 average and led the league with 43 doubles. Zernial hit 29 homers and drove in 100 runs. Scheib came back to post a record of 11-7. A hard-throwing righthander named Harry Byrd won 15 games and become American League rookie-of-the-year, although he had appeared in six games during a brief stint with the club in 1950. Jimmy Dykes smoked his ever-present cigars and told lots of funny stories to the press. And Bobby Shantz had a super season.

Bobby was great, winning 24, losing seven, with an earned run average of 2.48. It was the most any pitcher had won for the Athletics since Lefty Grove. Shantz dominated the year and was voted the most valuable player in his league. "He had unbelievable stuff," Joost said, "a good, moving fastball and a great curveball that was always around the plate." Shantz later said, "I got to a point where I could do just about anything I wanted to out there on the mound. Everything seemed to go right."[2]

Bobby even sparkled in the All-Star Game. The midsummer classic, played in Shibe Park in 1952, was led by the Nationals when Casey Stengel put Shantz in to pitch the fifth inning against the top of the batting order. Shantz struck out the Giants' Whitey Lockman, then Jackie Robinson, then Stan Musial. The fans in old Shibe Park were ecstatic;

the Athletics' lefthander could take aim the next inning at Carl Hubbell's famous record of consecutive All-Star strikeouts. But there was no next inning. A heavy rainstorm resulted in the game being called at that point, and Bobby Shantz pitched no more that day. But the 32,875 people there knew that they had witnessed a great pitcher at work.

The A's finished fourth in 1952, their first entry into the first division since 1948. With the batting champ, the most valuable player, and the rookie of the year, with the slugging feats of Zernial thrown in, the Athletics were still unable to draw more than 627,100 spectators to their home games. The Phillies also finished fourth in 1952 with the fading Whiz Kids, but their home attendance was 775,417. The handwriting was there on the wall for the Macks to read. Only on those days when Bobby Shantz was scheduled to pitch could a good crowd be expected. What would happen if hard luck should befall Shantz? In 1953, the A's found out.

The year 1953 was a bad one for Jimmy Dykes, the Mack family, and the whole franchise. As Dykes said later, "By May my hopes were shattered." Late in the '52 season, Shantz had broken two bones in his left wrist when hit by a pitch from Washington's Walt Masterson. In his first 1953 start, possibly favoring the wrist, Shantz tore a muscle in his shoulder and, as he said, "I wasn't worth a damn all year…. I just couldn't throw." His record slipped to 5-9, and, disastrously, his innings pitched fell from 275 to 109.[3]

Ferris Fain, preparing to defend his two consecutive batting titles, was traded off to the White Sox for first baseman Eddie Robinson, a big, slow-moving slugger, whose performance in Philadelphia was far below the standard established by Fain. Harry Byrd lost 20 games, and his earned run average ballooned to an unsightly 5.51.

The pitching as a whole was bad. The best pitcher on the squad was Kellner, at 11-12. A 29-year-old rookie named Marion Fricano had a mark of 9-12, just getting by with marginal stuff, and Morrie Martin came back from a sore arm to put up a record of 10-12. But that was all there was. Byrd had his bad year, Shantz had his bad year, Scheib was 3-7, Joe Coleman's comeback effort netted him no better than three wins and four losses, and a tall youngster named Charlie Bishop, used as both a starter and a reliever, was 3-14.

Eddie Joost, too, was wearing out. He could play in only 51 games

Pitcher Bobby Shantz: MVP in 1952 (The Falvey Collection, courtesy Philadelphia A's Historical Society Archives).

in 1953, and Joe "Froggy" DeMaestri, a light-hitting utility man obtained from Chicago in the Fain deal, played most of the year at shortstop, with help from Joost. "I learned a lot from him," DeMaestri said. "In fact, he was the first guy to actually take time to help me in the field."[4]

There were some good performances. Pete Suder was slowing down, but he hit a solid .286. Catcher Joe Astroth hit well, and Gus Zernial, with .284, 42 home runs, and 108 runs batted in, maintained his standing among the league's most feared sluggers. Eddie Robinson, though he hit only .247, drove in 102 runs, which was, after all, the reason

177

they traded for him. Dave Philley had his best season, hitting .303 and playing in every game.

The A's were involved in one of the more bizarre stories of the 1953 season when, on May 6, a tall rookie righthander from Georgia named Alva "Bobo" Holloman appeared on the mound against them, pitching for the St. Louis Browns. Holloman had been purchased from Syracuse on a conditional basis by Bill Veeck, the Browns' owner, and had been unimpressive. The Browns were going broke in St. Louis, having been turned down in efforts to move to either Milwaukee or Baltimore, and Veeck was anxious to return Holloman to Syracuse before he had to pay an additional $25,000 for the privilege of keeping him. Holloman pleaded for the chance to make one start, so Veeck and manager Marty Marion agreed to pitch him against the A's. Veeck wrote that "everything he threw was belted. And everywhere the ball went, there was a Brownie to catch it." Veeck, in his inimitable style, describes the improbable fielding plays of that evening, down to the last out in the ninth, a smash to first baseman Vic Wertz. "Big Bobo," Veeck said, "had pitched the quaintest no-hitter in the history of the game," and he, Veeck, was stuck with him; he couldn't ship an immortal back to the minors. It was the only complete game Bobo Holloman ever threw, in a big league career that ended later that season. These things seemed to happen to the Athletics.[5]

On September 13, 1953, a tall righthanded pitcher named Bob Trice made his debut with the Athletics and, in doing so, became the first black player to perform for a Philadelphia major league club. Trice, a 28-year-old from Georgia, began with the Homestead Grays in the Negro National League at the age of 22. He had compiled a 21-10 record for Ottawa in the International League earlier in '53. Dykes started Trice three times in the last couple weeks of the season, and he won two and lost one.

Still, the team slipped to seventh, winning 20 fewer games than in 1952. "We had no money to plug holes," Dykes said, "no bench strength."[6] Even more ominous, as the time for paying the mortgage came round, was the fact that the paid home attendance fell to 362,113, little more than half that of the year before. *That*, the A's discovered, was what happened when Bobby Shantz could no longer take his regular turn on the mound.

For 1954 there were no great hopes. The team looked bad, there was no money, and a new and final disaster never theretofore contemplated by A's fans became a menacing possibility. Just before the 1953 season began, Lou Perini moved his Boston National League franchise to Milwaukee, and the map of major league baseball, unchanged since the move of the Baltimores to New York in 1903, started to crack apart.

Perini's hand had been forced by Veeck, who tried to move his St. Louis Browns to the Wisconsin metropolis but was blocked by Perini's ownership of the Milwaukee minor league franchise and hence the territorial rights to the area. Since his Braves were dying in competition with the Red Sox in Boston, Perini exercised his rights to the Milwaukee area by making a hasty but tremendously successful move there. With players like Warren Spahn, Eddie Mathews, Joe Adcock, and rookie Henry Aaron, the new Milwaukee Braves finished in second place, drew a million and a half more fans than in their last year in Boston, and showed the way for any clubowner dissatisfied with his situation.[7]

Before the next season started, the American League clubowners pried the Browns loose from Veeck, forcing him to sell to a group which promptly moved the club to Baltimore, a move which Veeck, unpopular among his fellow owners, had been prevented from making. Attendance in the Maryland city far surpassed that of the hapless Browns.

In Philadelphia, loose talk was heard that the same fate might befall the Athletics, whose status paralleled that of the Braves and Browns: a poor team competing for customers in the same town against a better team with greater resources. No one expected the Mack family to leave Philadelphia, but anyone could recognize that their hold on the heavily mortgaged franchise had become precarious.

After the 1953 season, the Macks rid themselves of general manager Ehlers and field manager Dykes. Earle Mack made himself general manager and named Joost to run the team on the field. This was a saving of two salaries, since both men were already on the payroll. Ehlers and Dykes both went off to Baltimore.

Economics dictated another transaction. Dave Philley, after his good year, wanted to be paid in a manner befitting a .300 hitter. The club pointed out that there was no money in the till, but Philley refused to sign for what he was offered. In addition, Zernial said that Philley

From left to right: Eddie Joost, Earle Mack, and Roy Mack, as Joost signs to manage the team in 1954 (Urban Archives, Temple University, Philadelphia).

did not like Joost and said he would never play for him. The upshot was a trade to Cleveland, which needed Philley much less than the A's did, and consequently gave up only two minor league pitchers named Bill Upton and Leroy Wheat, neither of whom won a game for Philadelphia.[8]

Earlier, a big trade was negotiated with the Yankees. On December 16, 1953, the A's got rid of two of their bigger salaries, those of Harry Byrd and Eddie Robinson, for a lot of little ones, those of six minor leaguers or scrubs found wanting by New York. The Yankees threw in $25,000, and three of the Athletics' marginal performers were shipped off to the Yanks' farm system.[9]

Despite the changes, or perhaps because of them, the 1954 Philadelphia Athletics were a truly bad ball club. They won only 51 games and lost 103. They finished further from first place, 60 games, than any other A's team. Most of the games they lost were neither close nor interesting. With the new uniforms they adopted for the '54 season, they did not even look like the A's. The traditional "A" on the left chest was replaced with the word "Athletics" in script across the chest, something which had never been seen before, and the staid royal blue gave way to red and blue trim.

The team lost, home crowds dwindled, mortgagee made threatening noises, and there was talk of selling the franchise, of moving it to Kansas City or Los Angeles or someplace. A Chicago real estate mogul named Arnold Johnson said he wanted to buy the club in order to move it to Kansas City, and he was said to have close and extensive connections with Del Webb and Dan Topping, the owners of the Yankees.

Early in the season, as the rumbling grew louder, Mayor Joseph S. Clark, Jr., announced a campaign to "Save the A's." It was touched off with appropriate fanfare and affirmations of civic duty by interested citizens, businessmen, and other groups, but the mayor had little real interest in the effort and the campaign soon died away. The baseball fans of Philadelphia showed little desire to spend their money on a bad team in a lopsided league.

Jim Finigan, one of the acquisitions from the Yankees, played third base, hit .302, and represented the A's in the All-Star Game. The Athletics' only bright spot in 1954, Finigan never again played as well as he did that dismal season. First base was shared by ex-Yankee Don Bollweg and Lou Limmer, a product of the A's small minor league system, but neither mustered much offensive punch. Limmer had been touted for several years by the A's as an up-and-coming slugger, but major league pitching proved too much for him. "He is a bad memory," Joost said; "he was the nicest guy in the world, but he couldn't hit, he couldn't field, he couldn't run, and he couldn't throw."[10]

A little hustler named Forrest "Spook" Jacobs played second, hitting .258 with 17 stolen bases. Joost preferred Suder, but the aging Pete hit only .200 so Jacobs saw the bulk of the action. DeMaestri played shortstop most of the way. Manager Joost tried a few games early, found the results not commensurate with the effort, and retired to the dugout, to suffer his torments unseen.

Five men did most of the outfield work, Vic Power, Bill Renna, Valo, Zernial, and a midseason pickup from Chicago, Bill Wilson. Power was a flashy Puerto Rican who had been traded by the Yankees, some said, because he was too much of a hot dog to have the honor of being their first black player. Others said the staid Bronx Bombers peddled him because they disapproved of his dating white women. Power played acceptably in Philadelphia but the A's were playing the future star first baseman at the wrong position. Renna was a disappointment, and the oft-injured Valo hit poorly in limited action. Wilson, after coming over from the White Sox, batted only .238 and was swallowed up in the general mediocrity.

Zernial hit .250, with 14 home runs and 63 runs batted in for little over half a season, but one hot afternoon, as the team was absorbing a pounding from the Red Sox, he tripped over a hole for the sprinkler system while chasing a line drive and broke his shoulder, bringing his career in Philadelphia to a premature end. The fans had been on him for his fielding, and as he lay on the ground, Zernial said, "Thank God I don't have to come out here anymore." As big Gus was carted off the field on a stretcher, the disgusted fans rose up and booed, in one of those classic incidents always cited as evidence of the ultimate depravity of Philadelphia fandom.[11]

The catching was handled by Astroth, whose batting tailed off, and two light-hitting rookies, Al Robertson from the Yanks, and Wilmer Shantz, Bobby's kid brother.

The pitching was awful. Rookie Arnold Portocarrero, a big, burly New Yorker, could do no better than 9-18 and 4.06, and he was considered the ace of the staff. DeMaestri said that Portocarrero "was a big kid, but he wasn't strong. He had very thin arms and legs for a big man.... [H]is ball was too straight, with no movement on it."[12]

Alex Kellner, disappointing again, was 6-17 and 5.39. John Gray was 3-12, with an ERA over six and a half. Fricano was 5-11 and was involved in a nasty incident when he beaned and seriously injured Cass Michaels of the White Sox, a former A's teammate.

Carl Scheib lost the only game he pitched and was then sold to St. Louis. It was his 11th season with the A's, with one year out for the service, and he was still only twenty-seven.[13] Bobby Shantz, his arm badly out of kilter, worked in only two games all season. Trice was a disappointment, winning seven and losing eight with a high earned run average. None of Joost's pitchers accomplished anything noteworthy, and the monotony of the daily losses was soon obscured by the contention in the front office between Roy and Earle Mack and the increasing probability of the club's move.

Attendance for the year was only 304,666, and management went heavily into debt. Payment was never made for the new uniforms. Over the last part of the season there was more financial and corporate news about the A's than baseball news. For the long-suffering Athletic loyalists, whose numbers were steadily dwindling, the business picture was just as melancholy as the baseball scene.

And when the end came, it came in a tragicomedy of fits and starts, of sloppy, confusing procedures which left fans and supporters in both Philadelphia and Kansas City unhappy and disillusioned. It was as if the Athletics were cut off from the body of Philadelphia not with a surgeon's scalpel but with a rusty and jagged saw.

The whole sad story had overtones of an old-time melodrama. At one point, like the U.S. Cavalry charging to the rescue of an embattled wagon train, a "Philadelphia syndicate" was formed, a group of wealthy localites led by the Sylk brothers of Sun Ray Drugstore fame, joining together to bail out the Macks, the A's, and civic pride. Waiting in the wings, though, like the mustachioed villain in the black silk hat ready to foreclose the mortgage on the old homestead, was Arnold Johnson, supported by Webb and Topping of the Yankees, and eager to buy the club to move it to Kansas City. In the mid-1950s, what the powerful Yankees wanted was generally what happened.

The Sylk group was really Philadelphia's last chance to hang onto the A's: the Macks were done, old Connie weary and sick, Roy and Earle feuding and divided, none of them close to the kind of money needed to keep their ball club. In late July, Roy Mack made a strong effort to locate the cash to buy out his father and brother, to keep the team in town, but this failed. The "Philadelphia syndicate" reportedly raised two million dollars, but their offer was insufficient.

With Clark Griffith of Washington and Spike Briggs of Detroit adamantly opposed to a move of the Philadelphia franchise, the American League clubowners held an inconclusive meeting on September 28 in New York to wrestle with the situation. Roy Mack was given two weeks more to raise the money necessary to buy the club.

On October 12, the owners met again, in Chicago this time, and approved the sale to Johnson when Roy Mack tearfully told them he had failed to raise needed cash and the deal should go through. Johnson, however, still had to negotiate a final settlement with the three Macks.

Ironically, the one part of the transaction which was settled was the agreement of Bob Carpenter of the Phillies to buy the ball park from Johnson for $1,675,000, whenever Johnson should happen to come into possession of it.[14]

On October 15, the picture seemed to change again when eight prominent Philadelphia businessmen, led by wealthy auto dealer John P. Crisconi, announced that *they* had come up with money to buy the club. Arnold Johnson promptly announced his intention of suing the eight, but the three Macks entered into an agreement to sell to them.

Philadelphia's last chance died when the American League owners, led by Webb and Topping, turned down Crisconi and his group in a bitter six-hour meeting in New York on October 28. A league functionary told the press the Macks were free "to return to Philadelphia to work out their own problems," which meant they had no alternative to the sale to Johnson.[15]

Within a week, the sale was consummated, with Johnson paying Connie $604,000 for his 302 shares of stock and Roy and Earle $450,000 each for their blocs of 163 shares. He also assumed two million dollars' worth of debt, including the Connecticut General mortgage that did the Macks in. Red Smith wrote that "before this deplorable charade can be finished, the American League must meet again and, for the second time, approve of Johnson as the buyer and sanction his plan to move the club to Kansas City."[16]

The American League, brushing aside a West Coast proposal with which Bill Veeck was associated, gave its approval to the transfer. The league thus turned its back on its past, represented by Philadelphia, and its future, represented by Los Angeles, for some kind of indeterminate middle course. It is ironic that in 1968, after the National League had become well entrenched on the West Coast, the Athletics moved again, this time to Oakland.

In transferring the A's to Kansas City, the league did something else. It gave the back of the hand to one of its greatest figures, one of its founders, the Grand Old Man of Baseball. Johnson announced that Connie Mack would be the "honorary president" of the Kansas City club. But this was a meaningless gesture.

Earle Mack, who spurned the offer of a job in the Kansas City operation (brother Roy *took* the position offered him), spelled out what happened: "Dad was in the league fifty-four years, and only one time did he ask for a favor. He asked the other owners at the meeting in New York to keep the club in Philadelphia. He didn't care who owned the club as long as it stayed in Philadelphia. They turned him down. Fifty-four years in the league and they turned him down."[17]

With that transfer, the Athletics' part in the history of baseball in Philadelphia came to an end. On the whole, it had been the best part, with the early pennants, the great teams of Waddell, Plank, Lajoie and the $100,000 infield, and the mighty crew of Simmons, Cochrane, Grove, and Foxx. For most of the time the Athletics and Phillies shared the city, it had been the A's town. Even near the end, the 1948 contender and such favorites as Joost, Shantz, Johnson, Valo, Fain, and Zernial had given A's fans their share of glorious moments.

But the failure of the Mack family to keep up with changing times as well as the simple lack of resources with which to compete against the wealthy Carpenters condemned the franchise to exile. After World War II, with the ever-increasing costs of operating a modern franchise, most cities, Philadelphia included, simply did not have a fan base large enough to support two baseball teams. The Athletics, run with the purpose of supporting the Mack family and turning a modest profit, not necessarily winning a pennant, could not continue to function in the same old way in the postwar economy.

Connie Mack stayed on in Philadelphia, attending an occasional Phillies game at the old ballpark whose name had been changed to honor him, and on February 8, 1956, he died, the last connection to the early days of the game gone.

Connie Mack died as he had lived in those last years, a vague, shadowy relic of the game's past, a figure who had been the Grand Old Man of Baseball for as long as most Philadelphians could remember. In his day, though, Mack was a vital element in the city's life: a businessman who depended upon the Athletics for his livelihood and made decisions accordingly, a manager who accepted last place without complaint but also put together some of the best teams of all time, and a gentleman who was kindly, soft-spoken, and fondly remembered by most of those with whom he came in contact. Connie Mack was not a saint, certainly, but he was a good man who brought credit to his adopted city and made a major impression upon his place and time.

The baseball team he created and nurtured over a half-century disappeared even before Connie Mack did, but its achievements were real and substantial, many of its heroes legendary, and it was missed by a great number of people in the Philadelphia region—many of whom had neglected to come out to Shibe Park for too long a time when the A's needed them most. More than forty years later, the old names—Jimmy Foxx, George Earnshaw, Sam Chapman, Lefty Grove, Bob Johnson, Eddie Collins, "Black Jack" Barry, Buddy Rosar, Chief Bender, Russ Christopher, Stuffy McInnis, and so many others—still resonate in Philadelphia's collective memory.

Epilogue:
The Wanderers

The Kansas City Athletics were warmly greeted by the fans of their new hometown, and in 1955 they won 12 more games than their Philadelphia predecessors had the year before. Arnold Johnson, the new owner, broke his word to Joost and replaced him as manager with Lou Boudreau, because, he told Joost, "he wanted a name for when the team moved to Kansas City."[1]

Under Boudreau the Athletics finished sixth and, with the enthusiasm surrounding the unfamiliar appearance of major league baseball, drew 1,393,054 in attendance. In the 13 years the club stayed in Kansas City, it would never finish as high as sixth again, and it would never draw as many fans to its park. Not once would the team win as many games as it lost. For a couple of seasons the names appearing in the box scores were familiar to fans back in Philadelphia—names like Zernial, Valo, Shantz, Astroth, and Suder—but soon these names faded out, and new and unfamiliar ones succeeded them. After a while only Joe DeMaestri was left.

The Kansas City Athletics under Johnson became a thinly disguised farm club for the New York Yankees. It seemed like a return to the "syndicate baseball" of the 1890s as the Yankees plucked every promising player off the Kansas City roster. In the steady stream of transactions between the two clubs, it was soon recognized around the league that any good player who showed up in Kansas City would shortly be in New York. When Cleveland traded a promising young slugger named Roger Maris to KC in June 1958, everyone in baseball assumed that he was just stopping off on his way to Yankee Stadium. Sure enough, on December 11, 1959, Maris was traded with DeMaestri and another player to New York for four players the Yankees were ready to discard, including a first baseman named Marv Throneberry. The rest is history.

In 1961 a Chicago insurance man named Charles O. Finley bought the club from the deceased Arnold Johnson's estate. The Yankee connection ended, but Finley was unable to improve things in the Missouri metropolis. After the 1967 season, he received permission from the league to transfer the franchise to Oakland, California. In three of the last four years in Kansas City, the Athletics managed to accomplish something they never did in Philadelphia: they finished in tenth place.

Finley was gathering some high-quality baseball players, and in 1971 the Oakland Athletics won the western division crown, although they were blown out by the Baltimore Orioles in the league championship series, three games to none.[2] In the next three years the Athletics won both the American League title and the World Series, behind stars such as Reggie Jackson, Joe Rudi, Jim "Catfish" Hunter, Rollie Fingers, and Sal Bando. In 1975 the A's were the western winners, losing to Boston in the LCS.

After the Finley era, the Athletics had another stretch of three consecutive pennants, in 1988, 1989, and 1990, with a world's championship in 1989, and a division winner in 1992, all under manager Tony LaRussa. It was slightly reminiscent of Connie Mack's dynasties, particularly after management restored the historic elephant to the team's uniform, albeit in green and yellow rather than white.

The eeriest parallel with the club's Philadelphia forebears came when Finley, strapped for cash as he headed into the new realm of free agency with high-powered but aging champions, started to sell them off for cash. Rudi, Jackson, Hunter, Bando, Vida Blue—Finley worked out a series of deals to sell them for large cash prices, because he knew he could not meet the market when these stars became free agents. Finley's plan went awry when Commissioner Bowie Kuhn intervened and set the sales aside as "not in the best interests of baseball." He soon lost those players anyway, as he had foreseen, without getting *anything* for them.

Charles O. Finley, brash, innovative, crude, and outspoken, was about as far removed from Connie Mack as one individual could be from another. Yet he had shown that when placed in a situation similar to that of Mack in 1914 his reaction was to do almost exactly the same thing Mack had done in 1914-15. It was uncanny, and it seems a fitting place to end the tale of the storied franchise Connie Mack, Frank Hough, and Ben Shibe created from scratch back in 1901.

Notes

Prologue

1. Russell F. Weigley, ed., *Philadelphia: A 300-Year History* (New York: W.W. Norton, 1982), 471, in a chapter by Nathaniel Burt and Wallace E. Davies. Much of what follows in the next few pages is based upon the Burt & Davies chapter.

2. Michael P. McCarthy, "The Unprogressive City: Philadelphia and Urban Stereotypes at the Turn of the Century," *Pennsylvania History*, October 1987, 265.

3. *Ibid.*, 266–67.

4. Frederick G. Lieb and Stan Baumgartner, *The Philadelphia Phillies* (New York: G.P. Putnam's, 1953), 58. It should be noted that Lieb was adept at manufacturing just the right quote for a situation, but this one sounds like Rogers.

Chapter 1

1. It has been asserted by some that the name "Mack" was routinely utilized by the family; see *Philadelphia Inquirer*, June 13, 1997.

2. *Philadelphia Inquirer*, Dec. 5, 1900. The National Agreement, originally between the National League and the American Association, defined the relations between and among the National League and the several minor leagues.

3. *Philadelphia Inquirer*, Dec. 6, 1900. Rogers added that if the new league intended to stay independent, "it will naturally mean war ... the survival of the fittest."

4. *Daily Evening Telegraph*, Jan. 7, 21, 1901; *Philadelphia Inquirer*, Feb. 28,

1901. It was not long before Brush and Rogers were at each other's throats over who was to blame for the demise of their captive minor league.

5. Mack hired Billy Sharsig, former manager of the old Association team from 1886 to 1891, as business manager. On December 11, Somers told the press in Philadelphia that gilt edged backing had been obtained for the local team and that "an option has been secured on a first class grounds." *Philadelphia Inquirer*, Dec. 12, 1900. Neither statement happened to be true at the time.

6. Weigley, ed., *op. cit* ., 474.

7. *Daily Evening Telegraph*, Jan. 23, 1901. Mack, it was said, was "very well pleased" with arrangements for his new park.

8. *Philadelphia Inquirer*, Feb. 20, 1901. Hough, the *Inquirer* writer, did not disclose any financial interest in the new club, and when he was named a defendant in the Phillies' lawsuits the paper simply identified him as an "agent" of the club, mentioning no connection with the newspaper; *Philadelphia Inquirer*, March 28, 1901.

9. Lawrence Ritter, *The Glory of Their Times* (New York: William Morrow, 1984, orig. pub. by Macmillan, 1966), 33.

10. J.M. Murphy, "Napoleon Lajoie: Modern Baseball's First Superstar," *The National Pastime*, spring 1988, 14–15. Lajoie detailed the story of his 1900 contract in his testimony in court on April 20, 1901, reported in the *Inquirer* of April 21. Marc Mandell, in "Baseball's First Free Agent," *The Pennsylvania Lawyer*, May/June 1997, says Lajoie was signed for $5500. The author of the latter article seems unaware that John I. Rogers, who he says was hired by the Phillies with Johnson to plead their case, was actually co-owner of the club.

11. Connie Mack, *My 66 Years in the Big Leagues* (n.p.: Universal House, 1950), 28.

12. Mack played in his final 27 games with Milwaukee in 1897, batting .254.

13. *Daily Evening Telegraph*, April 9, 1901.

14. *Philadelphia Inquirer*, Dec. 21, 1900 (Melba). The Queen's death (and the succession of Edward VII) took place on January 21, 1901; Harrison died March 13, 1901.

15. *Daily Evening Telegraph*, April 26, 1901.

16. *Ibid*. The first batter for the Athletics was outfielder Jack Hayden, who walked.

17. Ritter, *op. cit.*, 241.

18. Mack, *op. cit.*, 32–33.

Chapter 2

1. *Philadelphia Ball Club, Limited, v. Lajoie*, 202 Pa. 210, 217, 219, 221 (1902).

2. *N.Y. Times*, April 22, 23, 1902.

3. *Public Ledger*, April 22, 1902.

4. *Public Ledger*, April 24, 1902.

5. *N.Y. Times*, April 24, 1902; Mack, *op. cit.*, 29. The Athletics won their opener, 8–1, behind Bernhard.

6. "I am going to obey the law," said Fraser when he joined the Phillies. "The courts have ruled that I shall work for the Philadelphia National League team, and I see no chance to escape;" *Public Ledger*, May 17, 1902.

7. On May 27, Lajoie told a reporter, "If I play anywhere in the American League it will be with Cleveland. Will I go back to Colonel Rogers? I hardly think I will. He had his chance to get me, and failed to take advantage of the opportunity" (*Public Ledger*, May 28, 1902). The contract Lajoie signed with Cleveland has been variously reported as $25,000 for three years or $30,000 for four (Murphy, *loc. cit.*, 24). Even before Lajoie signed, the first time Cleveland came into Philadelphia, the club left Flick behind, although he had not been sued.

8. *Public Ledger*, May 12, 1902. "For the preservation of the game as a national pastime," the writer said, "the two leagues must arbitrate their differences."

9. J.G. Taylor Spink in *The Sporting News* (hereinafter cited as *TSN*), Nov. 12, 1942.

10. Ritter, *op. cit.*, 49, 51. "They never made another like him," Crawford said.

11. Mack, *op. cit.*, 93–95. As they waited, the reporters put in items like this: "Waddell still fails to put in an appearance, but he is expected on every train;" *Public Ledger*, June 17, 1902.

12. Mack had signed Husting for his Milwaukee club before he was asked by Ban Johnson to move to Philadelphia. Husting became a lawyer and was appointed by President Franklin Roosevelt U.S. Attorney for the Eastern District of Wisconsin, serving from 1933 to 1944; *Philadelphia Inquirer*, Sept. 4, 1948 (after Husting's death on September 3).

13. *Philadelphia Inquirer*, Sept. 1, 1902.

14. *Philadelphia Inquirer*, Sept. 2, 1902.

15. *Philadelphia Inquirer*, Sept. 3, 1902.

16. *Philadelphia Inquirer*, Sept. 10, 1902.

17. "Just how many people would have been in evidence had not President Shibe peremptorily ordered the discontinuance of the sale of tickets there is no telling" (*Philadelphia Inquirer*, Sept. 21, 1902).

18. Also, curiously enough, on a wild pitch, by Guy Hecker of the Louisville Eclipse. *Philadelphia Inquirer*, Sept. 24, 1902 ("order the pole").

19. *Philadelphia Inquirer*, Sept. 25, 1902.

Chapter 3

1. Ritter, *op. cit.*, 201.

2. "That crowd was certainly a corker! It broke all records for a gather-

ing of base ball enthusiasts and there was not an inch of space that it could spread itself over, cling to, stand upon or rubber from of which it didn't take advantage" (*Philadelphia Inquirer*, Oct. 1, 1905).

3. *Ibid.*

4. *Philadelphia Inquirer*, Oct. 3, 1905.

5. *Philadelphia Inquirer*, Oct. 6, 1905.

6. *Philadelphia Inquirer*, Oct. 8, 1905.

7. *Public Ledger*, Oct. 9, 1905.

8. *Ibid.*

9. *Philadelphia Inquirer*, Oct. 10, 1905.

10. *Public Ledger*, Oct. 10, 1905.

11. *Public Ledger*, Oct. 11, 1905. This was a little more restrained than the *Inquirer* writer the same day who said "the big copper-skinned athlete ... had the speed of an arrow shot from the bow of a Chippewa marksman, he was cool as an Esquimaux in a snowhut, and his aim was as good as that of Davy Crockett when that hunter was wont to hit a squirrel in the eye."

12. *Public Ledger*, Oct. 14, 1905.

13. *Public Ledger*, Oct. 16, 1905.

Chapter 4

1. The 1906 White Sox won the pennant by three games despite their league-low .230 batting average, which won them their nickname. They had splendid pitching, and they defeated their crosstown rivals, Frank Chance's Cubs, in the World Series in six games.

2. *TSN*, Feb. 26, 1931. Collins said football was his favorite sport in school, not baseball.

Chapter 5

1. Bruce Kuklick, *To Every Thing a Season: Shibe Park and Urban Philadelphia 1909–1976* (Princeton, NJ: Princeton University Press, 1991), 28.

2. Bobby Shantz, "There Used to Be a Ballpark: Shibe Park Philadelphia," *The Diamond*, June 1993.

3. Wilfrid Sheed, *My Life As a Fan* (New York: Simon & Schuster, 1993), 37.

4. Kuklick, *op. cit.*, 29.

5. *Ibid.*, 30.

6. Charles C. Alexander, *Ty Cobb* (New York and Oxford: Oxford University Press, 1984), 81. Sportswriter Fogel, who was soon to become president of the Phillies, had, curiously enough, been manager of the Indianapolis team in the National League in 1887 and the New York Giants in 1902.

7. *Philadelphia Inquirer*, Aug. 13, 1910.

8. Russell had a record of 0–3 and 7.67 in 1911, 0–2 and 7.27 in 1912, and then left the big leagues. It was Russell who was offered a 1911 contract by the Athletics for $1800, less than he was making in the minor leagues the year before; he had to hold out all winter to receive finally $2400.

9. *Philadelphia Inquirer*, Oct. 19, 1910.

10. *Philadelphia Inquirer*, Oct. 20, 1910.

11. *Philadelphia Inquirer*, Oct. 24, 1910. Each member of the victorious Athletics received a Series share of $2062.74.

12. *Philadelphia Inquirer*, Oct. 25, 1910.

Chapter 6

1. *Philadelphia Inquirer*, Sept. 4, 6, 1911.

2. *Philadelphia Inquirer*, Oct. 14, 1911.

3. *Philadelphia Inquirer*, Oct. 17, 1911.

4. *Ibid.*

5. *Philadelphia Inquirer*, Oct. 18, 19, 1911.

6. *Philadelphia Inquirer*, Oct. 19, 1911. Hal Chase was considered one of the best fielding first basemen of all time, but he turned his sharp yet warped intelligence to so many nefarious schemes, throwing games or using other players to rig the outcome of games, that he was finally driven from Organized Baseball.

7. *Philadelphia Inquirer*, Oct. 22, 1911.

8. Weigley, ed., *op. cit.*, 556.

9. *Philadelphia Inquirer*, Nov. 17, 1912.

10. *Ibid.*

11. Ritter, *op. cit.*, 191 (Bressler), 113 (Crawford); Ben Yagoda, "The Legend of Connie Mack," *PhillySport*, August 1989, 62; Jimmie Dykes and Charles O. Dexter, *You Can't Steal First Base* (Philadelphia and New York: J.B. Lippincott Co., 1967), 17. Dykes went on to say that Mack "was, without seeming so, a strict disciplinarian. He'd lay into miscreants with quiet sarcasm. If the offense was repeated, the offender would soon be handed a railroad ticket to some other destination." *Ibid.*

Chapter 7

1. *Philadelphia Inquirer*, Oct. 6, 1914.

2. *Philadelphia Inquirer*, Oct. 5, 8, 1914. "The Old Sport" was a penname used by Frank Hough, the former part-owner of the Athletics.

3. *Philadelphia Inquirer*, Oct. 9, 1914. Stallings went on to say, "I will

settle this affair with Mack after the series are over and if Mack wants to keep out of trouble he had better keep out of my way" (*Evening Bulletin*, Oct. 9, 1914).

4. *Philadelphia Inquirer*, Oct. 5, 22, 1914. Rube Bressler said, "Overconfidence was the thing that did us in more than anything else. We thought it would be a pushover" (Ritter, *op. cit.*, 192).

5. *Philadelphia Inquirer*, Oct. 10, 1914.

6. *Evening Bulletin*, Oct. 10, 1914.

7. *Philadelphia Inquirer*, Oct. 11, 1914.

8. *Philadelphia Inquirer*, Oct. 12, 1914; *Evening Bulletin*, Oct. 12, 1914.

9. *Philadelphia Inquirer*, Oct. 13, 1914.

10. *Evening Bulletin*, Oct. 13, 1914. Rube Oldring said, "I am so sore at myself for the way I have been playing that if anybody tried to cross me I'd eat him alive" (*ibid*). Oldring was harassed during the Series by a woman claiming to be his wife, apparently after his Series share. "What chance had I," he said, "to play good ball when everyone in Boston was yelling that I deserted my wife?" Harold Seymour, *Baseball: The Golden Years* (New York: Oxford University Press, 1971), 102.

11. *Philadelphia Inquirer*, Oct. 14, 1914. Bender, the writer said, "could hardly be trusted with the work of another contest."

12. *Philadelphia Inquirer*, Oct. 15, 1914; *Evening Bulletin*, Oct. 14, 1914. Mack made a curious statement: "I really am glad that in losing we were beaten four straight games. It is the best thing that could have happened to baseball. It proves the honesty of the game, which comes before everything else" (*ibid*). The twenty-four A's players received losing Series shares of $2031.68 each.

13. *Evening Bulletin*, Oct. 13, 1914.

14. *Philadelphia Inquirer*, Nov. 1, 1914. The story of the three pitchers on the waiver list had been leaked to the press by manager Hugh Jennings of Detroit, which angered Mack. Waivers are supposed to be confidential, he said, "but this much could not be expected of Jennings, who devotes six months of the year to baseball and the other six months to his vaudeville act."

15. *Philadelphia Inquirer*, Oct. 25, 1914, for the report of Plank's visit to New York. After his release, Plank confirmed that he was the one who told Mack a few days earlier about "a strong offer from the Federal League" (*Philadelphia Inquirer*, Nov. 1, 1914).

16. *Philadelphia Inquirer*, Dec. 5, 1914. Shawkey thought Coombs "will come back," based on a hunting trip the two of them had taken to Maine, just before Shawkey's wedding.

17. *Philadelphia Inquirer*, Dec. 6, 1914.

18. *Philadelphia Inquirer*, Dec. 9, 1914. "At present, I haven't any definite plans for Collins' successor," Mack said, "but I guess the team will be strong in that position next season" (*ibid*).

19. *Ibid*.

20. *Ibid*.

21. *Philadelphia Inquirer*, Dec. 10, 1914.

22. *Evening Bulletin*, Apr. 7, 1915.
23. Murphy, *loc. cit.*, 58.

Chapter 8

1. After Nabors's 1-25 record, even Connie Mack admitted, "Nabors has been a disappointment to me and I am not counting upon him." But then he added, charitably, "Jack may come back suddenly and prove a star. In fact I look for him to come through yet as he has every attribute necessary" (*Philadelphia Inquirer*, Apr. 10, 1917). Sheehan pitched with more success a few years later with Cincinnati and Pittsburgh, became a longtime scout, and in 1960 managed the San Francisco Giants.

2. *Ibid.* He said he needed only one or two men for "the foundation for the greatest team I have ever had, and I expect to have them before long..." Connie Mack, with all his virtues, was a buncombe artist first class.

3. On Strunk's suspension, see *Philadelphia Inquirer*, Apr. 7, 9, 10, 1917. In announcing that Strunk had been sent home, Mack said, "I am through with this player until he explains the cause of his actions toward me."

4. *Philadelphia Inquirer*, Apr. 12, 1918. Their Opening Day baseball performance was less noteworthy; Walter Johnson of the Senators blanked them on three hits, 3-0. Sportswriter D.L. Reeves noted "the one thing more than any other" which aroused public suspicion of the motives of the ball player was "his desire to serve the country in a capacity which at the same time would permit him to pick up a little easy money playing ball" (*Public Ledger*, Sept. 22, 1918).

5. *Public Ledger*, July 22, 1918.

6. *Public Ledger*, July 22, 27, Aug. 24, 1918.

7. Dykes and Dexter, *op. cit.*, 16.

8. *Public Ledger*, July 21, 1918.

9. *Philadelphia Inquirer*, May 2, 1918.

10. *Philadelphia Inquirer*, June 13, 1918. Voting for the Braves were National League president John K. Tener, Cincinnati Reds president Garry Herrmann (the chairman of the commission), and John H. Farrell, secretary of the National Association (the minor leagues' umbrella organization). Voting for Mack were Ban Johnson and R.H. Bough, president of the Southern Association. Vila later wrote, "The idea of allowing two minor league men to decide the dispute between the Athletics and Braves over Perry is one of the painful jokes which are hurting the national game" (*Philadelphia Inquirer*, June 21, 1918).

11. *Philadelphia Inquirer*, June 16, 1918, in a long article written by Joe S. Jackson, the president of the Baseball Writers of America.

12. *Philadelphia Inquirer*, June 18, 20, 1918. Griffith later called the commission's decision on Perry "the rawest thing ever pulled off in Organized Baseball" (*Philadelphia Inquirer*, June 21, 1918).

13. *Philadelphia Inquirer*, June 24, July 11, 1918.

14. *Philadelphia Inquirer*, July 10, 1918; *Public Ledger* (article by D.L. Reeves), July 15, 1918.

15. *Public Ledger*, July 18, 1918.

16. *Public Ledger*, Aug. 7, 1918; *Philadelphia Inquirer*, Oct. 18, 1918.

17. *Philadelphia Inquirer*, Oct. 21, 1918.

18. James C. Isaminger in *TSN*, Jan. 6, 1921. Burrus hit even more poorly in 1920 (.185) and Mack sent him to Columbus after the season, "the greatest disappointment Mack has had in many years." Burrus reappeared with the Boston Braves in 1925 and gave them four relatively productive seasons.

19. On Perry and Rogers, *Philadelphia Inquirer*, Aug. 13, 1919.

20. Established spitball pitchers were "grandfathered" and allowed to use the damp pitch for the balance of their careers. Seventeen pitchers were placed in this category in 1921.

21. *TSN*, Feb. 10, June 23, July 14, 1921.

22. *Ibid.*

Chapter 9

1. *Philadelphia Inquirer*, Oct. 28, 1978 (Walberg's obituary).

2. Dykes and Dexter, *op. cit.*, 26.

3. *TSN*, June 6, 1935. Mack did not disclose what the bad play was.

4. *Ibid.*, 30.

5. Gordon S. Cochrane, *Baseball: The Fan's Game* (Cleveland: Society for American Baseball Research, 1992, orig. pub. 1939), 13.

6. Bob Gorman, *Double X* (Camden, NJ: Holy Name Society, 1990), 22.

7. The Cobb-Speaker case was a murky situation regarding an alleged fixed game near the end of the 1919 season, and the two great stars do not come off well in the story. The principal witness against them, ex-pitcher Hub Leonard, refused to come east to testify, perhaps intimidated by Cobb, and, without Leonard's testimony, Landis seemed relieved not to have to ban two more greats. See J.G. Taylor Spink, *Judge Landis and 25 Years of Baseball* (New York: Thomas Y. Crowell, 1947), 154–163, for a description of the affair.

8. Alexander, *op. cit.*, 196.

Chapter 10

1. Dykes and Dexter, *op. cit.*, 35.

2. *Philadelphia Inquirer*, Aug. 13, 1928.

3. *Ibid.*

4. *Philadelphia Inquirer*, Aug. 14, 1928.

5. *Philadelphia Inquirer*, Sept. 2, 1928.

6. *Philadelphia Inquirer*, Sept. 10, 1928.

7. *Ibid.*

8. *Philadelphia Inquirer*, Sept. 2, 1928.

9. Gorman, *op. cit.*, 29 (Mack on Foxx), 24 (Foxx on Cobb).

10. *N.Y. Evening Post*, Sept. 26, 1929.

11. Donald Honig, *Baseball Between the Lines* (New York: Coward, McCann & Geoghegan, 1976), 27 (for Henrich on Simmons).

12. *Philadelphia Record*, Aug. 1, 1929.

13. *Philadelphia Record*, Aug. 2, 1929.

14. *Philadelphia Record*, Aug. 20, 1929.

15. *Philadelphia Inquirer*, Sept. 11, 1929.

16. *Philadelphia Inquirer*, Sept. 15, 1929.

17. *Philadelphia Inquirer*, Sept. 14, 1929.

18. *Philadelphia Inquirer*, Sept. 8, 1929.

19. *Philadelphia Inquirer*, Oct. 10, 1929. Fred Lieb said that Mack told him later, "I've thought since what people might have said if I had lost that game—with Earnshaw, Grove, and Walberg sitting on my bench." Frederick G. Lieb, *Connie Mack: Grand Old Man of Baseball* (New York: G.P. Putnam's Sons, 1945), 225.

20. *N.Y. Evening Post*, Oct. 16, 1929.

21. *N.Y. Times*, Oct. 11, 1929.

22. Homer Thorne on the contention over the rooftop bleachers: *N.Y. Evening Post*, Oct. 14, 1929.

23. *N.Y. Times*, Oct. 14, 1929.

24. *N.Y. Times*, Oct. 13, 1929.

25. *Ibid.*

26. *Evening Bulletin* and *Philadelphia Public Ledger*, both Oct. 15, 1929. Several writers have attributed to the crowd at this game an incident which actually took place two years later, the Prohibition-hating Philadelphia fans screaming at Hoover, "Beer! Beer! We want beer!" Lieb cites it on pp. 228–29 and quotes Mack calling it "a most regrettable occurrence." The story is also mentioned in Kuklich, *op. cit.*, 61, who cites Lieb in the *Bulletin* for October 11 and 12, a couple of days before the Hoover incident is alleged to have occurred, and cites an article in the Nov. 2, 1929, *Literary Digest* entitled "President Hoover's Trials at the World Series" which says not a word about any "beer" shouts. David Voigt, *American Baseball, Vol. II: From the Commissioners to Continental Expansion* (University Park, Pa., and London: Pennsylvania State University Press, 1983, orig. pub. 1966–1970), 207, also mentions the "beer" incident as being in the '29 Series, citing only the *Literary Digest* article.

27. William Nack, "Lost in History," *Sports Illustrated*, Aug. 19, 1996.

28. *Philadelphia Public Ledger*, Oct. 15, 1929. When McCarthy stepped into the A's clubhouse to congratulate Mack on his victory, the Athletics' leader said graciously, "I hope to live to see the day when you will win a World Championship, Joe" (*Evening Bulletin*, Oct. 15, 1929). Little did he know.

29. *Ibid.*

Chapter 11

1. *Philadelphia Inquirer*, Oct. 9, 1930.
2. *Philadelphia Inquirer*, Oct. 3, 1930. Flint Rhem, the Cardinal starter, was a South Carolinian celebrated for his alcoholic feats. In one of the more bizarre tales of the game, Rhem had disappeared before a key mid-September game he was scheduled to start against Brooklyn. When he showed up later, he allegedly told a story of being kidnapped by two gunmen in front of the team's Manhattan hotel, being driven to a house in New Jersey, and being forced at gunpoint "to drink whisky all day … glass after glass of liquor—rye, or maybe Scotch, I wouldn't know. It might have been gin," he said. "It was terrible, Sarge," he told manager Gabby Street. Years later, Rhem said that he had simply been sick from overindulging at a party the night before. John Thom, "The Kidnapping of Flint Rhem," *The National Pastime*, 1990.
3. *Philadelphia Inquirer* and *N.Y. Times*, both Oct. 9, 1930.
4. *TSN*, Feb. 12, 1931.
5. *TSN*, Oct. 8, 1931.
6. *TSN*, Oct. 15, 1931.
7. *TSN*, Oct. 8, 1931.
8. *TSN*, Oct. 15, 1931.

Chapter 12

1. "It is a curious fact, demonstrated over and over again," Mack wrote in his autobiography, "that Philadelphians will turn out in greater numbers to see their home team fight to become champions than they will to see them fight to remain champions" (Mack, *op. cit.*, 42).
2. *Evening Bulletin*, Sept. 29, 1932. During the winter Mack attended a testimonial dinner for Dykes and said, "If there is ever a time that you need help, I don't care what it is, if you'll come to me you'll get it" (*TSN*, Feb. 2, 1933).
3. *Philadelphia Inquirer*, July 22, 1918.
4. John A. Lucas, "The Unholy Experiment: Professional Baseball's Struggle Against Pennsylvania Sunday Blue Laws 1926–1934," *Pennsylvania History*, April 1971, 168. The Supreme Court decision was handed down on June 25, 1927, in *Commonwealth v. American Baseball Club of Philadelphia*, 290 Pa. 136. Although the court's vote was 7-2, the two dissenters disagreed on procedural grounds, agreeing with the majority that playing professional baseball was "worldly employment."
5. *TSN*, Jan. 12, 1933.
6. It was on this expedition that Cleveland catcher Moe Berg, the linguistically gifted Princeton grad, photographed key military, industrial, and transportation facilities in Tokyo, films which were allegedly used in planning Jimmy Doolittle's famous 1942 bombing raid. Berg's latest biographer, how-

ever, says "no archival or trustworthy published evidence has emerged to suggest that Berg's films were put to any use during World War II"; Nicholas Dawidoff, *The Catcher Was a Spy: The Mysterious Life of Moe Berg* (New York: Pantheon, 1994), 135.

7. Gordon Mackay in *TSN*, Jan. 17, 1935.

8. Article by New York writer Dan Daniel in *TSN*, Jan. 17, 1935.

9. C. William Duncan in *TSN*, Feb. 7, 1935; *TSN*, March 21, 1935.

10. "A victory should be scored for the Shibe Park razzers, for they took the responsibility for chasing Dib Williams off the team," Jimmy Isaminger wrote (*TSN*, May 9, 1935).

11. *TSN*, Sept. 12, 1935.

12. *TSN*, Jan. 3, Aug. 22, 1935.

13. *TSN*, June 6, 1935. Cascarella returned to the majors and was 14-27 over the next three seasons with the Red Sox, Senators, and Reds.

14. *TSN*, April 18, 1935. Ironically, by the time Shibe's "spite fence" went up, there were no longer many occasions for filling the rooftops with spectators.

15. *TSN*, Aug. 1, 1935.

16. *Philadelphia Inquirer*, April 18, 1939.

17. Kuklick, *op. cit.*, 47. Kuklick points out correctly that geographical considerations, which made the big difference in fan allegiance in other multi-team cities like Chicago and New York, were absent in Philadelphia, where the two ballparks were only seven blocks apart. From 1938 on, the A's and Phillies shared the same stadium.

18. F.C. Lane, in *Baseball Magazine*, May 1937 (on spring training jaunt).

19. Lieb, *op. cit.*, vi.

20. *Philadelphia Record*, June 27, 1938.

21. *Philadelphia Record*, June 25, 1938.

22. *Philadelphia Record*, July 2, 1938.

23. Jimmy Isaminger in *TSN*, Apr. 6, 1939. Higgins batted over .300 for Boston in each of the two seasons that Werber played third for the A's.

24. Yagoda, *loc. cit.*, 58.

25. Curt Smith, *Voices of the Game* (South Bend, Indiana: Diamond Communications, 1987), 88.

26. Kuklick, *op. cit.*, 76; Isaminger in *TSN*, April 27, 1939.

27. *TSN*, Jan. 5, 1939. A couple of weeks later Miles was said to be "dissatisfied with coming here ...[but the] fans don't care whether he reports or not" (*TSN*, Jan. 26, 1939).

28. Jay Feldman, "Benny McCoy," *The National Pastime*, 1994, 41.

29. Weigley, ed., *op. cit.*, 636.

Chapter 13

1. One observer commented sourly that "Philadelphia baseball became the greatest of all escapes from the war, since our wartime teams looked exactly like our peacetime ones" (Sheed, *op. cit.*, 125).

2. *Philadelphia Record*, Dec. 9, 1941.

3. *Philadelphia Record*, Jan. 17, 1942.

4. *Philadelphia Record*, Jan. 2, 1942.

5. *Philadelphia Record*, Dec. 18, 1941. There is no doubt that Connie Mack sincerely believed this, but his players, with their wages barely above subsistence levels, must have choked on reading his statement.

6. *Philadelphia Record*, Jan. 16, 1942.

7. *Philadelphia Record*, April 1, 1943; interview with Charlie Metro, June 13, 1991, University of Kentucky Library A.B. Chandler Oral History Project (Black). Metro added that Don Black was always "meticulous in dress."

8. *Philadelphia Inquirer*, Nov. 4, 1943.

9. Harrington E. Crissey, Jr., *Teenagers, Graybeards and 4-F's* (Philadelphia: n.p., 1982),v.2, 67–68.

10. *Philadelphia Inquirer*, Nov. 24, 1943. Connie Mack, who shared ownership of the Wilmington Blue Rocks Interstate League franchise with the new Phillies president, said of the Carpenters, "They are one of the finest families in the country" (*ibid*).

11. *Philadelphia Inquirer*, Aug. 5, 1944.

12. Crissey, v. 2, *op. cit.*, 111, 118, 131; Metro interview, *op. cit.*; interview with George Kell, June 4, 1988, University of Kentucky Library A.B. Chandler Oral History Project.

13. Crissey, v. 2, *op. cit.*, 105; Metro felt that Estalella, who he said was clearly part African in descent, really integrated the A's during the war (Metro interview, *op. cit*).

14. Crissey, v. 2, *op. cit.*, 103.

15. Mack owned the Wilmington club in the Interstate League but also had an arrangement with the Lancaster owner, to whom he had loaned money, that he had first refusal of any two Red Rose players. Mack chose Kell and Lew Flick (Kell interview, *op. cit*).

16. *Philadelphia Inquirer*, July 20, 1945.

17. Crissey, v. 2, *op. cit.*, 128–29. George, who added, "I hated most of the umpires in the American League," was suspended for ninety days, which extended well into the 1946 season. After George punched Rue, the umpire hit him with his mask (Kell interview, *op. cit*).

18. *Philadelphia Inquirer*, July 23, 1945. The game started at 3 p.m. and was called at 7:48 p.m. Berry, the little relief pitcher, had hurled three innings the night before, a warm-up for his eleven-inning stant.

19. Interview with Hall, April 26, 1997. Although Shibe Park was equipped with lights, the rules of the day forbade turning them on for a day game.

20. *Philadelphia Inquirer*, July 23, 1945.

Chapter 14

1. Infielder Al Brancato, a Philadelphian who had played for the A's before the war, was discharged in time to join the club in September 1945 and

played ten games. Because of that his protection under the Federal rule had ended and Mack sold him to Toronto over the winter; he never made it back to the majors (Crissey, *op. cit.*, v. 2, 100–101).

2. *Philadelphia Inquirer*, July 26, 1946. There were like stories concerning the Browns.

3. See, for example, the Kell and Metro interviews (*op. cit*).

4. *Philadelphia Inquirer*, April 23, 24, 1946.

5. *TSN*, Jan. 22, 1947. McQuinn, signed as a free agent by the Yankees after the A's let him go, hit .304 with 24 homers and 80 runs batted in for Bucky Harris's 1947 pennant-winners.

6. *Philadelphia Inquirer*, June 4, 1946. Newsom signed with the Washington Senators.

7. *Philadelphia Inquirer*, June 7, 1946.

8. Danny Peary, ed., *We Played the Game* (New York: Hyperion, 1994), 40.

9. *Sports Illustrated*, June 12, 1989. See also Kell interview, *op. cit.*

10. *TSN*, Feb. 5, 1947.

11. Mack, *op. cit.*, 33 (on Thomas); *Philadelphia Inquirer*, Feb. 1, 1911 (Warner). George Kell said, "Mr. Mack would see some kid that was ready to go to college, and a good kid, and he'd send him there [Duke] without signing him, with the understanding [that] if he made it, then he could sign him" (Kell interview, *op. cit*). Such a practice, of course, would be illegal today.

12. *Evening Bulletin*, June 17, 1948. Brucker, who attended Palmyra and Pitman high schools in New Jersey as well as Germantown Academy in Philadelphia, had spent much of his youth around the ballpark with his father.

13. Soon after the end of spring training in 1949, the Athletics in effect gave up on young Brucker, selling him outright to Martinsville of the Class B Carolina League; *Evening Bulletin*, April 16, 1949. Brucker hit .284 with nineteen home runs for Martinsville and had a fairly lengthy minor league career, but he never again appeared in the major leagues.

14. Ira Berkow, *Red: A Biography of Red Smith* (New York: Times Books, 1986), 109.

15. "Ferris Fain was his own worst enemy," Eddie Joost said. "He had a lifestyle of his own and would do exactly what he wanted to do. There were many things the players didn't like about him" (Peary, ed., *op. cit.*, 41). McCosky said that Fain "couldn't get along with anybody" but was "a good hustling ball player" (interview with Barney McCosky, March 16, 1988, University of Kentucky Library A.B. Chandler Oral History Project).

16. Peary, ed., *op. cit.*, 41.

Chapter 15

1. Kevin Kerrane, *Dollar Sign on the Muscle* (New York: Avon Books, 1985, orig. pub. 1984), 63. Johnson claimed that "I could have gotten Larry Doby

and Minnie Minoso, too," but since both were already in the American League that cannot be true (John B. Holway, "Judy Johnson a True Hot Corner Hotshot," *The Baseball Research Journal*, 1986).

2. *Evening Bulletin*, March 13, 1948.

3. Peary, ed., *op. cit.*, 72–73.

4. *N.Y. Times*, Oct. 23, 1985.

5. The Potter and Dietrich stories can be followed in the *Bulletin*, and to a lesser extent the *Inquirer*, from June 14, 1948, until Potter went to Boston. The quote at Potter's 1941 sale is by Red Smith in his syndicated column in the *Bulletin* on June 17, 1948, and obviously may not be exact. Brissie's comment to the author was Nov. 1, 1997.

6. *Philadelphia Inquirer*, Aug. 3, 1948.

7. *Philadelphia Inquirer*, Aug. 6, 1948. Frank Papish was the victim of the A's late scoring.

8. *Philadelphia Inquirer*, Aug. 13, 1948.

9. *Philadelphia Inquirer*, Aug. 17, 1948. This was also the day that Alger Hiss appeared before a secret session of the House Un-American Activities Committee and swore to his innocence of the spying charges which had been leveled against him by Whittaker Chambers.

10. *Philadelphia Inquirer*, Aug. 20, 1948. The X-rays were taken at Graduate Hospital in Philadelphia.

11. *Philadelphia Inquirer*, Aug. 23, 1948. Raschi pitched a four-hitter to beat Bill McCahan easily.

12. *Philadelphia Inquirer*, Aug. 24, 1948. Joost, Art Morrow pointed out, until now "has been the iron man of American League shortstops since joining the Macks."

13. *Philadelphia Inquirer*, Aug. 28, 1948.

14. *Philadelphia Inquirer*, Sept. 1, 1948.

15. Peary, ed., *op. cit.*, 100 (Joost on Nellie Fox). Fox, of course, was voted into the Hall of Fame in 1997, for his play with the White Sox, not the Athletics.

Chapter 16

1. Earle, born in 1892, played ten years in the minors with limited success, appeared in five A's games between 1910 and 1914 (batting .125 with 2-for-16), and managed eight years in the North Carolina, Blue Ridge, and Three-I leagues before assuming his coaching job with the Athletics in 1924.

2. *Evening Bulletin*, April 11, 1950.

3. *Ibid.*

4. *Evening Bulletin*, May 2, 1950.

5. Peary, ed., *op. cit.*, 127.

6. *Philadelphia Inquirer*, May 13, 1950.

7. "My son Earle will succeed me as manager of the Philadelphia Athletics," Mr. Mack wrote in his autobiography, published earlier that year (Mack, *op. cit.*, 5). The old man also wrote, "It is my desire always to have a Mack-Shibe combination in our national game. For this purpose I have trained my sons to keep the tradition going, and I hope they will train their sons to follow in the path of their grandfather—and so on all through the Mack line" (*ibid*). Reading this must have sent a cold shudder through many good A's fans. For the comments of Metro and McCosky, see the interviews with them (*op. cit*).

8. *Philadelphia Inquirer*, May 27, 1950.

9. *Philadelphia Inquirer*, June 9, 10, 13, 1950. Clark and his group, unable to purchase the Athletics, who might have been saved for Philadelphia by them, went on instead to buy the pro football Eagles.

10. *Philadelphia Tribune*, July 15, 1950. Jones came to the majors in 1951 and won 102 games over a 12-year career.

11. *Philadelphia Inquirer*, July 20, 21, 1950.

Chapter 17

1. Peary, ed., *op. cit.*, 133, 159.

2. Peary, ed., *op. cit.*, 193; Honig, *op. cit,*, 150.

3. Dykes and Dexter, *op. cit.*, 109; Honig, *op. cit.*, 151.

4. Peary, ed., *op. cit.*, 228. Joe DeMaestri was the last former Philadelphia Athletic to play for the Kansas City Athletics, through the 1959 season.

5. Bill Veeck with Ed Linn, *Veeck—As in Wreck* (New York: G.P. Putnam's Sons, 1962), 296–97. Les Moss, who caught Holloman's gem for the Browns, said, "All I remember was Billy Hunter making two outstanding plays at short. It was a legitimate no-hitter"; Peary, ed., *op. cit.*, 230. Holloman's record for the year was 3-7; he had nine additional starts.

6. Dykes and Dexter, *op. cit.*, 109.

7. See Veeck and Linn, *op. cit.*, 279–81, for a graphic (and perhaps slightly overblown) description of the process by which the Braves ended up in Milwaukee.

8. Zernial in Peary, ed., *op. cit.*, 264. Big Gus said, "Philley didn't like Eddie, but he didn't like a lot of guys."

9. "I hated that deal," Joost said. "I didn't want us to get a reputation for being a dumping ground for the Yankees" (*ibid.*, 263).

10. *Ibid.*

11. *Ibid.*, 264 (Joost's version), 265 (Zernial's story), 268 (the Zernial fall as seen by Bill Wilson, playing center field that day).

12. *Ibid.*, 265.

13. Scheib worked three games for the Cardinals, lost one, and his major league career came to an end.

14. Interestingly enough, Connie Mack, reputed to be cheap and grasp-

ing, refrained from cluttering his outfield walls with advertising. As soon as the ballpark was purchased by the more well-endowed Carpenter, the walls were covered with signs.

15. *Sports Illustrated*, Nov. 8, 1954.
16. *Philadelphia Inquirer*, Nov. 5, 1954.
17. *Sports Illustrated*, Nov. 15, 1954.

Epilogue

1. Peary, ed., *op. cit.*, 264. "I wasn't too upset," Joost said, and he signed to play for the Red Sox, for whom he played 55 games in 1955.
2. That is, the descendants of the St. Louis Browns playing the former Philadelphia A's.

Bibliography

Periodicals

Baseball History
Baseball Hobby News
Baseball Magazine
Baseball Research Journal
Literary Digest
Newsweek
New York Evening Post
New York Times
(Philadelphia) *Daily Evening Telegraph*
Philadelphia Daily News

(Philadelphia) *Evening Bulletin*
Philadelphia Inquirer
Philadelphia Magazine
(Philadelphia) *Public Ledger*
Philadelphia Record
PhillySport
Sports Illustrated
The National Pastime
The Sporting News
(Wilmington, Del.) *Journal-Every Evening*

Books and Articles

Alexander, Charles C. *Ty Cobb*, New York and Oxford: Oxford University Press, 1984.

Berkow, Ira. *Red: A Biography of Red Smith*, New York: Times Books, 1986.

Casway, Jerrold. "Locating Philadelphia's Historic Ballfields," *The National Pastime*, 1993.

Cochrane, Gordon S. "Mickey," *Baseball: The Fan's Game*, Cleveland: Society for American Baseball Research, 1992.

Crissey, Harrington E., Jr. *Teenagers, Graybeards and 4-Fs*, 2 vols., Trenton, NJ: n.p., 1982.

Curtis, Gerald R. *Factors That Affect the Attendance of a Major League Base-*

ball Club, unpublished M.B.A. thesis, Wharton School, University of Pennsylvania, 1951.

Dawidoff, Nicholas. *The Catcher Was a Spy: The Mysterious Life of Moe Berg*, New York: Pantheon, 1994.

Dittmar, Joseph. "Doc Powers' Shocking End," *The National Pastime*, 1993.

Dykes, Jimmie, and Charles O. Dexter. *You Can't Steal First Base*, Philadelphia and New York: J.B. Lippincott Co., 1967.

Feldman, Jay. "Benny McCoy," *The National Pastime*, 1994.

Gibson, Campbell. "Simon Nicholls: Gentleman, Farmer, Ballplayer," *Baseball Research Journal*, 1989.

Gorman, Bob. *Double X: The Story of Jimmie Foxx—Baseball's Forgotten Slugger*, Camden, NJ: Holy Name Society, 1990.

Honig, Donald. *Baseball Between the Lines: Baseball in the '40s and '50s as Told by the Men Who Played It*, New York: Coward, McCann & Geoghegan, 1976.

Kerrane, Kevin. *Dollar Sign on the Muscle: The World of Baseball Scouting*, New York: Avon, 1985.

Kochanowicz, George. "Why Connie Mack's Hair Turned White," *The National Pastime*, 1992.

Krevisky, Steve. "'XX' and Hoosier Chuck," *The National Pastime*, 1993.

Kuklick, Bruce. *To Every Thing A Season: Shibe Park and Urban Philadelphia 1909-1976*, Princeton, NJ: Princeton University Press, 1991.

Lieb, Frederick G. *Connie Mack: Grand Old Man of Baseball*, New York: Putnam, 1945.

Longert, Scott. "Elmer Flick," *The National Pastime*, 1995.

Lowry, Philip J. *Green Cathedrals*, Reading, Mass.: Addison-Wesley, 1992.

Lucas, John A. "The Unholy Experiment: Professional Baseball's Struggle Against Pennsylvania's Sunday Blue Laws 1926-1934," *Pennsylvania History*, April 1971.

Mack, Connie. *My 66 Years in the Big Leagues*, Universal House, 1950.

Mandell, Marc. "Baseball's First Free Agent," *The Pennsylvania Lawyer*, May/June 1997.

Masterson, Dave, and Tim Boyle. *Baseball's Best: The MVPs*, Chicago: Contemporary Books, 1985.

McCarthy, Michael P. "The Unprogressive City: Philadelphia and Urban Stereotypes at the Turn of the Century," *Pennsylvania History*, October 1987.

Morris, Joe Alex. *The Richardson Dilworth Story*, Philadelphia: Mercury Books, Inc., 1962.

Murphy, J.M. "Napoleon Lajoie: Modern Baseball's First Superstar," *The National Pastime*, 1988.

Nack, William. "Lost In History," *Sports Illustrated*, August 19, 1996.

Neft, David S., Richard M. Cohen, and Jordan A. Deutsch, *The Sports Encyclopedia: Baseball*, New York: Grosset & Dunlap, 1981.

Okkonen, Marc. *Baseball Uniforms of the 20th Century: The Official Major League Baseball Guide*, New York: Sterling, 1991.

_____. *The Federal League of 1914-1915: Baseball's Third Major League*, Garrett Park, MD: SABR, 1989.

Parrott, Harold. *The Lords of Baseball*, New York: Praeger, 1976.

Peary, Danny, ed. *We Played the Game*, New York: Hyperion, 1994.

Philadelphia Ball Club, Limited v. Lajoie, 202 Pennsylvania Reports 210, 1902.

Ritter, Lawrence. *The Glory of Their Times*, New York: Morrow, 1984, orig. pub. 1966.

_____. *Lost Ballparks: A Celebration of Baseball's Legendary Fields*, New York: Viking, 1992.

Robinson, George, and Charles Salzberg. *On a Clear Day They Could See Seventh Place: Baseball's Worst Teams,* New York: Dell, 1991.

Romanowski, Jerome C. *The Mackmen*, Delair, NJ: n.p., 1979.

Rubenstein, Bruce A. "Don't Let the Rain Come Down: The 1911 World Series," *Pennsylvania History*, Fall 1995.

Scott, Joe A. "The Rube Arrives," *The National Pastime*, 1990.

Seymour, Harold. *Baseball: The Early Years*, New York: Oxford University Press, 1960.

_____. *Baseball: The Golden Years*, New York: Oxford University Press, 1971.

Shantz, Bobby. "There Used To Be a Ballpark: Shibe Park, Philadelphia," *The Diamond*, June 1993.

Shearon, Jim. "The Underrated Dick Fowler," *Baseball Research Journal*, 1993.

Sheed, Wilfrid. *My Life As a Fan*, New York: Simon & Schuster, 1993.

Smith, Curt. *Voices of the Game*, South Bend, Ind.: Diamond Communications, 1987.

Spink, J.G. Taylor. *Judge Landis and 25 Years of Baseball*, New York: Thomas Y. Crowell, 1947.

Tekulsky, Joseph D. "Russ Christopher—Courageous Athlete," *The National Pastime*, 1995.

Tholkes, Robert. "Chief Bender—The Early Years," *Baseball Research Journal*, 1983.

Thorn, John, ed. *The National Pastime*, New York: Warner Books, 1987.

_____, and Pete Palmer, eds. *Total Baseball*, New York: Warner, 1989.

Tygiel, Jules. *Baseball's Great Experiment: Jackie Robinson and His Legacy*, New York: Oxford University Press, 1983.

Veeck, Bill, with Ed Linn. *Veeck—As in Wreck*, New York: Putnam, 1962.

Voigt, David Quentin. *American Baseball*, 3 vols., University Park, Pa., & London: Pennsylvania State University Press, 1983.

Weigley, Russell F., ed. *Philadelphia: A 300-Year History*, New York: Norton, 1982.

Yagoda, Ben. "The Legend of Connie Mack," *PhillySport,* August 1989.

Yuetter, Frank. "He's No Ordinary Player," *Baseball Magazine*, May 1942.

Mention should be made of the University of Kentucky Library A.B. Chandler Oral History Project, for interviews with former Athletics players Charlie Metro, George Kell, and Barney McCosky. In addition, much use has been made of the annual publications of *The Sporting News*, such as the *Baseball Register, Baseball Guide, One for the Book*, and *The Dope Book*, and such other annual publications as *The Little Red Book of Baseball* for various seasons. There have also been scorecards, yearbooks and other publications issued by the Athletics. Basic statistics have, for the most part, come from successive editions of *The Baseball Encyclopedia*, published by Macmillan, and *Total Baseball*, edited by John Thorn and Pete Palmer.

Index

Aaron, Henry 152, 179
Abbott, Bud 135
Abernathy, Talmadge 131
Abernethy, Lloyd 57
Academy of Music 18, 131, 162
Adams, Sparky 109
Adcock, Joe 179
Albany club 158
Alexander, Grover Cleveland 63, 73, 82
Alexander, Dale 116
All-Star Game 119, 134, 136, 170, 175, 181
Altrock, Nick 28
Ambler, Wayne 145
American Association 9, 14, 16, 20, 28, 191
American Baseball Guild 141
American League 12, 14, 19, 22–24, 40, 42, 45, 47 48, 57, 59, 66, 70, 75, 81, 93, 107, 116, 119, 127, 133–34, 144, 156, 158, 164–65, 169, 174, 179, 184, 188, 202, 204
Ames, Leon 54–55
Archer, Jimmy 49–50
Armstrong, Dick 170
Arntzen, Orie 131
Arthur, Doug 166
Ashbridge, Samuel H. 19
Ashburn, Richie 163

Associated Press 15
Astroth, Joe 2, 170, 177, 182, 187
Athletics (original) 9, 14, 16, 28
Atlanta club 77, 80, 122

Babich, Johnny 132
Baker, Frank 40, 45–46, 48, 51–57, 58 (photo), 60–64, 66–67, 69, 72, 76, 90, 145
Baker, Newton D. 78, 81
Baker, William 73
Baker Bowl 2, 84, 93, 115, 126
Baldwin Locomotive Works 6–7
Baltimore Orioles 10, 26–28, 69, 188
Bancroft, Dave 63
Bando, Sal 188
Bankhead, Dan 146
Barry, Jack 20, 40, 45, 50, 54–57, 58 (photo) 60–61, 66–69, 72, 83, 147, 186
Baumgartner, Stan 90, 146
Bay, Harry 32
Becker, Beals 53
Bender, Charles Albert "Chief" 30, 31 (photo), 33–37, 40, 46, 48–49, 51–56, 58, 60–64, 66,

68, 70–72, 82, 135, 186, 196
Bennett Park 27, 47
Benton, Al 123
Berg, Moe 200–01
Berra, Lawrence "Yogi" 159, 161, 170
Berry, Charley 120
Berry, Jonas "Jittery Joe" 131, 136, 139, 202
Bernhard, Bill 17, 19–20, 22–24, 28, 193
Binks, George 155
Birmingham club 145
Bishop, Charlie 176
Bishop, Max 88, 91, 98–99, 104 05, 109 10, 112–14, 118, 120
Black, Don 133, 136, 202
Black Sox 38, 82, 138
Blades, Ray 109
Blair, Buddy 132
Blake, Sheriff 104
Blankenburg, Rudolph 56–57
Blue, Vida 188
"Blue laws" 119
Blue Ridge League 204
Bodie, Ping 77
Boley, Joe 94, 97, 99, 104–05, 111, 115, 135
Bollweg, Don 181
Bonner, Frank 24
Borowy, Hank 135

Boston Braves 2, 64–69, 73, 80–82, 88, 147, 155, 179, 197–98, 205
Boston (A.L.) team 26–28, 30, 32–33, 38–39, 44–45, 48, 52, 58, 60, 64, 69, 72–74, 76, 79, 81, 83–85, 90, 97–98, 120, 123, 131, 143, 153–54, 156, 159–61, 167, 179, 182, 188, 206
Bottomley, Sunny Jim 108, 112
Boudreau, Lou 154, 161, 187
Bough, R. H. 197
Bradley, Bill 32
Brancato, Al 132, 202
Braves Field 64
Breadon, Sam 125
Bressler, Rube 30, 59, 64, 73, 196
Briggs, Spike 184
Briggs Stadium 44
Brissie, Lou 153–55, 157–60, 162, 166, 168, 170, 173
Broad Street Station 6, 27, 34, 50
Brooklyn (N.L.) Dodgers 10, 20, 70, 95, 138, 140–41, 146, 175
Brooklyn Federals 63
Brotherhood 9, 11–12
Brown, Carroll "Boardwalk" 58, 60
Brown, Moose 77
Brown, Mordecai "Three-Finger" 48–50
Brown, Willard 146
Brucker, Earle 164
Brucker, Earle, Jr. "Gidge" 145–46, 203
Brush, John T. 10, 14, 192
Buffalo (P.L.) club 11
Burns, George 77, 79, 82, 104
Burrus, Maurice 82, 198
Busch, Edgar 131, 136
Bush, Donie 45
Bush, Guy 102–03
Bush, Joe 60–62, 64, 67–68, 76–77, 79, 135

Butler, Smedley D. 88
Byrd, Harry 167, 175–76, 181

Cahall, Walter 109
Cain, Merritt 118, 121, 123
Carolina League 47, 203
Carpenter, Lew 141
Carpenter, Robert R.M. 134, 202
Carpenter, Robert R.M., Jr. 134, 184–85, 202, 206
Carr, Charlie 19
Carrigan, Bill 74
Cascarella, Joe 121, 123, 201
Cassatt, Alexander 6
Caster, George 125
Castro, Jud 24
Cavarretta, Phil 140
Century of Progress Exposition 119
Chambers, Whittaker 204
Chance, Frank 48–50, 194
Chandler, Albert B. 140, 142
Chandler, Spud 143
Chapman, Ben 146
Chapman, Sam 20, 126–28, 132, 143, 148, 149 (photo), 152, 155, 157–58, 161, 167–68, 170, 174, 186
Chase, Hal 54, 195
Chattanooga club 128
Chestnut Street Opera House 18
Chicago Cubs 22, 47–50, 75, 95, 102–05, 109, 126, 138, 194
Chicago White Sox 26, 28, 32–34, 37–38, 47, 72, 76–77, 82, 87, 90, 93, 95, 102, 118–19, 132, 143, 156–58, 160, 165, 168, 173–74, 182–83, 194, 204
Christopher, Russ 132–33, 136, 138–39, 143, 148, 154, 186
Cicero, Joe 131

Cincinnati Reds 14, 95, 147, 175, 197
City Hall 6, 57, 88
Clark, James P. 169, 205
Clark, Joseph S., Jr. 162–63, 181
Cleveland American League team 23–24, 27–28, 32, 38, 40, 47, 58, 73, 78–79, 81, 83, 95, 99, 119, 135, 138, 143, 146, 154, 156–61, 167, 170, 173–75, 180, 188, 193, 200
Cleveland Spiders 10, 12
Coakley, Andy 28, 33–35, 37
Coan, Gil 166
Cobb, Tyrus R. 39, 45–47, 69, 71, 79, 93, 97, 99–100, 126–27, 198
Cochrane, Mickey 20, 91–92, 94–95, 99–101, 100 (photo), 103–05, 108–12, 114, 116, 118, 120, 164, 168–69, 171, 185
Cole, Leonard "King" 48
Coleman, Joe 148, 153, 157, 160–61, 166–69, 175–76
Coleman, Ray 155
Collins, Eddie 20, 37–38, 40, 45–46, 48–49, 51–54, 57, 58 (photo), 61–64, 67, 69, 71, 82, 93, 186, 194, 196
Collins, Jimmy 30, 32, 39, 41
Columbia College 37–38
Columbia Park 15, 23, 28, 35, 38–40, 42, 44
Columbus team 198
Comiskey, Charles 12, 23, 26, 63
Comiskey Park 44, 119, 157
Connecticut General Life Insurance Co. 171–72, 184
Connecticut State League 11, 24
Connolly, Joe 68
Coombs, Jack 20, 37, 39,

212

45–46, 48–55, 57, 60, 64, 70–71, 145, 196
Corum, Bill 114
Costello, Lou 135
Cotten, Joseph 166
Coveleskie, Stanley 81
Cox, William 134
Cramer, Roger "Doc" 59, 107, 114–16, 121, 123–24
Cramp Shipbuilding Co. 7
Cravath, Clifford "Gavvy" 63, 73
Crawford, Sam 25, 39, 45, 59, 64, 193
Crisconi, John P. 184
Crisham, Pat 19
Cross, Lafayette "Lave" 19, 24, 33, 35–36
Cross, Monte 21, 23–24, 33, 36, 39
Crowell, Minot 77
Cuyler, Kiki 102–03, 105

Dahlgren, Ellsworth "Babe" 134
Daily Evening Telegraph 18
Dale, Richard L. 17
Damrosch, Walter 8
Davis, Harry 19, 24, 32–34, 36, 39–41, 45, 49, 51, 53, 55
Davis, Judge 22
Davis, Phoebe 18
Deal, Charlie 65–66, 69
Dean, Chubby 145
Delahanty, Ed 9, 16–17, 21
Delahanty, Jim 52
DeMaestri, Joe "Froggy" 2, 177, 182, 187–88, 205
Demaree, Al 60–61
DeMars, Billy 157
Democratic National Convention 125, 161
Democrats 7, 57, 125, 148, 161–63
Dempsey, Jack 93
de Reszke, Edouard 18
Derringer, Paul 112–13
Detroit Tigers 14, 27, 38–40, 45–47, 51–52, 83, 93, 97, 101, 111, 128, 134,

139, 141, 144, 155, 158, 160, 162,167, 170, 196
Devore, Josh 53, 68
Dewey, Thomas E. 161
DeWitt, Bill 165
Dietrich, Bill 121, 123, 154–55, 204
Dillinger, Bob 165–67, 170–71
Dilworth, Richardson 123, 148–49, 162–63
DiMaggio, Dominic 161
DiMaggio, Joe 158–59, 161
Dinneen, Bill 28
Doby, Larry 146, 203
Doerr, Bobby 161, 167
Dolan, Joe 17
Donaghey, Don 146
Donovan, Wild Bill 39–40, 45
Doolittle, Jimmy 200
Dooly, Bill 110, 119
Dougherty, Dennis J. 119
Douthit, Taylor 109, 112
Doyle, Larry 52, 54–55
Dugan, Joe 79, 83, 85
Duggleby, Bill 21, 23, 28
Duke University 145, 203
Dunn, Jack 69, 88, 90, 94
Dunn, James 78, 81
Durham, Israel 7
Dyer, Bill 124
Dygert, Jimmy 39–40
Dykes, Jimmy 59, 79, 83, 88, 90–92, 94–97, 99–101, 103–05, 108–14, 118–19, 124, 164, 168–172, 175–76, 178–79, 195, 200

Earle, George H., Jr. 56–57
Earnshaw, George 20, 96–103, 108–14, 120–21, 186, 199
Eastern League 158
Easton (Md.) team 90
Ebbets Field 44
Ehlers, Arthur H. 145, 172–73, 179
Ehmke, Howard 92, 94, 97–105, 109, 111, 135

Elliott, Bob 140
English, Woody 102, 105
Ennis, Del 163
Equity, The 8
Estalella, Bobby 136, 138, 141–42, 202
Evening Bulletin 46, 65–66, 72, 104, 146, 166
Evers, Johnny 48, 64, 67–68
Excelsiors 8

Fain, Ferris 1, 146–48, 152, 156–58, 160–61, 167, 170, 173–77, 174 (photo), 185, 203
Farrell, John H. 197
Federal League 63, 69–72, 75, 196
Feller, Bob 158, 161
Fels, Joseph 15
Fenway Park 44, 65, 67–68, 98, 154, 167
Ferrell, Wes 101, 108
Ferrick, Tom 129
Fingers, Rollie 188
Finigan, Jim 181
Finley, Charles O. 188–89
Finney, Lou 118, 122
Flick, Elmer 21–24, 28, 32, 47, 193
Flick, Lew 202
Flores, Jesse 133, 136, 144, 148
Fogel, Horace 46, 194
Forbes Field 44
Foster, James 15
Fowler, Dick 132, 139, 144, 148, 153, 157–60, 162, 166–70, 175
Fox, Nelson 162–64, 204
Foxx, James E. 90, 92, 94, 96–97, 99–105, 107, 109 14, 116 18, 117 (photo), 120, 122–24, 142, 173, 185–86
Franklin, Murray 141
Franks, Herman 152, 157
Fraser, Chick 17, 19–20, 22–23, 193
Frazee, Harry 81
Freedman, Andrew 10
Freeman, Buck

Index

Freitas, Tony 116
French, Walter 92, 94, 105
Fricano, Marion 176, 182
Frisch, Frankie 108
Fultz, Dave 20, 25, 28

Galehouse, Denny 159
Galloway, Chick 85, 87, 91, 94, 153
Gardner, Isabella Stewart 27
Gardner, Larry 79
Garner, John Nance 125
Garrison, Ford 143
Garver, Ned 170
Gassaway, Charlie 131
Gehrig, Lou 94, 96
Gelbert, Charley 109
George, Charlie "Greek" 131, 138, 202
Gimbel's 65
Glade, Fred 34
Golden Jubilee 164–65, 167, 169, 171–72
Gopadze, Ilarion I., M.D. 152
Gordon, Joe 161
Gounod, Charles 18
Gowdy, Hank 64, 66, 68
Gowen, Franklin 6
Graduate Hospital 157, 159, 204
Grauley, S.O. 102
Gray, John 182
Gray, Sam 91–92, 96
Gray, Ted 158
Greenberg, Hank 122
Griàth, Clark 81, 184, 197
Grimes, Burleigh 109–10, 112–14
Grimm, Charlie 77, 102
Grove, Robert M. "Lefty" 3, 90–92, 94–95, 97 (photo), 97–105, 108–114, 116, 118–121, 124, 175, 185–86, 199
Guerra, Fermin "Mike" 148, 152, 159

Haas, George "Mule" 96–97, 100–01, 105, 108–09, 112, 116, 118–19
Hafey, Chick 109

Haines, Jesse 109–10
Hale, Sammy 87, 90–92, 94, 97, 99, 107
Hall, Irvin 139
Hall of Fame 9, 38, 47, 109, 204
Hallahan, "Wild Bill" 109–10, 112–14
Hamilton, Billy 9
Hamner, Granny 163
Handley, Gene 143
Haring, Claude 165–66
Harper, Jack 192
Harris, Charles "Bubba" 154–55, 158, 160
Harris, Luman 2, 132–33, 136, 144
Harris, Stanley "Bucky" 92, 154, 156, 203
Harrison, Benjamin 18, 192
Harriss, Slim 84, 91–92
Hart, James A. 12
Hartzel, Topsy 25, 27–29, 33, 36, 41
Hasty, Bob 84
Hauser, Joe 85, 87, 90–91, 94, 97, 99–100
Hayden, Jack 192
Hayes, Frankie 2, 121, 124, 126–28, 133, 136, 138
Healey, Thomas 104
Hecker, Guy 193
Heilmann, Harry 94
Heimach, Fred 90, 92
Henley, Weldon 30, 33–34
Henrich, Tommy 101
Herrmann, Garry 30, 81, 197
Herzog, Buck 52–53
Heving, Johnny 111
Higgins, Mike "Pinky" 118, 121–22, 124–26, 201
High, Andy 114
Hiss, Alger 204
Hitchcock, Billy 163–64, 174
Hoffman, Danny 33
Holliday, Billie 166
Holloman, Alva "Bobo" 178, 205
Homestead Grays 178

Hooks, Alex 122
Hooper, Bob 3, 168, 175
Hooper, Harry 58, 72
Hoover, Herbert C. 104, 109, 199
Hornsby, Rogers 102–03, 105
Houck, Byron "Duke" 60
Hough, Frank 15–16, 58, 189, 192, 195
Houston, Henry 6
Houtteman, Art 167
Hoyt, Waite 95, 111–13
Hubbell, Carl 176
Huggins, Miller 95, 99
Hughson, Cecil "Tex" 134
Hulbert, William 9
Hunter, Billy 205
Hunter, Jim "Catfish" 188
Husting, Pete 26–27, 193

Indianapolis Clowns 152
Indianapolis N.L. club 194
International League 178
Isaminger, James 84, 97, 102, 128, 198, 201

Jackson, Joe S. 197
Jackson, Reggie 188
Jackson, "Shoeless Joe" 47, 82
Jacobs, Forrest "Spook" 182
Jacobson, William "Baby Doll" 92
James, Bill 64, 66–67
Jefferson Street Grounds 9
Jenkins, Tom 92
Jennings, Hughie 19, 38, 45, 196
Johns Hopkins Hospital 169
Johnson, Arnold 181, 183–85, 187–88
Johnson, Ban 5, 12–15, 19, 22, 30, 78, 81–82, 93, 193, 197
Johnson, Bob 118, 121, 123, 124 (photo), 124–28, 132–33, 185–86
Johnson, Hank 99
Johnson, Jing 78, 83

Johnson, John G. 17, 192
Johnson, Walter 40, 46,
  108, 135, 197
Johnson, William "Judy"
  152, 203
Jones, Davy 39
Jones, Fielder 32–33,
  37
Jones, Sam 170, 205
Jones, Samuel "Butch"
  15–16, 58
Joost, Eddie 2, 147–48,
  152–53, 155, 157–62,
  167–68, 170, 173–74,
  176–77, 179–83, 180
  (photo), 185, 187, 203–
  04, 205–06
Joss, Addie 32

Kansas City Athletics
  187–88, 205
Kell, George 136, 138,
  143–44, 152–53, 162,
  203
Kelley, Harry 124–25
Kellner, Alex 161, 166–67,
  175–76, 182
Kelly, Ray 166
Keltner, Ken 161
Kendrick, W. Freeland 87
Kent, Atwater 15
Kerns, James N. 8
Kerr, W.W. 12
Keystones 8
Killian, Ed 39
Kinney, Walt 83
Klein, Lou 141
Klem, Bill 55
Klieman, Ed 165
Kling, Johnny 48–50
Knerr, Luther 131, 136,
  144
Knott, Jack 129, 132
Koenig, Mark 99
Koufax, Sandy 30
Krause, Harry 45–46, 58
Kuhn, Bowie 188

Lajoie, Napoleon "Larry"
  16–17, 19–24, 28, 32, 47,
  73, 76, 107, 185, 192–93
Lamar, "Good Time Bill"
  90–92, 94

Lancaster club 136, 141,
  202
Landis, Kenesaw Moun-
  tain 93, 128, 131, 133–
  34, 137, 140, 145, 198
Lanier, Max 141
Lannin, Joseph 69
Lanning, Les 77
Lapp, Jack 50, 53, 55, 57,
  60–61, 76
LaRussa, Tony 188
Lazzeri, Tony 96, 121
Leach, Tommy 16
League Park 32
Lehner, Paul 155, 165,
  167–68, 173
Lemon, Bob 1, 161
Leonard, Emil "Dutch"
  134
Leonard, Hubert "Dutch"
  198
Lewis, Duffy 58
Lieb, Fred 100, 191, 199
Limmer, Lou 2, 181
Lindstrom, Axel 77
Livingston, Paddy 45
Lockman, Whitey 175
Lopat, Eddie 159
Lord, Bristol 33, 35–36,
  47, 49–51, 55
Louisville Eclipse 193
Louisville N.L. club 10
Lowry, Sam 136

McAleer, Jimmy 28, 34
"McAllister, Jack" (Andy
  Coakley) 28
McCahan, Bill 20, 145,
  148, 153, 155, 157, 159–
  60, 204
McCarthy, Joe 95, 102–
  04, 115, 154, 199
McCarthy, Joseph R. 164
McCosky, Barney 143–44,
  148, 149 (photo), 152,
  157, 160–61, 168, 174,
  203
McCoy, Benny 128, 132,
  142
McCrabb, Les 141
McCracken, Robert T.
  128
McFarland, Ben 151, 158

McGillicuddy, Mrs. Cor-
  nelius 142, 171
McGinnity, Joe 35–36
McGraw, John 26, 34–36,
  52, 54–56, 60–61, 119
McInnis, John "Stuffy"
  51–53, 55–57, 58
  (photo), 60, 64, 69, 73,
  76–77, 79, 186
McIntire, Harry 49
Mack, Connie (Cornelius
  McGillicuddy) 1–3, 5,
  11–12, 13 (photo), 14–30,
  32–34, 37–42, 45–52,
  54–65, 67–73,75–79,
  81–85, 87–111, 113–15,
  117–23, 125–130, 132–
  39, 137 (photo), 141–48,
  151–56, 158–60, 162–66,
  168–70,172, 183–86,
  188–89, 192, 195–200,
  202–03, 205
Mack, Connie, Jr. 142,
  155, 169, 171
Mack, Earle 64, 128, 142,
  155, 164, 167–69, 171–
  72, 179, 180 (photo),
  183 85, 204 05
Mack, Roy 142, 169, 171–
  72, 180 (photo), 183 85
McKechnie, Bill 147
Mackey, Harry 104–05
McKinley, William 18
McLean, Larry 61
McLinn, Stoney 92
McNair, Eric 3, 107–08,
  111, 121–23
McNichol, James P. 57
McQuinn, George 121,
  142–43, 146, 203
McShain, John 171
Maglie, Sal 141
Mahaffey, Roy 107–08,
  112–13, 116, 118
Majeski, Hank 147–48,
  152, 157–58, 160–61,
  165, 174
Malone, Pat 102–05
Mann, Les 66, 68
Maranville, Rabbit 64
Marchildon, Phil 129, 132,
  144, 148, 152–53, 155–
  59, 161

Marcum, Johnny 118, 121, 123
Marion, Marty 140, 178
Maris, Roger 188
Marquard, Richard "Rube" 52–55, 60–61
Martin, Billy 55
Martin, David 7
Martin, Fred 141
Martin, John "Pepper" 112–14, 116
Martin, Morrie 175–76
Martinsville club 203
Masterson, Walter 176
Mathews, Bobby 9
Mathews, Eddie 179
Mathewson, Christy 35–36, 52–54, 60–61
Mauch, Gene 55
Mayo, Eddie 134
Meehan, Austin 162
Melba, Nellie 18
Mercantiles 8
Meriden (Ct.) team 11
Merkle, Fred 52, 55, 61
Metro, Charlie 136, 168, 202
Meusel, Bob 98
Mexican League 140, 142
Meyers, Chief 52
Michaels, Cass 183
Miles, Dee 128, 201
Miller, Bing 85, 87, 89, 91–92, 95–97, 99–101, 104–05, 108, 110, 112–15, 118, 120–21, 164
Milwaukee A.L. club 14, 193
Milwaukee Braves 179
Milwaukee N.L. club 17
Milwaukee Western League club 12, 15
Minervas 8
Minoso, Orestes "Minnie" 173, 203
Mitchell, Fred 26–27
Mitterling, Ralph 77
Moore, J. Hampton 83
Moore, Jimmy 111
Moore, Wilcy 95
Moran, Herb 68–69
Moran, Pat 63, 73

Morgan, Cy 45–46, 51–52, 56, 58
Morrow, Art 157, 204
Moses, Wally 3, 122–28, 132, 162
Moss, Les 205
Mueller, Les 137
Mullin, George 39, 45–46, 52
Murphy, Charles W., Estate of 126
Murphy, Danny 24, 26, 28, 32–33, 35, 38–41, 45–46, 49–51, 54–56, 58 (photo), 60, 63, 70
Murphy, Eddie 60–61, 67–68, 72
Murphy, Mike 77
Murphy, Robert 141
Murray, Ray 173
Murray, Red 55, 61
Musial, Stan 141, 175
Myers, Elmer 76

Nabors, Jack 76, 197
National Agreement 12, 191
National Association 9, 197
National Commission 30, 80–81
National League 9–13, 16, 20–21, 30, 42, 47–48, 53, 65, 75, 80–81, 90, 107, 115, 119, 147, 152, 185, 191, 197
Navin Field 44
Naylor, Rollie 83–84
Negro American League 152
Negro National League 178
Nehf, Art 104
Nelson, Lynn 125–26, 128
New York Evening World 54
New York Giants 24, 34–36, 52–55, 60–61, 87, 95, 122, 141, 175, 194
New York Yankees (Highlanders) 1, 46–48, 51, 54, 64, 72, 76–77, 84, 90, 92, 94–99, 101–02,

111, 114–16, 121–22, 132, 138, 143, 147–48, 152, 154, 156–61, 170, 180–82, 187–88, 203, 205
Newark Bears 121
Newhouser, Hal 1, 134, 140–41, 160
Newsom, Louis "Bobo" 135–36, 138, 143, 203
Nicholls, Simon 39
North Carolina League 204
Northern League 38
Northwestern General Hospital 44
Noyes, Win 78
Nugent, Gerald P. 2, 125–26, 128, 134
Nuxhall, Joe 134

Oakland Athletics 26, 188
Oldring, Rube 3, 37, 39, 41, 46, 48, 51, 53, 57, 60–61, 67, 69, 76, 135, 196
Olmo, Luis 141
O'Loughlin, Silk 39–40
Olympics 8
Organized Baseball 130–31, 136–37, 195, 197
Orions 8
Orsatti, Ernie 114
Orth, Al 21
Orwoll, Ossie 96–99
Ottawa club 178
Overall, Orvie 48
Owen, Mickey 140

Pacific Coast League 88
Paige, Leroy "Satchel" 158
Papish, Frank 204
Parker, Ace 145
Pasek, Johnny 120
Pasquel, Bernardo 140–41
Pasquel, Jorge 140–41
Pate, Joe 93
Peck, Hal 143
Pellagrini, Ed 155
Pennock, Herb 58, 69, 72, 95
Pennsylvania Railroad 6, 43, 64

Pennsylvania Supreme
Court 21, 24, 119, 200
Penrose, Boies 7, 57
Perini, Lou 179
Perkins, Ralph "Cy" 79,
83, 87, 91, 100
Perry, Scott 80–83, 85,
197–98
Pezzola, Francesco ("Ping
Bodie") 77
Philadelphia Athletics
(A's) 1–3, 14, 16–30,
32–94, 96–115, 117–28,
130–36, 138–39, 141–48,
150–73, 175–76,178–83,
185–88, 192–93, 195–97,
199, 201–06
Philadelphia Award 105
Philadelphia Eagles 205
Philadelphia Inquirer 15–
16, 18, 26, 28, 34, 50,
52–53, 65, 67–68, 71,
81, 84, 90, 96–98, 102,
109, 146, 157,159, 171,
192, 194
Philadelphia Orchestra 57
Philadelphia Phillies 1–2,
5, 9, 13–14, 17–18, 20–
24, 32, 63, 65, 73–75,
82, 84, 93, 125–28, 130,
133–35, 138, 144, 146,
160–62, 164–68, 171–72,
176, 185, 192–94, 201
Philadelphia Record 101,
126
Philadelphia Transporta-
tion Co. 135
Philley, Dave 173–74,
178–80, 205
Piatt, Wiley 17, 19
Picinich, Val 77
Pillion, Squiz 3, 73
Pinchot, Gifford 119
Pipgras, George 95, 98
Pittsburgh Pirates 12, 19,
29, 170, 197
Plank, Eddie 20, 25, 27–
30, 33–37, 39–40, 44–
47, 51–53, 55, 57, 60–
64, 66–67, 70–71, 185,
196
Players League 11–12, 20
Podres, Johnny 95

Pollock, Ed 105
Polo Grounds 35–36, 44,
52–53, 60–61
Poole, Jim 91–92
Portland Beavers 87, 91,
107, 118
Portocarrero, Arnold 2,
182
Potter, Nelson 154–55,
160, 204
Potter, William P. 21–22
Power, Vic 182
Powers, Michael "Doc"
20, 25, 44–45
Progressive Party 161
Prohibition 119, 199
Public Ledger 35–36, 104
Pythians 8

Quakers 9
Quinn, John 147
Quinn, John Picus 92, 94,
97–101, 103, 108–09

"Rags" 122
Ralston, Robert 17, 22–23
Raschi, Vic 158, 161, 204
Reach, Alfred J. 9, 15–16
Reading club 40
Reading Railroad 6, 43
Reeves, D.L. 197
Renna, Bill 2, 182
Republican National Con-
vention 128, 161
Republicans 7, 56, 84,
125, 148, 150, 161
Reulbach, Ed 48–49
Reyburn, John E. 44, 50
Rhem, Flint 109, 200
Rice, Grantland 103, 108
Richards, Paul 122
Richardson, Jack 77
Richmond, Don 132
Rickey, Branch 145–46
Rizzuto, Phil 154, 161
Roberts, Robin 163
Robertson, Al 182
Robinson, Eddie 176–77,
181
Robinson, Jackie 146, 175
Rogers, John I. 9–10, 13–
14, 16–17, 19, 21–23,
191–93

Rogers, Tom 83, 198
Rommel, Eddie 79, 83–
86, 90–92, 94–95, 97–
101, 103, 108, 112, 115,
121
Roosevelt, Franklin D.
125, 128, 131, 135, 193
Roosevelt, Theodore 18,
56
Root, Charlie 102, 104
Rosar, Warren V. "Buddy"
138, 143–44, 148, 152,
159, 161, 163–64, 186
Rossman, Claude 40
Rowe, Harland 77
Rudi, Joe 188
Rudolph, Dick 64, 66–
69
Rue, Joe 138, 202
Ruàng, Charles "Red"
97–98, 116
Russell, Clarence "Lefty"
48, 195
Russell, Jane 166
Ruth, George Herman
"Babe" 69, 79, 84, 90,
94, 96, 98–99, 116, 121,
135, 159

Saam, Byrum 127, 165–66
Saint Columba's Church
43
St. Louis Browns 2, 26–
28, 33–34, 40, 46, 51,
75, 77, 92, 96, 107, 111,
122, 125, 127, 133, 135–
36, 139–41, 143–44, 146,
154, 157–58, 160, 162,
165, 167, 170, 172, 178–
79, 203, 206
St. Louis Cardinals 95,
108–10, 112–15, 125, 133,
141, 183, 200
Sally League 47, 153
Samuel, Bernard 149–50
San Francisco Giants 197
San Francisco Seals 146
Savage, Bob 144, 148,
154–55, 160
Savannah club 153
Schang, Wally 60–61, 67–
69, 73, 76–77, 79, 107
Scheib, Carl 131, 134, 153,

157–60, 162, 166–67, 175–76, 183, 205
Schmidt, Christian 15
Schreckengost, Ossie 24, 33, 40–41
Schulte, Frank "Wildfire" 48–49
Schultz, Joe 155
Scott, Hugh 161
Seerey, Pat 157
Sesquicentennial 93
Seybold, Ralph "Socks" 19–20, 24, 29, 33–34, 36, 38, 145
Shantz, Bobby 2, 43, 162, 167–69, 175–76, 177 (photo), 178, 183, 185, 187
Shantz, Wilmer 182
Sharsig, Billy 192
Shawkey, Bob 60, 64, 68–70, 72, 95, 196
Shearing, George 166
Sheckard, Jimmy 48–49
Sheehan, Clancy 76, 197
Sherman, Joe 73
Shettsline, Billy 22
Shibe, Mrs. Ben 137 (photo)
Shibe, Benjamin F. 15–16, 18, 22, 26–28, 41–43, 59, 62, 69, 72–73, 189, 193
Shibe, John 42, 123–24, 127–28, 149, 201
Shibe, Tom 42, 124
Shibe Park 2, 43–45, 48–49, 52–54, 61, 65–66, 73, 87, 93, 101, 103, 111–12, 117, 122–23, 126–27, 131, 135, 138–39, 142, 146, 156 (photo), 159, 173, 175, 186, 201–02
Shocker, Urban 95, 98
Shores, Bill 100–01, 108–09
Siebert, Dick 1, 127–28, 132–34, 136, 142
Simmons, Al 88–89, 89 (photo), 91–93, 96–97, 99–105, 107–14, 116, 118–19, 124, 135, 142, 164, 185

Sisler, George 135
Skardon, Jim 138–39
Smith, Edgar 125
Smith, James "Red" 65
Smith, Walter "Red" 126, 146, 184, 204
Snodgrass, Fred 52, 54–55
Soden, Arthur 10
Somers, Charles W. 12, 14, 16, 19, 22–23, 47, 192
Sousa, John Philip 8
South End Grounds 64
Southern Association 77, 145, 197
Southern League 47
Southworth, Billy 95, 155
Spahn, Warren 179
Sparks, Tully 28
Speaker, Tris 58, 93, 96–97, 198
The Sporting News 113, 123
Sportsman's Park 109, 112–13, 116, 136
Stage Door Canteen 131
Stahl, Jake 58
Staller, George 136
Stallings, George 64–65, 68, 73, 80, 88, 195
Stanky, Eddie 140
Steele, William 43
Steffens, Lincoln 15, 56
Stengel, Casey 147, 175
Stephano brothers 15
Stephens, Vernon 140, 161, 167
Stephenson, Riggs 102, 104
Stetson, John B. 15
Stokowski, Leopold 57
Stovey, Harry 9
Strand, Paul 88–89
Street, Gabby 109, 110, 112, 114, 200
Strunk, Amos 48–49, 57, 61, 66, 73, 76–77, 79, 83, 90, 197
Suder, Pete 147, 152, 157–58, 161–62, 177, 182, 187
"Sullivan, Eddie" (Eddie Collins) 37–38
Summers, Bill 139

Susnek, Otto 139
Swift, Bob 134
Swiftfoot, the 8
Sylk brothers 183
"Syndicate baseball" 10, 187
Syracuse club 178

Taft, William Howard 46
Tebbetts, George "Birdie" 159
Tener, John K. 81, 197
Tesreau, Jeff 60–61
Texas League 122
Thomas, Ira 45, 54, 135, 145
Thompson, Henry 146
Thompson, Sam 9
Three-I League 204
Throneberry, Marv 188
Tiger Stadium 44
Tinker, Joe 48, 102
Tipton, Eric 145
Tipton, Joe 162–64
Todt, Phil 111
Tokyo Giants 121
Topping, Dan 181, 183–84
Toronto club 203
Townsend, Jack 21
Trice, Bob 178, 183
Tri-State League 40
Trout, Paul "Dizzy" 139
Truman, Harry S 161, 166
Tulsa club 122
Tunney, Gene 93
Turner, Tink 73
Turner, William Jay 17
Twentieth Steet House-holders Association 103
Tyler, George "Lefty" 64, 67–68

Upton, Bill 180

Valo, Elmer 1, 143, 148, 149 (photo), 152, 158, 160, 167–68, 174, 182, 185, 187
Vare brothers 7, 57
Vare, William S. 56, 83, 93
Vaughn, Porter 132
Veeck, Bill 178–79, 184

Vickers, Rube 40
Victoria, Queen 18, 192
Vila, Joe 80–81, 197

Waddell, George "Rube"
  25–30, 33 34, 36 37,
  39–40, 185, 193
Wagner brothers 9
Wagner, Hal 133, 145
Wagner, Honus 135
Wahl, Kermit 174
Walberg, George "Rube"
  87, 92, 94–95, 97–103,
  108–09, 111–13, 116, 118,
  120–21, 199
Walker, Clarence "Tilly"
  79, 82–83, 85
Walker, Jimmy 98
Wallace, Henry A. 161
Wallaesa, Jack 141, 143,
  157
Walsh, Ed 32
Walsh, Jimmy 60
War Labor Board 135
Warner, Herman 145
Warstler, Rabbit 121
Washington N.L. club 10–
  11
Washington Senators 14,
  17–19, 21, 34, 40, 46,
  60, 75, 81 82, 92 93,
  96–98, 108, 111, 118, 122,
  124, 148, 157–58, 162,
  166, 172, 197, 203
Watkins, George 109, 114

Webb, Del 181, 183–84
Webb, Jim "Skeeter" 157,
  160
Webster, John 171
Welch, Frank 87
Welles, Orson 166
Werber, Billy 125–26, 201
Wertz, Vic 178
West Side Grounds 49
Western League 12, 20, 25
Weygandt, Cornelius 8
Wheat, Leroy 180
Wheat, Zack 93, 96
Wheaton, Woody 135
White, Doc 32
White, Don 157, 160
White, Joyner "Jo Jo" 133
Whittaker, Walt 77
WIBG 165–66
Wilkes-Barre club 170
Williams, Dibrell 107, 111–
  12, 114, 118, 122, 201
Williams, Marshall 77
Williams, Ted 153, 159,
  161, 167
Willkie, Wendell 128
Wilmington Blue Rocks
  202
Wilson, Art 55
Wilson, Bill 182
Wilson, Hack 102–03, 105
Wilson, Howard 26–28
Wilson, Jimmy 110
Wiltse, George "Hooks"
  55

Wiltse, Lewis "Snake" 26,
  28
Wolfe, Edgar 67
Wolff, Roger 1, 132–33
Wolverton, Harry 21
Wood, Smoky Joe 48,
  58
Worcester club 82
Worcester N.L. club 9
World Series 36, 45, 47–
  48, 52–53, 60–61, 65–
  67, 69–70, 73, 78, 82,
  102–03, 105, 108, 112–15,
  158, 188, 196
World War I 78
World War II 92, 124, 130,
  133, 185
WPEN 165
Wrigley Field 44, 102
Wyckoff, Weldon 73,
  76
Wyse, Henry 167, 170

Yankee Stadium 158, 160,
  188
Yawkey, Thomas A. 38,
  63, 123
York, Rudy 157
Young, Denton "Cy" 27–
  28, 32 33

Zernial, Gus 173, 175–77,
  179, 182, 185, 187, 205
Zimmerman, Heinie 48
Zoldak, Sam 173